There Are No Answers Here, Only Questions

*A Memoir of Two Life-Altering Events
and the Transformation from Their Unlikely Collision*

by Charles Bruce McIntyre

Book design by Diana Wade
Cover art and line illustrations by Darcy Wade

ISBN: 9781088082805

The author has tried to recreate events, locales, and conversations from his memories of them. This is a memoir and has been written from memory and notes. The author has confirmed each detail where possible, but as with any story, if there were eight eyewitnesses, there may be eight different accounts. Yet while written words can be imperfect, spoken words are more so. Either way, try as the author might, he cannot escape his point of view. For this reason, the author has attempted to understand the "why" and the "what," and to understand everything happening in its own sliver of time. None of the names have been changed, but some timelines have been altered to fit the narrative. If the actual date is given, that was the date. This story, to the best of the author's ability, is true.

*To Joyce, for riding shotgun all these years, always
with her eyes on the road, whether wide or narrow,
dry or wet, straight or crooked. Whether the road went
around blind corners or down dead-end alleys,
she has always been the guard rail
keeping me out of the ditch.*

Author's Note

Everyone Has a Story

The book you are holding is memoir, and like all memoirs, the story is true. But unlike many books of memory, this one contains two. For that reason, there are twice as many dates, events, and characters to keep up with, yet each plays a role, and once I began including some, there became more because where do you draw the line when the story includes friends?

The two stories could be told separately, but I am telling them together because, oddly enough, both started and ended in the same weeks, four months apart.

This is a story I have wanted to write for over ten years, and while I have often spoken of these four months in 2010, pen to paper is best.

One story is of selling the business I built over thirty years and was preparing to turn over to its new owner. The other story is of my battle with cancer and the difficulties in my fight. Each is its own story, but they are magnified by their simultaneous occurrence.

And while these two life-altering events happened together, I will need to take you back in my life to where things began. Then we will look a few years ahead, so you can understand the cathartic changes they brought with them, many of which had already begun to take place.

The title, *There Are No Answers Here, Only Questions*, comes from the story. Whenever I thought I'd found an answer to why something happened, I only uncovered more questions and came to appreciate questions more than answers.

As for me as a person, you may know me from family, business, or community. But you don't know me as anyone famous. I've never done anything remarkable, nothing different from what you would have done if you were me. But you're not me, and that's how it should be because you have your own story. And if you're as old as I am, or even if you're not, my one piece of advice is to share your story with others while you still can. Speak your story out loud or write it down, but either way, share. Tell not just the who, what, when, where, and why but also the meaning in each. Tell us what you thought then, along with what you know now. That's the story of transformation, and that's what readers want to hear.

So, that's the story I hope to tell. Because it's in the telling that I find answers. Thanks for reading my story.

—Bruce

The real voyage of discovery
consists not in seeking new landscapes
but in having new eyes.

—Marcel Proust

Chapter 1

Waiting Till Ready Is Waiting Too Long

April 15, 2010

The sun had just begun to reach the top of the tall oaks along the sixth fairway when I stepped out the back door that Thursday. I paused, but only for a moment, to think about the life I had built and how happy I was with how things had turned out. There were times I was fearful, but not anymore.

Today was going to be one of those defining moments people often dream about but rarely see happen. It was the day talks would begin with the buyer of my company, a company that had started with nothing and grown over the past thirty years to where it is today. Taking a deep breath of spring air, a second cup of coffee in my hand, I started across the terrace, surveying the rolling back lawn, savoring the peaceful setting we had chosen to live out the rest of our lives. We bought the house a half dozen years back, and the work we had done on the landscaping was already paying off. The grass had filled in after the grading, and the azaleas were now coming into bloom. I'd pruned the nandina in February, hoping to have more berries this season. I was proud of our work on our home

1

and knew my parents would be as well if they were still alive.

Walking down the steps to the freshly cut lawn, I headed toward the shop and garage. I had been breathing deeper recently, perhaps preparing for the day I would blow out all sixty-nine candles with a single breath when the family gathered for my birthday.

For the umpteenth time that morning, I ran my left hand over the side of my neck. I had discovered the lump, about the size of a double-A battery, Tuesday evening. It was probably just a clogged saliva gland like the oral surgeon said on Wednesday when he prescribed the antibiotics. I'd taken the first only yesterday and one this morning, so there were still eight in the vial. He said it could take several days for my immune system to calm down, so all I could do was keep taking the pills and wait. "Be patient," Joyce had said. But being patient was something I had never done well.

When I reached the driveway pavers, I stomped the grass clippings from my shoes, then walked to the side door. I paused before entering to glance at the teak bench under the giant oak. I often sat on the weathered bench, watching the morning sun fill the sky and thinking about how things had turned out and how the life I wanted was possible when I believed hard enough.

Few knew me when it all started, yet here I was, surrounded by more than I had ever imagined. And while many said I was self-made and should be proud, I knew it was only with the help of so many guiding hands, the people putting their shoulders to my wheel, adding drops to the overflowing bucket of my life that had gotten me to where I was today. *Self-made*, I laughed to myself. *There's no such thing.*

I had been working from home more the last few months, and while I had an office in the house, my best work was done in the shop. I could spread papers on the butcher-block island in front of the long workbench. I could step through one of the double glass doors into the garage, admire the shine of my old Porsche, or check the oil in my truck. These diversions allowed me to think of what should come next.

From the butcher block, I gathered the papers I'd studied the night before—the financial statement I'd read and reread, my copy of the nondisclosure everyone had signed—and put them into my soft leather briefcase, along with a fresh legal pad and my laptop. One last look around. No, I hadn't forgotten anything. I'd be back that afternoon and still needed to put away the banner I'd used a few weeks back. It wasn't a fancy store-bought banner, just an old bed sheet, but it had saved my company back in '97, and it was now part of our culture, our DNA, and at the heart of our annual celebration of how, together, we could survive anything.

Leaving my empty cup on the workbench, I stepped outside, closed the door, and walked around to my car. I put my briefcase and blazer with its clover lapel pin on the back seat and slid behind the wheel. I lowered the visor and opened its lighted mirror. Yes, the lump was still there. "Antibiotics are fast, Bruce, but not that fast," I said to no one but myself.

Over Woodlawn Road, onto the Billy Graham Parkway, exit to Charlotte/Douglas International Airport. It's just Charlotte Route 4 from my driveway on Sharon Road to the airport, but even with the green pentagonal shield, and Charlotte's familiar crown logo above its number, no one thinks of it that way, or at least I don't.

My attorney was meeting my flight. We'd talked extensively about what papers to bring to the meeting, who would say what, and

3

even what to wear. "Bruce, I think you want to present a relaxed and casual appearance: successful and confident, but not aloof or stuffy. I'll wear a tie, of course, like I always do at meetings like these. But remember, I'm there as support; you're the lead in this play. So save the tie for church. Okay?"

I agreed, but everything did feel somber in a way. Not like a church service, but more like the first date for an arranged marriage where the questions sound like a job interview for the vacant life-partner position. So yes, it was sobering.

Was this potential buyer the right choice? Only one way to find out—go on the first date.

The security lines moved quickly, and as I sat in the gate area waiting for my flight to be called, I thought about the company I'd started in 1980. Back then, I wanted to be like the other food brokers I'd met across the country, who were selling groceries to the large chains.

But we were too small, so I found a niche that others had overlooked. My company began selling only to the distributors who serviced the restaurants, hotels, schools, and hospitals where food was consumed away from home, not to the grocers selling to families who would eat the food at home. Our niche—foodservice (not two words, but one I had learned)—was small when I began, but as more and more women entered the workforce and the pace of daily life picked up, eating out became more common, and our niche grew. Now households across the United States spent more on food away from home than all the money they spent in grocery stores.

After all these years of building the business from nothing to now employing fifty people, I was ready to sell, retire, and see what was next. I still felt young, so why not get out while I was ahead and

4

had time to enjoy the years I had left?

Joyce felt the same. Our children had worked in the business when they were younger, both made significant contributions, and I had hoped they would be there forever. Our daughter was creative with a knack for organization; our son was outgoing and a natural at sales. She could run the office, and he could do everything else. But each, in their own way and in their own time, saw how the business wasn't for them and moved on to build successful careers of their own. Then, I offered the vice presidents opportunities to take over, invest in the LLC that owned the building, and buy the company from its profits. But it was not to be. Perhaps they felt they would be safer with a larger organization, or were afraid of the risk, or other reasons they may have had but never told me.

So, I looked elsewhere.

There were only a handful of agency owners my age around the country. We had all started about the same time and had ridden the crest of a wave many called the "Golden Age" of foodservice. We all knew each other and talked often. Yes, this was the right thing to do.

Whether my company was merged or sold didn't matter to me. Either way, I'd be gone. Thirty years was long enough. I'd accomplished more than I ever thought possible, so why not get while the gettin's good? I'd worked for myself too long to take orders from somebody else. I'd take my money, give a speech, hug everyone, and walk out the door.

"Flight 609 to Baltimore/Washington now boarding all rows," the muffled voice on the loudspeaker announced.

I took my seat on the aisle, two rows back from the front cabin.

After takeoff, I removed the legal pad from my briefcase, lowered my tray table, and for the next several minutes only stared straight ahead. I knew then that if I waited until everything was ready, every light was green, I would wait too long. Better to start the process, then let things fall in place. Besides, our industry was consolidating, and if I missed the right moment, the value would fall—fast.

I began to write some words on the blank pad. The words weren't in any order; there was no structure, no outline. They were just words or initials scattered about. Some were circled, some had solid lines connecting the circles, some had dots, and some just stood alone, unconnected. It didn't mean anything to the person next to me, just scribbling, like a child using crayons on the freshly painted wall in the front hallway the evening before the guest arrived.

"Just water, thank you," I answered the flight attendant. I'd quit drinking things with sugar and had already had enough coffee. *Stay hydrated and remember to breathe* was my mantra that day.

I looked down at my pad. Some words were about today, who would do what, and what was next. But others were about the future. The initials HFH (Habitat for Humanity) were circled with a line connecting them to the initials E.S. (El Salvador). Then MPPC (Myers Park Presbyterian Church) was circled and connected to both. UMC (Urban Ministry Center) stood alone. There was the number 356 (the model of my Porsche). Then MPCC (Myers Park Country Club). Then there were names of cities Joyce and I wanted to visit. Would everything connect? After decades of business travel, I was used to being productive while flying at high altitudes in a long silver tube, but today, with so many unknowns, it was hard. I closed my eyes and took in a deep breath, hoping all I had sketched on the pad could be my new life.

"Ladies and gentlemen, U.S. Airways welcomes you to the greater Baltimore/Washington, D.C. area. The local time is 9:07 a.m."

I looked back at my pad. It's incredible how much you can think about in an hour and twenty minutes.

I ran my hand over the left side of my neck. I needed to make an appointment with my primary care doctor when I got home, so I made a note on my pad. Not that I would forget, but just to clear my mind. What if the lump was not an infected salivary gland? Perhaps it was a fatty tumor, like the one I'd had on my back a few years ago. Or could it be something else?

My mother had breast cancer when she was eighty but lived to be one hundred. My dad's cancer was different. His was in his lungs, and he died young. But I'd quit smoking thirty-five years ago. Yet, if the lump was not easily removed but more like my mom's or dad's, and if things didn't end well, what value would all the scribbled notes on my pad be?

My attorney was waiting when I walked out of BWI, but the sun was so bright my eyes needed time to adjust before spotting his car. I got in the front. I was on his right, so he could see my neck, but he was too busy pulling away from the curb and into traffic to notice.

Barry said the drive wouldn't take long, smiled over at me, and said, "Relax and enjoy the cherry blossoms, Bruce."

Relaxing had been hard lately. I'd always been an overthinker. "You worry too much," my parents said. I had a stomach ulcer before I was old enough to drive. The doctor said it was more common among children than most thought. He showed us the X-ray, and I spent years on a special diet. I had picked my fingernails down to the quick until they bled for as long as I could remember, picked my toenails too, and I hadn't stopped that habit until I was out of college and working for Procter & Gamble. Maybe the secure job made me relax, but from then on I tried not to worry, or at least not to let it show.

Barry Maloney, a Washington, D.C.-based lawyer, had been my attorney for almost twenty years. We met when I was asked to join the National Food Brokers Association board. The association started recognizing foodservice as a growing part of the industry and wanted someone like me on the Board of Directors. Barry was the association's legal counsel and attended all the meetings. When I acquired a small broker in Raleigh, I asked Barry for legal help. From then on, for a reasonable fee, he stayed involved. If I needed a lawyer, Barry was on my side.

Barry was more fun when we were alone like this. We usually talked about baseball or some other sport during breakfast at a convention. He was a Washington Nationals fan, and my team was St. Louis, and even though the Cardinals had more intense rivalries, a win is a win, even over the Nationals.

At a conference table, he was less talkative. But when he did speak, it was near the end and in a way that reduced the whole conversation to a few paragraphs, summarizing what actions would be taken for what and by whom and carefully recording them in the notes. "Deliverables," Barry called them.

Closer to our destination, Barry moved the conversation to how he thought today's meeting might go. I could tell his mind was shifting into the role of my attorney, helping me put together the biggest deal of my life.

Overall, he was optimistic and felt things should go well. Barry knew the potential buyer, Todd Furr, from various industry functions, plus they both lived in the same metropolitan area. Todd's business was like mine, only larger. And Todd, younger than I, was ambitious. Barry also knew the other attorney, but more by reputation than anything else, so he wanted to do most of the talking and he wanted to talk directly to Todd, who he knew better. I was to remain quiet, or as much as possible. I smiled, thinking how often I had gone on talking when being quiet would have said more.

I wondered if Barry had seen the lump I was hiding. Maybe his wanting to do the talking had nothing to do with my lump. Perhaps it was more about him leading the conversation. Barry's third-party position gave us the advantage if he could keep the other lawyer more on the sidelines.

Todd's offices were nice enough. It was rented space in a newer suburban complex with no flow or overall design, like thousands across the country. Just various offices with various mismatched furniture acquired over the years. Maybe that was all manufacturers expected from a broker. Perhaps all the thought and planning I had put into our office over the years was wasted time. Besides, there was no need to compare his building to ours; none of that mattered because the one thing, above all, that makes owning a small business unique is being able to choose. There isn't one right answer. It's about what works—for you.

As we were escorted to the conference room, I noticed how dreary and dark it looked. Ours was bright and cheerful. But here I was again, comparing my conference room to his. Did it matter?

Not in the least. If this conference room made Todd happy, I needed to just smile and go on.

There was bottled water was on the polished table, so I opened one and remembered today's mantra: *Stay hydrated and breathe.*

Todd came in, greeted us, and welcomed us to Baltimore, then introduced his attorney.

I introduced Barry, who quickly moved to the specifics of how powerful Todd would be with the Carolinas added to his territory, expanding Todd's reach from Maryland, Virginia, West Virginia, and the District of Columbia into North and South Carolina. This would allow Todd to control the entire Mid-Atlantic. If the East Coast ever expanded into one giant market running from Maine to Florida, as many said it would, Todd would then be in the perfect spot to make a move either north or south, or perhaps both, for subsequent acquisitions. Barry was positioning Todd's ego perfectly.

Barry asked if I had brought our latest financials (he knew I had and had already studied his copy before we went in). I pulled them from my briefcase; Barry took them and slid them across the table to Todd.

Todd studied the numbers for several minutes, then moved the papers to his lawyer, pointing to one line, then one more. I didn't know exactly what lines he had been pointing to, but I knew our numbers well enough to know he was looking at our pretax income, our profit. Todd's face didn't change much, but I saw a faint smile as he waited for his lawyer to review the numbers.

Our interests clearly lined up: Todd wanted control and would need my management team to stay in place; there were enough similarities in our manufacturers that even when some were forced out by conflicts, many remained. And most importantly, Todd said he could raise whatever amount of cash was necessary and was confident we could quickly come to terms.

There was an agreement, and that's all we needed. Barry said we'd work on the details and get back to them. We said our goodbyes.

As we walked to the car, Barry said he thought it had gone better than expected and that everything should fall in place if Todd and his lawyer followed up.

Barry would drop me at BWI, and I could get an earlier flight. "I'm not going into the office tomorrow, Bruce. I'm taking the day off, and my wife and I are going to our place on Lake Placid for a long weekend, so she'll be happy to get away early." Then he added, "Oh, let me give you her mobile number. I never answer mine when we're up there, but she's never without hers. So call her and say you need me."

"Thanks," I replied, getting out at the airport.

The lump had never come up; honestly, I'd nearly forgotten about it until now. Funny how one thing takes your mind off another.

All the flights were on schedule, and the skies up and down the East Coast were clear. I'd be home before dinner and have time after to get the small golf bag and some clubs I kept in the shop and walk a few holes before it got too dark. I'd play number six, then seven over the lake, walk back to number four, finish with the short par three, then into our backyard. Four holes in less than an hour was a nice finish to the day. But maybe I should skip the golf and spend the evening with Joyce, fill her in on the day. Yes, that would be a better choice. *I've got the rest of my life for golf,* I thought.

Chapter 2

Working Your Way Out of Work

April 15, 2010

Over dinner that evening, I told Joyce about the meeting with Todd, how we had an agreement, and how the lawyers would need to work on the details. I bragged on Barry, about how well he had handled everything, and how comfortable I felt with him on my side rather than the other.

"But nothing's done till it's done, right?" Joyce stated more than asked.

"Still, I feel pretty good about this getting done," I replied.

"No, the lump never came up," was my answer to her next question. I told her I'd call Dr. Lacouture, our primary care doc, first thing in the morning.

"Good," she said.

After dinner, we sat on the terrace and watched the sun go down. It was one of those spring evenings when the entire western sky was on fire, and you hoped everyone else was outside enjoying the layer after layer of yellows, reds, oranges, magentas, and purples.

As the sky grew darker, we talked about how lucky we'd been

over the years, how the business had grown and how it had given us a chance to see parts of the world we didn't even know about when we were young. We talked about our children and their families, about how fortunate we were to have them so close; how great it was that the four grandchildren were good friends and got along well together. When they first visited, I'd made a mark on the door frame in the new shop. Even six years later, they always wanted to stand against the frame, have me put a book on their head, then draw a line. Each line had a name and date. James had started at the bottom in 2004 and was now close to the top.

The "Cuz Club" had fixed up the loft over the shop. They'd painted the walls, or at least as high as they could reach. They had fashioned a table and four chairs so they could have meetings to discuss Cuz Club business.

"Will we still be able to travel as much?" Joyce asked.

"Yes, but it'll be different. Maybe we'll go to out-of-the-way places where the hotels aren't as nice, but there won't be the long dinners."

Many manufacturers had offered incentive trips for a successful product launch or reaching a particular sales goal. Perhaps our people liked having me out of the country and out of their hair, so we won most. We had cruised the Mediterranean from St. Tropez to Porto Ercole, with stops in Nice, Portofino, Portovenere, and Elba. We had been treated to Emma Ford teaching Joyce and me the skills of hunting with peregrines at Gleneagles Hotel near Auchterarder, Scotland. We visited the Andalusia region of Spain and enjoyed the five-star luxury of Hotel Alfonso XIII in Seville. We toured the Loire Valley, saw all the chateaus, and went on far too many wine tastings.

We won a ten-day trip to Sydney and the Great Barrier Reef, but Joyce asked not to go because of the long flight and suggested I take our son, who was about to graduate from high school. His teachers said it would be okay, but only if he wrote a report when he got home. I wish I still had a copy of K.B.'s essay, especially the part about accidentally walking onto a topless beach with his father by his side.

In the early years, being away from the office was worrisome. I was concerned that the work wouldn't get done or the bills wouldn't get paid—all things owners worry about when they are away. But as more and more good people joined, I discovered the work did get done, the bills did get paid, and all of it often better than when I was there.

George Howard had joined us in 1985, moved up through the ranks, and now oversaw sales. His office was right next to mine.

Kristi Philips had built a marketing team that none in the country could match. When I traveled to advisory meetings, people would say, "So, you're Bruce McIntyre; tell us about Kristi." Kristi's office was larger than mine, on the corner at the end of the hall.

Laura Bates was the office manager, or Director of Operations, the chart said. She kept things running inside while George, Kristi, and their people took care of business across the two states. I had reached a point where my being in the office didn't matter much. I'd worked my way out of a job, which was fine.

"We can use the place in Palm Springs more," Joyce said. I bought the two-bedroom timeshare at the Westin Mission Hills Resort when I was in Palm Springs for a meeting in 2005. We stayed there when I received the 2007 Jerry Waxler Award for my accomplishments on behalf of the Foodservice Sales & Marketing Association.

15

"We'll do that each year, for sure."

Before bed, I took our dog Caroline, a West Highland white terrier, for "last call" around the yard. It had been a long day, and I was tired, but it was refreshing to think about how much I had accomplished by going on the first date.

Chapter 3

It's Hard Times That Shape People and Companies

April 16, 2010

I didn't go to the office that Friday. I'd told Laura earlier in the week that I would work from home and check in throughout the day. Laura knew I always had my Blackberry with me, and she had talked with Glenda, the receptionist, months ago about how even if I wasn't there, she was to keep my door open with the lights on to make it look like I'd only stepped away for a moment. Glenda knew that if anyone called for me to say I was out and would be right back, and that she'd have me call them the moment I returned.

After breakfast, I had a second cup of coffee on the terrace and walked around the backyard with Caroline. It was still early but looked to be another lovely spring day. Some of the azaleas peaked a week ago, but many were only beginning to open. Joyce had taught me how to prune them correctly. I wouldn't say ours were as nice as the azaleas at the Master's Tournament I'd watched on TV last weekend, but Augusta is farther south. The leaves on two of our bushes had a tint of yellow in their leaves, maybe not enough lime. I'd ask Joyce.

Caroline and I sat on the teak bench together. I needed to help her up now that she was older. Her full name was Caroline Brave-heart McIntyre, and she was born in the highlands of North Carolina in Hildebran. Joyce and my mother had selected her from the litter in 1995, and Caroline rode back to Charlotte, asleep and as content as could be in my mother's lap as Joyce drove. Westies are a hardy lot, bred to go "to ground," chase critters, and bring them out of their burrows. Their long white tail is the handle you grab to pull them out clinching their prize. They seek the highest spot in the meadow, the advantage; clever like their Scot forebears who roamed the High-lands. She was a natural Westie, not a show dog. I've never under-stood the West Highland white terriers in dog shows; they look so unlike a Braveheart.

This morning was like yesterday, but I wasn't in a hurry to check voicemail or email; they'd wait. Instead, I could linger and reflect. I was doing that more, looking back as much as looking forward. Was I doing that because I was older? Perhaps, but also because my life was about to change. If McIntyre*Sales* wasn't me, who was I? What would I be? What would I do? How would I spend my days?

I remember my list from yesterday, all of the words I'd scribbled on my pad. Today, I'd fill in the blanks and talk with Joyce about our plans over dinner.

Sure, the deal wasn't done yet and would need to be right to get done, the dollars would need to add up, but Barry would work on that. My concern had been the safety of George, Kristi, Laura, and all the others, and Todd had made it clear he wanted them in place. The McIntyre*Sales* name would go away in time, but if everything else remained the same, I would be happy. Besides, nothing lasts forever.

Caroline hopped down to walk behind the azaleas along the

neighbor's fence as I leaned back on the bench and listened to the woodpecker excavating his nest. He was doing what all of nature does: preparing for the future. So as he was getting on with his work, I needed to get on with mine.

I walked toward the shop, entered the side door, and spread the papers from my briefcase over the island. "Call Lacouture" was first on my to-do list. Then the word, "Mason." Next, "Little Darlin'," and at the bottom were the words, "What's next?"

I called Dr. Lacouture's office. The nurse said his first appointment was late, so she put me through. I quickly explained to him my story, how I'd noticed the lump on Tuesday, saw the oral surgeon on Wednesday, started the antibiotics that same day, and how the lump was still there. And could he work me in later today?

"Hold on, Bruce," he said. "You've only been on the antibiotics a few days, right? Let's wait till Monday and see if they've made any difference, and if not, I'll see you then. That work?"

I was anxious to get this lump taken care of, but I couldn't argue his logic. I said I'd call him first thing Monday and we'd take it from there.

I dialed Bill Mason in Boston. Bill was a partner with The Hale Group, a consulting firm in Boston that I had been working with for five years. I'd met the founder, Bill Hale, years back at a conference. His firm worked with only two companies like ours, one in the Northeast and the other on the West Coast. The Hale Group's clientele were sizable international food manufacturers and national restaurant chains. They were the best at spotting emerging trends and helping clients position themselves for changing times. Bill Mason was Bill Hale's son-in-law, and well respected in the consulting world.

Bill answered on the second ring.

"Hi, Bruce. How'd it go?" Bill knew I'd been in Baltimore yesterday. He'd helped me narrow down my possible partners. Like the others who studied the industry more from looking at longer-term trends than day-to-day events, Bill knew the window of opportunity was about to close. Bill had warned that they didn't ring a bell when the time was right. "It's a curve that gradually moves up to the top, then suddenly falls off a cliff. Sell too soon, and you're short of the peak, but wait too long, and the value is in the toilet, with all the good deals done," he'd said, adding, "Think of it as being in the front row of a car on the roller coaster and being pulled gradually to the highest point until the chain lets go and the rapid race to the bottom begins."

I laughed at his roller coaster analogy, then said, "Yeah, I think the meeting went well. Have you talked to Barry?"

"No, I tried, but he's out today."

I went on to tell Bill how Barry and I had talked after the meeting, and we both thought everything went well. Barry would discuss some details with Todd's lawyer and get back to me.

Bill asked if EBITDA had come up. I said it hadn't, not exactly, but that I had given Todd our balance sheet in the meeting, and he had studied the numbers before giving them to his lawyer.

EBITDA (Earnings Before Interest, Taxes, Depreciation, and Amortization) is a wonky business school term that, if I ever knew it, I'd forgotten. It's the best measure of strength in a tightly held company. The earnings on a balance sheet could be used, not the massive size of the top line. Bill's Harvard MBA taught him that a multiple of EBITDA was the best way to set a price in deals like these. And besides, Bill had explained, if I didn't find a partner and remained on my own, a strong balance sheet would help me survive. Otherwise, mine wasn't a business, just a full-time hobby.

Bill and I had talked over the months about who might be interested; I had made it clear that I wanted someone who could write a check upfront, and let me walk out the door. I didn't want to stick around for the transition. I knew how painful it would be for me to take a back seat after being in charge. Bill understood, and agreed Todd was the best choice.

I told Bill to give me a call after he had talked to Barry.

The banner was still on the workbench, so I put it away.

The banner dated back thirteen years to a Friday afternoon telephone call. It was March 6, 1997, and the call was not good. Our largest manufacturer had chosen to go with their new parent company's broker. We were fired. They made it sound as nice as possible, but when I put down the receiver, we had lost 20 percent of our income—and the other broker was now that much richer.

I thought of every possible way to cut from our budget that Saturday. Reduce here, reduce there. Who could stay, and who would be let go? But by Sunday, I had a different plan. I found an old bedsheet we were no longer using and wrote out a few words. Words about how much we had to be grateful for. Words like *Great People, A Growing Market, Good Customers, Solid Manufacturers, Strong Relationships*, and all the rest. The plan would be simple, we'd just take the time we were spending on the manufacturer we'd lost, and spend it on the rest.

On Monday, that bedsheet was hanging over the door when our people walked in. No one lost their job, and we survived. We even grew by 10 percent that year and over 20 percent the next. Now, on that March anniversary, the banner is rehung, and the story retold.

It's hard times that shape people and companies. Unlike owners who only add workers when their pockets are full, the real job creators hold everyone together when times are hard. Job sustainers see things through—together.

I spent the rest of the morning polishing Little Darlin' with a special detail spray I'd ordered from a company on the West Coast. I'd given my 1958 Porsche her name in honor of Maurice Williams's hit single, "Little Darlin'," released the year after she rolled off the assembly line in Stuttgart, Germany.

Tomorrow was Little Darlin's birthday, April 17, and the grand-children planned to sit in the car and pretend to be on a long road trip with Ellie behind the wheel, taking them to who-knows-where, Disney World perhaps, and then everyone would have cake and ice cream in the shop. After the party, they would spend the night in the enormous beds in the guest bedroom.

Old Porsches are cars you can work on yourself without hooking everything up to a computer. Some say they look like upside-down bathtubs, but not to me—they've got the best lines of any car on the road today or yesterday. I owned my first when I was younger, so this was my second.

Porsches, like my 356, need to be driven. Regular performance keeps them young. I needed to drive her more in my retirement, so my plan was to take her to the mountains and let her enjoy the Blue Ridge Parkway. Maybe this fall. I would change the oil and adjust the valves later in the day, but a light dusting seemed almost therapeutic for now.

Barry's wife's cell number was still on the island. I doubted I'd need it this weekend, but better to keep it in my contacts than leave a scrap of paper on my always cluttered workbench. When I opened Barry's contact card on my laptop, I saw I already had much of his information listed. His office was on Wisconsin Avenue, about nine miles from Capitol Hill. I had his mobile number, his partner's mobile, and Barry's home number and address, so I keyed in his wife's cell. Then I scrolled down to Notes. "Corporate law, focus on partnerships, LLCs, trade and professional associations, tax-exempt organizations. Worked in Securities and Exchange Commission (CPA), Georgetown University, George Washington Law School. Approved to practice before Supreme Court." It's incredible how much information you can put on a computer. No wonder you need only a laptop and phone to do business these days.

When I started McIntyre and Company in 1980, there were retail food brokers in every market across the country. That was how business was done. Then, slowly, things began to change. Owners retired and sold to a local competitor, companies merged, and markets began consolidating. The Carolinas alone had seven different retail markets when I started. But now, there were only three major retail brokers for the whole country, each stretching from border to border, coast to coast, with thousands of employees and hundreds of offices. So now, over half the food sold in our nation's grocery stores was being controlled by three colossal companies. Imagine how much our once fragmented industry had changed. Could that happen to our side?

When I was the foodservice representative on the National Food Brokers Association board, one of our meetings was at the exclusive Del Monte Lodge in northern California. The group took a break and went shopping in Carmel-by-the-Sea so everyone could buy local artwork. I found a small pencil sketch of a fluffy dog curled up on a sofa. The dog looked like Jasper, a long-legged white cockapoo who was abused as a puppy but quickly became the happiest member of our family after being rescued by Joyce. Jasper was gone now, but I thought Joyce would like the sketch. The art the large retail brokers bought cost hundreds. The simple sketch I purchased cost only $75.

When the meeting was over, the president of one of the colossal companies and I were at the San Francisco airport ticket counter when a message came through on his phone. The text said he needed to be in Cleveland fast, so he wanted a first-class seat on the next flight.

His relentless deal-making meant constant travel and had earned him the top level in every frequent flyer club imaginable. As he shuffled through the cards from his wallet, the woman behind the counter made eye contact and said, "You don't have much of a life, do you?" It wasn't really a question, and he didn't answer, but I will never forget the look of pity in her eyes. His life was not the life I wanted. No, it was a young man's game now.

Chapter 4

Sometimes You Don't Call, You Go

April 19, 2010

On Monday, the lump was no better. I didn't call Dr. Lacouture; I drove straight to his office. "No, I don't have an appointment," I told his nurse when I walked in, "but I'll wait till he's free." It wasn't long until she said I could go back. I explained again what was wrong. He nodded toward the exam table, so I climbed up and unbuttoned my shirt.

"You're taking the antibiotics?"

"Yes, I've taken six. There are four to go."

After a few moments, my primary care physician, who knew every doctor in town, said, "I'd like someone to look at this. Name's Harley; he's from out east, Greenville or Kinston, someplace like that. He went to Brown before Harvard. Then spent time at the University of Pennsylvania for otolaryngology. And then a residency at Henry Ford Hospital before his head and neck surgery fellowship at Brigham and Women's Hospital in Boston. He's busy, but he's the best. Let me make a few calls and see what I can do. Okay?"

"Sure."

"We'll call you later today or tomorrow to tell you where and when."

"Thanks, Doc." I buttoned up my shirt and said goodbye. Because sometimes you don't call, you go.

Chapter 5

Three Words You Never Forget

April 23, 2010

The waiting room at Mecklenburg Ear, Nose, and Throat was sterile. The doctors planned it that way. People allergic to things are more comfortable without places for mold to hide, so there wasn't any carpeting and the chairs were not upholstered. There was the usual children's corner, with brightly painted tables and chairs, some toys, and story books, but again no carpet.

After checking in, I picked a chair where I could see the glass-paneled door leading to the exam rooms and waited.

A nurse later stepped into the lobby and called, "Charles." She called again. It had taken me years to get my mother to tell me why she gave me one name and then raised me by another. Realizing the nurse was calling me, I stood and walked in. She showed me into an exam room, saying Dr. Harley would be with me shortly.

I looked around. Yes, all the credentials Dr. Lacouture told me about were there.

Dr. Harley opened the door. "Charles?"

"Yes," I replied. Then added, "But actually, it's Bruce. I know the chart says Charles, but it's Charles Bruce, and I'd prefer Bruce if you don't mind, Doctor."

"What seems to be the problem?"

I explained the lump and how it was the size of a double-A battery when I first noticed it. And how the swelling hadn't changed even after the oral surgeon had given me the medicine. I had brought the now empty vial in case he wanted to look at the label, but he didn't seem interested in the antibiotics.

The doctor gently pressed on the lump a few times, then pulled a reflector mirror on his head, held in place by a leather strap that looked older than he was. Pulling a silver flashlight from his starched coat with one hand while taking a tongue depressor from a jar, he said, "Open wide, Bruce."

I gagged.

"Once more."

Better this time, but I struggled not to throw up.

"Not sure," he said. "Let's schedule an ultrasound biopsy at the hospital; we'll know more then."

He was almost out of the room when he turned to add, "The front desk will schedule you on the way out."

I'm not sure what I was looking for from my new doctor that day, maybe a pill that would make the lump vanish as quickly as it appeared. But one thing was for sure, Dr. Harley was a man of few words, and he wasn't going to give me any false hope.

The ultrasound biopsies at Presbyterian Hospital were negative, along with several needle probes done by another tech moments before. Everything was normal, yet something was wrong.

A few days later, the lump had swollen to the size of an orange, perhaps irritated by the poking about. I went to Presbyterian's Emergency Room, and after several examinations, Dr. Harley arrived. He studied the results, examined the swollen lump, and ordered an overnight stay with IV antibiotics.

The swelling went down, and I was allowed to go home, but this wasn't good.

Dr. Harley scheduled me for surgery on the next open date. He would put me to sleep so he could take a closer look.

May 13, 2010

A month later, I was in the hospital preparing for surgery. I don't remember much from that early morning; I wasn't allowed to eat or drink anything past midnight. I was dizzy and lightheaded, and the meds were kicking in as Joyce held my hand and said she loved me and that I would be okay. I was transferred to a gurney and rolled down the hall. A few fluorescent lights overhead flickered, probably something as simple as a loose wire or a bad ballast. One of the gurney's wheels needed oil. I closed my eyes.

Waking up, but only slowly, I would come around and then be gone again. The next time I opened my eyes, Dr. Harley was standing at the foot of my bed.

"Bruce, you have cancer."

I rolled over and went back to sleep. Acting like Scarlett O'Hara at the end of *Gone with the Wind,* who said, "I'll think about that tomorrow. Tomorrow is another day."

Joyce and our daughter Laura were waiting when Dr. Harley opened the door leading into the physicians' conference room that Thursday morning. They rose quickly, Laura knocking over the tissue box by her chair, as the tall, stoic doctor, still wearing light-green scrubs, motioned for them to sit. Everyone looked tired, even though the clock with its black numbers on the pale blue wall showed only a little past ten in the morning.

"The operation took longer than expected," Dr. Harley began. "The cells are so small they are not visible, but they're there. We have confirmed cancer. I've just come from telling Bruce."

Laura doubled over, and Joyce clung to her. They asked how I took it. "He seemed to take it okay," Dr. Harley replied. But it was not okay with them. They listened, huddled together nervously, as he continued. "The cancer is at the base of the tongue. We needed mirrors to locate the squamous cells and then take samples for pathology. The base of the tongue is the primary site, but it has also spread to the side of the tonsillar glandular area in his left throat. Two lymph nodes are affected. Stage 1 in one sample and stage 3 in the tongue sample. But, all in all, a good prognosis," said the doctor, according to Laura's notebook.

Dr. Harley had refused to accept six negative biopsies for an answer; he knew something was causing the inflammation. He could have sent me on my way weeks before. "Have a nice day," he could have said, but that was not the man I would come to know.

Chapter 6

Value Decisions Matter

2010

I now had a full-scale medical emergency on my hands, and while Todd seemed ready to buy my business, I needed to take a break. I replied to Barry's requests as he shuffled back and forth between Todd's lawyer and me, but I was also dealing with the cancer diagnosis and what to do next. And as I would try to look forward, I kept being pulled back, way back, to how it all began.

1979

It started as a values decision, really. A decision to make a permanent home for my family, and not be part of a large corporation always being moved about. It was 1979, and I was working for RJR Foods, in charge of sales for half the country, from Chicago to New Orleans and everything west, with Alaska and Hawaii thrown in. The Food Company, as we called ourselves, sold Hawaiian Punch, Patio Foods, Chun King, Brer Rabbit, and more through a network of food brokers. The brokers were managed by region managers, reporting to zone managers, who reported to Clint Owens for the East and me for the West. We lived in Winston-Salem with offices at international headquarters in Whittier Park, just across the street from where RJR Tobacco rolled out dollar bills. I was thirty-seven years old.

Food brokers were new to me. At Procter & Gamble, where my sales career began, we'd done everything in-house. But the idea of a broker was simple enough: contracting with a broker made sales a variable cost, rather than one that was fixed. Accountants tell you that's better. The business only pays for sales made with a commission, rather than a fixed amount for salesmen, who may or may not sell anything all week.

I'd watched food brokers operate over my many years in sales, and to me, they had never been anything but a "big car and credit card." But if it was a competition between my carefully prepared flip chart and the broker who took the buyer to a fancy lunch, you guessed it, the broker got the order. But now, I was managing these big-spender types and found them more skilled than I'd once thought. Some may have only been a glad hand and a slap on the back, but most were local businessmen and respected community leaders. And the important thing was that they knew their customers and their families inside and out. They knew their birthdays, anniversaries, and the names of their wives and children. My fixed-cost three-piece suit did flip charts; these guys sent get-well cards.

Joyce and I had been in Winston-Salem for three years when R. J. Reynolds, our parent company, bought Del Monte Foods. Top management decided to merge Del Monte into RJR Foods, relocating the Winston-Salem people to San Francisco and housing everything in Embarcadero Center.

Safeway Headquarters in Oakland had been my personal account for years, so I knew the Bay Area well. I could never schedule all the different people I needed to see on the same day, so I'd stay over, giving myself time to explore.

One favorite place to eat was The Tadich Grill. It was always filled with people and smoke from the Mesquite wood-fired seafood grill. I'd find a spot at the horseshoe-shaped bar and pretend to study the menu, but instead, I'd be watching the suited financial types who had just finished their day. They'd be celebrating a successful deal with friends before heading to the nearby Marina District or over the Golden Gate to their Marin County homes.

Were their deals only transactional, I wondered, over and done, and then on to the next? Or were the deals built on long-standing relationships? I was starting to think more about building relationships and not about chasing transactions. I had enjoyed relationships in my early days of selling with Procter & Gamble, and those were the feelings I wanted back.

"The usual Sand Dabs, mate?" the waiter with the Cockney accent asked. Tadich waiters remember their customers and what they like. It's all part of the culture, not just the wrap-around white aprons that go from the waist to below the knee, the white shirt, and a narrow black tie, but the caring they bring to their job as they hustle about the small, crowded restaurant.

"Yes, thanks." *The easiest choice is the one that's not different*, I thought, as I enjoyed my fish.

A few drinks at dinner, maybe one back at the hotel, then up to my room. It was a routine. I'd flip through the channels, then, finding nothing, I'd try to sleep. I'd doze off, then wake and wonder where I was. Every hotel room in America looks the same after a while. The soaps may smell different, but they're not.

So, while I told others I enjoyed my visits, I really didn't. I missed Joyce and the kids. Home with the family was more fun. Besides, we'd fallen in love with North Carolina after our years in Chicago and felt this could be our forever home. Funny, because when Joyce and I were dating in Indianapolis, back in the '60s, I'd told her how I was a "man of the corporate," and wherever they sent me was where I'd go. And if we were to marry, we'd be moving every few years, and that's how things would be. But now, as I think back, I was naively thinking only of what I saw for my life, without bothering to understand what she saw for hers.

If I took the job in San Francisco with the combined companies, it would be our fifth family home, and certainly not our last. I wanted a forever home, a spot in the community, not just a seat on a plane. I wanted to control my life and have time for my wife and children, to attend the events in their lives I was starting to miss. I wanted to go to ball games and school plays. I wanted them to grow up in the same place and not move so often, as I'd done as a child. We wanted to join a church and maybe even buy side-by-side cemetery plots.

But where? We had lived in Chicago before moving to North Carolina. But Chicago was big. Winston-Salem was nice, but too small.

I started to ask around. The Carolinas would be perfect, but the Carolinas were part of Clint's territory. I'd need to be cautious with my inquiries.

Marketing Concepts, Inc. (or MCI, as they preferred being called) was the RJR Foods broker in Raleigh and felt an office in

Charlotte would let them represent RJR there as well. They made me an offer. I talked to Clint. "That's not going to happen," he said. "You can join that MCI bunch if you like, but my broker in Charlotte is Bob McQuey. His team at Associated does a bang-up job, so you can tell Paul that if his Hawaiian Punch Drink Mix numbers aren't better next spring, it could be Bob McQuey representing RJR Foods in Raleigh. And he'll have one less thing to worry about."

MCI still wanted a Charlotte presence, despite what Clint said, and I was their man.

So, in the fall of 1979, we moved to Charlotte. We bought a house in Myers Park, enrolled the kids in public school, and settled in. Our home in Winston-Salem had been new with all the latest features, but the Charlotte home was old, built in 1928, and without things like a garbage disposal or dishwasher. The kitchen had dark linoleum countertops with a metal edge to hold down the linoleum and was as up-to-date as any in the '50s, but it was almost 1980. The two bathrooms had not been updated since they were built. There wasn't central heating and air. Instead, noisy radiators kept the house warm in the winter, and large window units tried to keep up with the summer heat.

While most of the homes in Myers Park were occupied by only one family, others had been modified to allow multiple families to live in the same house. The real estate agent said that would all change if and when the neighborhood was zoned for single-family dwellings only. We liked the large rooms and what the agent called "curb appeal." Plus, it was close to shopping, so we took a chance.

I hung a rope swing in the tall oak outside the dining room window and put up a basketball hoop in the driveway. Joyce could

35

keep an eye on the swing, but the view of the driveway was blocked by the window unit that cooled the first floor. Laura and K.B. began making new friends.

I rented office space in an old house on East Boulevard and put an ad in the *Charlotte Observer* for an executive secretary. Pat was experienced, personable, and typed sixty words a minute. I bought office furniture and sent the bills to Raleigh.

The MCI folks in Raleigh, especially Paul, kept asking about RJR. Each day my answer was the same. Dreams built on false hopes don't last. Clint Owens had made that clear.

MCI was losing money in Charlotte, and maybe elsewhere as well. Early Monday, May 12, 1980, Paul drove over from Raleigh and was waiting at the office when I walked in. I was fired. I went home and told Joyce. Somehow, she wasn't surprised. "Now what?" she asked.

I thought about her question the rest of the day, and by Tuesday morning, I had my answer. Going back to the corporate world wouldn't solve anything, and finding a job with another broker would only give me more of the same. I needed to step out on my own—do it my way.

We liked Charlotte and were learning our way around our new city with streets that changed names for no reason and intersections like Providence and Queens, where the former turns right, the latter turns left, and neither ever cross.

Yes, staying in Charlotte and stepping out on my own was the answer.

I'd name my new business McIntyre and Company. I sketched out a business card with two lines intersecting at right angles, like a cross-road. The card would be on cream-colored paper with green ink.

On Wednesday, Pat showed up at our house on Hertford Road. She said she had walked out right after I was fired and had no plans to return. "You'll need help with your new business, so I'll work for you."

How did she know a new business was now my plan? We'd never talked about anything like that. All I could say was, "We'll see." So we left it at that.

I found space in the Key Man Building. It looked old, even then. One furnished room, but it would do. The building had a conference room I could use, and a copier; they took in the mail and answered the phone after a few rings if I wasn't there.

That afternoon, as I was getting settled, Pat walked in. "Which desk is mine?" she asked. I told her I didn't know how much I could pay her or anything else.

"You'll work it out," she said.

Six Months Earlier

New adventures bring new relationships and friendships. One evening the first week after we moved into our home on Hertford Road, I was in the side yard surveying what needed work that winter and what would be better left till spring, when the fellow who lived just around the corner on Norton Road tossed the weeds he'd been pulling into a plastic bucket and walked over. He pulled the glove off his right hand and stuck it out, "Hey Padna-Padna, welcome to the neighborhood. I'm Tillman."

That meeting and the complex relationship that followed over the years influenced my life in ways I'm only now beginning to understand.

Tillman King sold insurance, graduated from Chapel Hill, and had been a good hitter on the college baseball team. His family was in the barbecue business out East in his hometown of Kinston. Everything about Tillman was Southern in a way only the coastal plains of North Carolina understands. I don't know if he was terrible with names or just didn't use them, but if you were male, you were "Padna-Padna," and if female, you'd be "Baby Girl."

Selling insurance meant being part of the community, which meant church and the club. Both were places Tillman said I belonged. On Sundays, he was the head usher, knew where everyone sat, walked families down the center aisle, and escorted single women to their spots and waited in the aisle for them to get settled before returning to his post.

You didn't see Tillman in the service much other than getting you seated and collecting your money, all in the orderly Presbyterian way.

Learning we shared his faith, Tillman said we needed to join, and we could all walk to church together each Sunday. He even had a spot for me on his usher team. "Be good for you, Bruce; you'll meet some nice people. Get seen, be part of things." When I said I'd think about it, he replied, "It's not hard, I'll teach you, and if you remember to keep your coat buttoned, you'll do fine."

When Tillman wasn't at church on Sunday mornings, he played golf at the club. If he didn't have a game, he'd have his large leather bag strapped on the back of a cart and play open holes, hopscotching around. Tillman might join a group, especially if the group was all women, and play along for a hole or two. He'd step up to the tee, casually toss his cigarette to the ground, quickly adjust his stance, and then hit long and straight down the fairway like the good base-ball player he had been. He'd pose long enough at the finish of his swing, but before the ball landed, pick up his cigarette and walk with his signature swagger back to the cart. He'd put his club away, slide in behind the wheel, and take another drink from the large Styrofoam cup that got refilled at the turn.

Tillman always wore long pants, never shorts, even on the hottest of Charlotte summer days. And if he saw anyone leave a ciga-rette butt on the course, he was quick to show them how, as he called it, to "field strip" the discarded cigarette by stripping the remaining paper away, scattering what tobacco was left to the wind, and putting the tiny roll of paper and filter in a pocket. Smoking was acceptable (as was using Styrofoam cups), but just don't litter—all in the strange way country clubs care for the environment.

One day when we were visiting in the side yard, I asked Tillman where I should shop for clothes. He didn't hesitate, "There're a few spots you might like, Padna-Padna, but you look like the kind who would trade with Jack Wood. He's Uptown. I'll call and tell him to expect you." There was one thing about Tillman, he could often be wrong, but he was never in doubt. "You'll like Jack. He's a connector."

I wasn't exactly sure what a connector was, but I quickly learned Jack was an institution in my new home city. Jack, about thirty years older than I, had gotten his start when young men came back from the war in the mid-forties. They got office jobs in the tall buildings and needed to look presentable. Jack would go floor by floor, door to door in the towers and measure the young men for a blue blazer. They already had khaki pants from the Army, so with a new blazer, one white shirt, the other blue, and a necktie, they were set.

That became Charlotte's uniform. Khakis and a blazer are always good, even if you're not still young and just home from the war.

Jack Wood's store was at the corner of South Tryon Street and West Third Street, in the center of an area Jack insisted on calling "Uptown."

Charlotte had grown from two intersecting trading paths, crossroads later named Trade and Tryon. Those old Indian paths crossed at the crest of a small hill. So to get there, Jack reasoned, one needed to go up, so his word, "Uptown," stuck.

My old suits, many with vests, were fine when I ushered, but they didn't fit with the grocery people I was meeting. A sport coat would be best.

I picked up my new sport coat as soon as the alterations were finished.

"I'm sure this Winston-Salem check is good, Bruce. But you'll be wanting a local bank," Jack said when I paid him, adding, "Why not leave the coat here, and we'll have it in a travel bag for you when we get back from meeting Bootie, your new banker." I had no idea what was happening as I followed Jack out the front door.

Bootie? I thought, as we walked the few doors south on Tryon, past Latta Arcade, then through the front door of the bank building. *That's no name for a banker.*

"Bruce, meet Oscar Cranz, your new banker. Bootie, say hey to Bruce."

I sat in the chair across the desk from Bootie. The bank was Branch Bank and Trust, and they were over a hundred years old but new to Charlotte. Their home office was in Wilson, North Carolina, and Bootie had joined them when he graduated from UNC. He'd done an excellent job in Kinston, his hometown, so they sent him to Charlotte and expected him to do the same here. He was always happy to have new customers, especially anyone Jack Wood brought in for a visit.

Bootie had played basketball at UNC and knew Tillman, not from UNC but from his family in Kinston. They'd belonged to different fraternities and now played golf at different country clubs, but everyone knows everyone when the circles are small. Bootie had an office but spent most of his time at a desk with the vice presidents in the lobby's center. Everyone had matching desks with a leather chair and two side chairs. Each desk had a nameplate with their BB&T title below, except Bootie. His name was spelled out in gold leaf on his office door and said Branch President. Bootie's pants matched his jacket, the vice presidents wore their blue blazers and khakis, while Jack Wood always wore a tweed jacket and looked like he was dressed for pheasant hunting in Scotland.

Relationships can start with a handshake while pulling weeds, a simple checking account, or a sport coat so well made I still wear it today, even to Jack's funeral in 2000 when everyone else wore dark gray or navy. I think Jack would have been proud I'd worn it and that it still fit.

Tillman wrote our insurance, both home and business over the years. He'd send a bill, and we'd pay. Years later, I was able to hire a book-keeper. Bookkeepers ask questions—that's their job. She never told me what to do, she just asked questions. So when she got Tillman's bill, she asked.

I called Tillman, "I know you look out for us, but how do I know this is the best coverage and price?"

"Trust me, Padna-Padna, we've been together for years. Our people gather the info, get the quotes, then send you a bill. Simple as that. Want to play Saturday?"

I told my bookkeeper everything was fine. She said, "Right." *What does that mean?* I wondered. Does *right* mean okay, or does it mean there is doubt?

I called Tillman back. "No, Tillman, I don't want to play Saturday, and let me take another look at your bill."

Another agent I knew, Bill Lowry, had been knocking on our door for months. I called Bill.

Maybe we all get lazy after a while, both Tillman and me. Tillman should have been shopping the market and I should have been getting other quotes, but sometimes we all get comfortable, take too much for granted. Easy just gets, well, easy.

Tillman had moved from around the corner, stopped drinking, and was on his third wife when he stopped by the office years later. He apologized in his best coastal plains manner, but it was over. He died not long after. I thumbtacked his obituary over my workbench, looking out at the golf course near the bay window. *His losing our business was good for him*, I thought. *You can't bounce back until you hit the floor.*

May 1980

In the first year of McIntyre and Company, more money was going out each month than coming in, and I needed cash. I called Bootie from my one-room office in the Key Man building. He said yes, BB&T would loan me part of the equity in our Myers Park home with no problem. But, since I was still new in town, the rate would be two points over prime, but he was sure I'd understand. "Pay it back regularly, and we can look at the rate again in a year or so if you like."

I'd never borrowed that kind of money before, but Bootie was like Tillman, Jack, and the others I was meeting in this capital of the New South. They were all pleasant, all "connectors," and all knew each other. They had broad smiles and never a bad word for anyone.

As the loan was being processed, I cobbled together a few things to sell. A company appointed us to sell a glue they said was "just like Permabond." We sold their glue to drug stores, but it didn't stick (on projects or in the stores). We also had shampoo in various colors. The label read "wash and repeat," but no one ever did. Repeat, that is.

We sold roast beef, corned beef, and pastrami for a company in New York City. It tasted good enough if you sliced it thin enough. Pace Picante Sauce and 2-Alarm Chili would both be stars someday, but in 1980 no one in the Carolinas had heard of either, so Murray Distributing put them in the gourmet food section with our green noodles and black popcorn.

Our largest line came from my friend Harry Knight. We'd worked together years before. He persuaded Hood Dairies to appoint me for Harris Teeters' private label fresh orange juice. Buddy Law, the buyer, never liked the deal and placed his weekly truckload orders directly with the plant in Dunedin, Florida. But no worries, Harry said, the commission checks would still come to McIntyre and Company.

All in all, we had four divisions: General Merchandise, Health & Beauty Aids, Grocery, and Foodservice.

I was happy to have something to sell, but selling to four different business sectors was a nightmare. Each day, I packed extra sample bags and visited various headquarters. I was trying to do too much and I was too small. The largest distributor customer in the Carolinas couldn't even remember my name.

I had an office and secretary, but it didn't take long to realize I didn't need sixty words a minute; I needed sixty sales calls. Orders were what mattered, not perfect letters.

"I can try," Pat said, and that became her new job: my first sales rep. I gave her some names and addresses to call on, and off she went. She made a few sales, but buying gas for her Buick Riviera was more than I could afford. So, I shopped around and found a Plymouth Horizon. The four-door hatchback design let her load everything she needed for the day in the back, and the stick shift was fun to drive. It was yellow and an economical choice.

She hated everything about it.

Pat drove the little yellow Plymouth for work, but her '72 silver "Boat-Tail" Riviera was always the car of choice for evenings and weekends.

Every new business is just one step away from its first big break—or at least that's what I kept telling myself.

I got word from a friend that a Danish importer called Prima

Foods was in town. I tracked the representative down and persuaded him to stop by. Prima Foods imported not only Danish hams, but something I'd never heard of—Danish baby back ribs.

I was ready when Steen Elgaar walked in. Pat was out making sales calls but had put together a new brochure. I had straightened up our small office. His chair gave him the best view of our most attractive blank wall. I could have rented the conference room, but there were just the two of us, and besides, it was $20 an hour.

"This says you have four divisions—that right?" Steen asked in his Danish accent. "Who runs the four divisions?"

"I do."

"Impossible. You need to figure out what you're doing, then do it right to be a success today," Steen said in his Danish way of pronouncing only small bits of each word and then compressing it in his soft voice. But whatever his words and however they were said was not important. What was important was their impact on me that day. My head was spinning. We weren't paying the bills with four divisions, how would we survive with just one?

Steen told me about a company in New England that specialized in foodservice, and did it in a way like no other. "Food Dynamics spends their time with the end user: the restaurants, hotels, and schools where the food is consumed. They get them to request, even demand, that the distributor stock the brand the end user wants."

To Food Dynamics, the lowly operator was king, not the big distributor. "It's the little tail that wags the big dog," Steen said, adding, "of course, you'll need to get rid of all this other stuff."

"I'll think about it, but for now, tell me about your hams and ribs," was all I could say.

With that, Steen launched into his presentation, telling me how Danish pigs differed from their American cousins, how they were raised, cared for, and what they ate. All things that would make your mouth water or make you a vegetarian. He even told me how Danish pigs had thirteen ribs, not just twelve like the pigs in my country, and said their long, lean Danish bodies increased the space between their ribs. "They've got more intercostal tissue to enjoy."

There was no risk for Steen to sign me up as his broker, so he drew up a contract naming McIntyre and Company the Prima Foods exclusive sales agent for the Carolinas.

The next week I was in Winston-Salem, calling on a small distributor who was beginning to sell our roast beef and pastrami. On my way back to Charlotte, I stopped in the Hanes Outlet for some socks and underwear before turning over to I-40 and home.

The once-popular but now-closed Sagebrush Steakhouse sign came on me fast. I was past it before the words registered. "Danish Baby Back Ribs—Coming Soon."

I turned around, yanked the car into the parking lot, and ran into the restaurant that was still under construction. Spotting what looked like the owner, I rushed over. He didn't seem happy to be interrupted from his conversation with the architect, but I blurted out my question anyway.

"Where are you getting your ribs?"

I got a cold stare, then his reply. "Who knows, we get 'em up in Allentown, but down here, everything is different. Nobody's even heard of Danish hogs, let alone baby back ribs!"

"I have, and I have them!" I said.

That billboard, that stop, those words changed everything.

"How can I get them and when?" he asked, his face brightening and without a word about price.

This was my big break. I was now Brian Lechner's hero, and he was mine.

O'Brian's, named for Brian Lechner, the owner, opened more and more restaurants across the Carolinas in the next few years, and I had several items on the menu. I went to every opening, often helping in the kitchen. I'd prepare the ribs, remove the membrane after they were par-cooked in the steamer, then put them in Cattlemen's Smoky Base barbecue sauce to marinate in the cooler before putting them on the chargrill.

With red-and-white checkered tablecloths, heaping bread baskets, friendly waitresses calling everyone "sweetie," and ribs that smelled and tasted like they just came off the oak smoke pit out back, O'Brian's Rip Roarin' Ribs was a hit.

Steen and I would travel the Carolina byways in my gray Cutlass sedan, making calls and selling ribs. When we couldn't find a radio station we liked, we'd sing Steen's favorite song at the top of our lungs. "We're in the Money" is a Depression-era song about having what it takes to get by, how the sky is sunny, and when we see the landlord, we can look that guy right in the eye, because "We're in the Money." Then we'd laugh and talk about how it started when we first met. I was crazy to think I could do so much when I had so little, and it was only when I got rid of the things holding me down that I could fly.

And yet, while we were singing, "We're in the Money," I knew we weren't. Sure, we were making more, but also spending more, and I had continued to borrow from Bootie. Yet, at least, that large distributor customer who once couldn't remember my name now had a new card in his Rolodex, and the card was mine.

The paradigm shift was working. By focusing on the restaurants and others who put the food on the tables to satisfy hungry diners, we could get our products in distribution where once only tradition kept us out.

My choice to only focus on foodservice, and do it like the New England company, would mean walking away from the other three segments and the established rules of the game. It was exciting and frightening all at the same time.

Gone was the glue that didn't stick, the shampoo that smelled funny, even Pace Picante Sauce, 2-Alarm Chili, Vemco green noodles, and Black Jewel popcorn.

The most painful call was to my friend Harry. We talked about my decision, and he understood. He even suggested a thirty-day notice, so the weekly truckloads of orange juice Harris Teeter was buying were credited to me. I'm sure Harris Teeter never knew.

I didn't resign the roast beef, corned beef, and pastrami. That was foodservice, and after all, that's what we did—now.

Chapter 7

Make the Numbers, and You'll Be Fine

2010

Things with the sale moved quickly in the three weeks after my visit to Baltimore. Todd's attorney called Barry to emphasize a few points. The attorney said Todd would be in control of the business. He could run everything from Baltimore and make a few trips to Charlotte each month. "He's a good manager," the Baltimore lawyer said, "and he wants the key McIntyre people to stay; he doesn't want them run off. We'll need contracts on all that," was his final request.

Barry listened, taking notes. "Got it. We'll get back to you."

"Another thing," Todd's attorney added, "Todd wants Bruce to go through his list of manufacturers and see who would be forced out if this deal happens. That way, Todd will know how much income he will be losing. Bruce will understand what that means."

Barry knew precisely what Todd needed, and we had already made those calculations.

When a food manufacturer appoints an exclusive sales agent for any geography, they expect that agency not to represent other competitive manufacturers. They encourage their agents to have

49

complementary manufacturers, but not head-to-head competitors. So a protein company would want us to have potatoes and gravy with vegetables, coffee or tea, and dessert, but not another manufacturer with the same protein. Early in the '80s and '90s, before consolidation, things were more straightforward. Manufacturers only did one or two things. Tyson did chicken, and that was it. Then things started to change. Tyson began buying other chicken companies, turning to other proteins when they ran out of those. Tyson later added beef, pork, and more.

Sara Lee had been a bakery in Chicago when it started buying other bakeries. Then pork, beef, sausage, and corn dogs. It's a long and complicated history of mergers and acquisitions.

Every manufacturer takes a different view of conflicts. Some are very rigid, but some are more understanding and will look the other way as long as the sales agent does a good job. "Make the numbers, and you're fine," they say. Some even publish a list of "hard" and "soft" conflicts. Hard conflicts are a red light, soft conflicts only a flashing yellow.

We'd run the numbers, and while there was some fallout, there wasn't much. Many of our manufacturers, like Smucker's and Reckitt & Colman (the French's mustard, Frank's Red Hot, and Cattlemen's Barbecue Sauce people) were the same.

Todd represented Tyson while we sold King's Delight—schools and other institutions bought more of our chicken than Tyson. But overall, Tyson was larger. King's Delight would be a casualty, unless Todd could assure them there would be no exchange of information between the Carolinas and Virginia. That might work. Better yet, Todd believed he could get Tyson to appoint his new combined company for both Carolinas, leaving their old broker behind. That would give Todd a power-play positioned perfectly between the Northeast and Southeast for the entire Mid-Atlantic regions. *Wishful thinking,* I thought, *but if that dream made Todd sleep better, so be it.*

Chapter 8

We're Not Poor; We Just Don't Have Any Money

2010

That night after my phone call with Barry, I walked around the yard with Caroline. I thought about how much the company had grown over the years when we had run out of money the second time and Bootie had given me the last of the equity in our house.

I'd borrowed money before, but never that much, only for repairs around the house, a new washer-dryer. Those loans were repaid with money my employer automatically deposited in my bank account like clockwork on the first and fifteenth of each month. But now that I was self-employed, my company's income, and thus mine, came in no particular order, and payments, when they did arrive, were in different amounts, and sometimes there wasn't any check at all. I'd call the manufacturer but only be told they'd look into it and get me what I was owed next month. There was no way of knowing what each month would bring.

When I thought about the money BB&T had loaned me, I realized it was really only the profit I'd made from selling our first home in Kansas City, then from selling our house in Chicago, and from the one in Winston Salem. The profit from the sale of our three homes had been the down payment for the house in Myers Park. Bootie was charging me money on my money. And, if that wasn't bad enough, the Federal Reserve took the lending rate higher and higher that year, until it hit an all-time record of 21.5 percent in December 1980. Add two points, and I was giving up almost twenty-five cents on every dollar of the money I used before I even began to pay it back.

Maybe the bank hadn't read the Old Testament Book of Exodus, where it says charging interest to poor people is wrong. Or maybe Bootie didn't consider me poor.

Perhaps it was like the conversation I'd heard when our daughter had a sleepover with her new friends, and I listened at her door as she explained, "We're not poor; we just don't have any money right now."

Chapter 9

Where Are You in This, Bruce?

1981

The Key Man Building had dozens of individual offices like mine, with only one or two occupants in each. Most left their doors open so people could come and go. A fellow upstairs sold paper bags to grocery chains in the Southeast. He sat in his office and made phone calls all day. He didn't make much on each bag, only fractions of a penny, but think of how many he sold. I began to think more about volume. Sell enough of anything, and even if the slice of the profit is small, it adds up. It made sense. Sell to the elite and dine with the masses, or sell to the masses and dine with the elite.

Jim Zervakis's office was next door to mine; his family owned the Epicurean Restaurant catty-corner across Scott Avenue. Jim sold advertising specialties: coffee mugs, key chains, T-shirts, and other brightly-colored trinkets companies put their logo on to improve sales. Jim always stuck his head in with his latest ideas. Maybe I should have listened; instead, I pretended to be busy.

I enjoyed the visits with a young graphic artist from across the hall. Joel Tevebaugh worked for a company that published a guide to apartments in Charlotte. His job was to make everyone look happy living in their temporary space.

Many small offices were decorated with travel posters from Paris or Rome thumbtacked to the wall. But I didn't think that fit what we were doing. Instead, I had a bright poster, published by the Food Marketing Institute in the late '70s, showing the scope of the entire food industry. Joel took a look at it one day.

In the foreground were restaurants, hotels, schools, hospitals, grocery stores, small neighborhood markets, convenience stores, even an Army PX. The food came in the back doors from various vendors and distributors who got the food from the manufacturers, packing plants, and canners. They, in turn, were supplied by farmers, ranchers, fishing fleets, and others. The poster even had sunshine nourishing the fields of grain and rain falling on the orchards. There was a large import/export terminal on the coast. Joel was fascinated as I explained each step. Then, he asked, "Where are you in this, Bruce?"

"I'm in the middle, between the people who make it, grow it, or catch it, and the ones distributing the food to the people who eat it." That seemed to make sense to him. Joel asked if he could borrow my poster.

A few days later, he returned. "They left out the most important part," Joel said. In the center, carefully pasted over what once was a small shop, was an office with a fellow who looked like me sitting at his desk, feet propped up, and talking on the phone. Joel had drawn a sign above the one-room shop, "McIntyre and Company."

That poster has been in my office ever since. It's nicely framed now, and I've used it thousands of times to explain my niche in our giant food system.

Chapter 10

Two Scotch-Irish Lads Selling Italian Food to Greeks

May 1981

I was still taking more out of the credit line than I was putting back. Pat reached her first anniversary and was still making $400 a month. She turned in her resignation. I didn't blame her.

I wanted to hire a young man I had met, but he was with another broker, so I needed to be careful when I called. When I finally got Chic Cariaga on the phone, I used the same approach headhunters had used on me over the years. I described what I was looking for and then asked if he knew anyone who might be interested. Of course, I'd hoped he would take the hint, but he didn't. Maybe I was too suave and subtle for my own good.

Chic fired back a name: Don Hemby would be perfect, he said. "Don has a food science degree from NC State, but he's hanging billboards for an outdoor advertising company these days. He'd love a chance to use his degree." I called Don, and we met. He'd get the yellow Plymouth and the $400 when he started the following week.

Don was everything Pat was not, and that was perfect. Don was young and enthusiastic, never overdressed, and fit in kitchens well.

Pat's high heels may have worked in board rooms, but Don's rubber-soled oxfords were better on slick kitchen floors. Don told everyone he was the "and Company" at McIntyre, and he was.

More manufacturers came on board. Manufacturers back then were called "packers" or "lines" or other names. Later I would call them clients. That sounded important, and they liked it. So client it was. And if they were our Client, they got a capital C. We were brokers, middlemen, but I used the word "agent." Funny how what you call something makes it different.

When Angelo Palmari called, I had trouble understanding what he said, what he wanted, and what his company did. After several minutes I figured out he was Italian, and the company, Rotanelli Frozen Foods, sold frozen Italian specialty items: manicotti, ravioli, stuffed shells, gnocchi, and breaded eggplant cutlets.

Angelo had heard of us and wanted to come by that afternoon. Don and I listened as Angelo explained each item. I started to get the hang of the language after a bit. To Angelo, it was "man-a-cot." Just cut the word off before it was over, and you sounded Italian.

We were hired. Two Scotch-Irish lads selling Italian food to restaurants in the Carolinas, most of which were owned by Greeks. Is this a great country, or what?

Angelo said we didn't need samples; the food would sell itself when we showed customers the pictures in the red trifold brochure, like the one he kept in his coat pocket. Don sold "man-a-cot" to Clemson University. They had a distributor in Greensboro from

Boston who knew Angelo, even the little red "silent salesmen," as Angelo called his pamphlet. A few days later, Clemson called with a complaint. The frozen manicotti was clogging their fryers—it wouldn't work. "No, you don't *fry* it; you bake it and cover it with marinara sauce. Remember?" Don said.

Education can be the hardest part. How many things fail simply because they were done wrong in the beginning?

Biggers Brothers, the largest distributor in the Carolinas, would need more than the little red "silent salesman" to get them on board with Rotanelli. They wanted a full-blown sampling, complete with checkered tablecloths and Italian bread—a full meal. I got some advice from Joyce, then put everything together, and headed to their warehouse.

I had the main room set and all of the food coming out of the ovens as Mr. Biggers and the others walked in. I talked about how more and more people from the North were moving South. Everyone enjoyed the food, and I finished my pitch by saying, "Why not sell them the food they grew up on and make money doing it?" That sounded good to Mr. Biggers. He and Kay Simmons, his buyer, talked in the corner—or he talked, and she listened. Kay's speech was slow and she spoke with a stutter, so she was better at listening than talking. A trait I'm still working on.

When everything was finished and I was cleaning up the kitchen, Kay came in. She told me Mr. Biggers would give my Italian food a try since I'd been working so hard to sell them my roast beef and pastrami and had never gotten to first base, other than the ribs. It would be a small order to start, and I'd need to work with their salesmen (there were no saleswomen back then) to teach them how to sell it; and, oh yeah, one more thing. The product must have a thirty-day guarantee. "If it doesn't sell, it goes back where it came from. Okay?"

When I called Angelo with Mr. Biggers' demand, his English was perfectly clear. "No," he said, explaining how Don and I would ride along with the Biggers Brothers salesmen as they made their sales calls, how the food was wonderful, and how Don and I would use the little red silent salesman.

"Remember them, Bruce?"

"Yes. Yes, Angelo, I remember. Got it; the order is not guaranteed to sell."

My conversation with Kay was different. "Kay, we're all set. I've placed the minimum order, two thousand pounds, and it will be here next week. And, yes, it's all guaranteed."

That evening I told Joyce we had just gotten our first big break at Biggers Brothers and how everything would be fine. When actually if it wasn't fine, we'd be eating Italian food for the next year.

To my relief, Rotanelli did well, very well. More people in the Carolinas had moved here from up North than any of the good ole boys understood.

I'd taken a chance, but it was a chance on which I was certain. Certainty isn't about being right or knowing it all; it's only about being certain. It's about knowing you can make it, even when others say you can't. There was a business to be built, and I would build it. Of that, I was certain.

Chapter 11

Debating Only Divides, Decisions Unite

Spring 2010

For the next several weeks, I debated which should come first: my cancer treatment, without knowing yet what it entailed, or the sale of my business, not knowing how long it would take. If Todd could raise the cash for the purchase as he said he could, this whole thing could be finished in a few months, and I'd be free to tackle my cancer in the fall.

Or, since Dr. Harley said the prognosis was good, maybe I should get cancer quickly behind me and then return to Todd and finish the deal. He was an eager buyer; he should hold.

But what if while I was getting treatment, Todd found one of my competitors in the Carolinas he liked better? Others would be cheaper to buy, not as good, but cheaper, and price is a powerful motivator.

My tongue sample was stage 3 and spreading. How fast does cancer spread? Maybe treatment should come first?

I looked up the stages. Stage 0 cancer can be detected, but has not spread to nearby tissue. A surgeon can remove the stage 0 tumor and the work is done. In stage 1 the cancer has spread into nearby tissue, but not deeply, and has not spread to the lymph nodes or other parts of the body. Stage 2 and stage 3 are similar, one only more advanced than the other. In these stages the cancer has grown more deeply into nearby tissue and may have spread to lymph nodes. And then, I read about stage 4, where cancer spreads to other organs and throughout the body. Stage 4 patients are labeled "advanced," and I wasn't ready for that. I was thankful mine had not made it that far.

But if I treated my cancer and didn't attend to the deal-making, and Todd found another partner, who would I partner with? Could I be left to run a company squeezed from all sides by competitors growing larger as the East Coast continually consolidated while I aged past any opportunity for retirement?

It was as though deciding what to do was the ball in a tennis rally, and I was watching the ball fly back and forth over the net. This rally had gone long enough, and as my mother would say, "You can talk till the cows come home," but what difference does it make without a decision?

Chapter 12

Both/And Is Better than Either/Or

2010

Todd and his attorney were moving ahead, and Dr. Harley had established my treatment path. Something needed to be put on hold. But what, and for how long?

Every morning, unless it was raining, I sat on the weathered bench in the backyard, watching the sun fill the sky, and thought about how making a choice and following it to completion had always been easy for me. It was always a simple "either/or" decision. My choices had turned out well, perhaps it was good luck, but good nonetheless. Why was this one so hard?

But maybe I was going at it all wrong? Perhaps instead of picking only one, I should pick both? If I could do one right, why not two? Could this be the time "both/and" was better?

Just like that, the answer was clear. I'd fight cancer *and* complete the sale at the same time. Thinking I needed to choose one over the other was wrong, not only as an outcome, but as a way of thinking. It was better to start with the idea that many good results can come from one right start. Dr. Harley was going for a cure; that might change if I waited. Todd was ready now, so why make him wait?

Sometimes it's only about the first step, so get on with it, I thought.

But this time, I'd need to lean back as others leaned in. And that can be hard for people who are used to being in control. Power clouds one's vision, making it hard to see the ideas of others. But Barry was an excellent attorney. He'd successfully done bigger deals than mine, and Dr. Harley had my complete confidence. Everyone would do better if I got out of my own way.

I'd do one day at a time. When it was time to think about the sale, that would be my focus. And then, when it was time for treatment, I'd concentrate on my cure. One kept my mind off the other, and distraction is the best cure for worry.

Dr. Harley assured me when we last talked that my cancer didn't come from anything I had done. I'd quit smoking thirty-five years ago and hadn't touched alcohol for almost as long. "These things just happen sometimes," he said. My father kept a Rudyard Kipling poem in a simple frame over his dresser. A few lines came to mind. "If you can meet with triumph and disaster and treat those two impostors just the same . . . you'll be a man, my son."

Was I to treat the horror of my cancer the same as my success in the business? After all, so many helped build the company, and just as many would be fighting my cancer.

I thought about the helium balloons that were inflated each year for the Macy's Thanksgiving Day Parade, gliding down the wide streets of New York City, those giants and the invisible wires held tightly by loving hands directing the journey. So many invisible hands. Tillman King took me to church and had me ushering within the first month. Jack Wood, who introduced me to Bootie at the bank, and then there was Puny Mann. . . .

Charlotte was different back when I met Puny. The buildings weren't as tall, and important people lived closer to the ground—they got out and about more, ate in the same restaurants as their workers, and shopped in the same stores. They socialized more and didn't need appointments to visit each other. So it wasn't a surprise when an unannounced visitor walked into my office that morning. Puny was a Native American, standing every bit of six feet three inches. He looked like he had played football when he was younger. I got his company's name right but needed help with his own. "Yes, the name's Puny. Puny Mann." The contrast between his size and his name was funny in a way that made it easy to remember.

Puny was the top salesman at 610 AM WAYS, the famous "Big WAYS" station created by Sis and Stan Kaplan, now known as WFNZ. Puny had stopped in to visit because he knew I was selling groceries, and grocery stores and grocery brands were big advertisers on Big WAYS. He invited me to join him for the monthly meeting of the area food dealers, offering to introduce me to a few of his friends.

The day of the meeting, I arrived early, wrote out my "Hello, I'm Bruce" nametag, then stepped to one side. I didn't know anyone, but Puny was a connector. Before long, he had everyone gathered around, all telling stories of their first days in Charlotte, how they had started, and what they were doing now. I'd exchanged business cards with half a dozen new friends by the end of the evening.

Those monthly meetings always ended with a drawing for small prizes, but you had to be present to win. I could hear Puny yelling from the back of the room, "Shake 'em up!" He wanted the tickets evenly distributed and for everyone who stayed in the game to have a chance to win.

Thinking about those evenings with Puny thirty years ago, I found the advice I needed today: keep things evenly distributed, the good and the bad. Stay in the game until the end and give myself a chance to win.

Chapter 13

Bankers Will Loan You an Umbrella Until It Rains

1981

Even with our success, there was still more going out than coming in each month, and soon the second half of the loan money ran out. I needed to go back to the bank. Bootie had moved on, and Bill Cowden had taken his place.

Bill had the file on his desk when I sat down. The meeting didn't take long. No was his answer. His advice was to find an equity partner, someone who would join me. He didn't say, "Your house is on the line," but that's what I heard.

Joyce had come to the office and was waiting with Don, the "and Company" of McIntyre, when I walked in. I don't know if Don saw the look on my face, but Joyce did. She asked how it went. "We'll just need to sell more groceries," was all I could say.

I was all-in. I'd pushed every chip I owned into the center of the table and could only wait for all the cards to be played. I went to Tom Cummings, the attorney who filed the articles of incorporation when I started the company. "Bankers will loan you an umbrella until it rains," were Tom's words, maybe paraphrasing Mark Twain, but the meaning was clear. He told me there was "street money" he could find, but if I thought the bank rates were high, I'd need to think again.

My mother had visited often from St. Louis and knew what I was going through. She'd never approved of me leaving my secure job with Procter & Gamble. Dad had been with the same company his entire life. If it was good enough for him, why not me?

Mother called one evening from St. Louis to tell us her plan. She'd been looking around her two-bedroom home. Joyce and I could have the front bedroom, and the kids could share my old room in the back. She'd put her bed in the basement. There was only one bath, but it would all work out. "Kenny says he can use someone at the filling station to pump gas and do oil changes. It won't be much, but we'll get by." She and Dad made it through the Depression; we could do the same.

Was she right? Was it time? I'd spent many a sleepless night staring at the ceiling with its paint peeling off where the plaster needed patching. Was it over?

Or maybe I'd find someone like me with a lovely home who would sign it over to the bank, all for the opportunity to join a failing business. Nope, that wasn't going to happen.

Maybe I'd find a corporate job again. I'd need to travel, but we could stay in Charlotte. Laura was twelve, K.B. was nine. They were doing well in school and making friends, we were becoming more involved in the church, and Joyce was happy, although she still felt the kitchen needed work. So, all in all, Charlotte had been a good choice. We could stay.

I'd need to make enough for us to live, of course. And, I'd need to pay back the bank and the two points over prime. Or let them have the house. Then we could rent a small apartment, because I wouldn't be able to pull together the down payment for another home.

No, the only answer was to make this work. So each Monday evening, Don would come to the house for dinner. Joyce would pull together a meal from the day's leftover sales samples, and Don would join us. After dinner, the two of us would go back to the office and make phone calls to the distributor salespeople to see if they had any questions, how we could help, and how they could sell more of the products we sold them. It was a logical plan, but the people we called had been out selling all day and didn't like our calling after dinner to ask them to sell more. Obviously, that wasn't the answer. Oh well, Joyce's meals were good and Don appreciated them.

I read trade magazines for industry news in the evening, mainly looking at manufacturers' ads. If it was a big ad, I wouldn't call because they usually had representation, and we were too small; plus long-distance calls were expensive. Little ads were different—they clearly needed help. If they made a quality product at a fair price, they might need us as much as we needed them.

One day, I called Casa di Bertacchi and spoke to the sales manager. It didn't take long to figure out that Larry, a New Jersey native, wasn't interested in talking to some small-time Southern broker like me.

Casa di Bertacchi made meatballs. I asked Larry if he needed sales in the Carolinas. "Sure, how many salespeople ya got on the street?" I had learned that you get your chops busted and fast if you didn't give it right back to people like Larry.

"Larry, first, tell me how much business ya got in the Carolinas?"

"None," snapped Larry.

"I win! You got no business, but I got one person; let me tell you where to ship the samples and mail my contract."

That was the start of a long and wonderful relationship. We made two cents a pound on paid sales. That meant we had to be the collection agent as well.

Casa di Bertacchi was in Vineland, New Jersey, and made the best meatballs in the world. There were different sizes, but the one-ounce, smaller than a golf ball and measuring only one inch in diameter, was the most popular. You could take a small bite or put the entire thing in your mouth at one time if you were hungry. It was the perfect size for appetizers. They also made braciola, thin slices of steak rolled around a cheese and bread crumb mixture, then cooked in a tomato sauce, or "gravy," as Larry called it. But we never sold any. The Carolinas weren't ready.

As I got to know Larry, I learned he wasn't Italian, but Irish. He was raised in an Italian neighborhood and grew up in their culture and speech patterns. My parents and I had lived in New Jersey years ago, in Newark, Kearney actually, during the war, and Dad rode the train to and from Manhattan every day. I was just a little boy then, so I don't know the difference between what I actually remember and what I was later told. But I do know my mother couldn't get out of New Jersey fast enough. She and the butcher where she shopped finally reached an agreement. She'd point to what she wanted, and he'd wrap it up, all without speaking. When asked if she'd ever gone back, she'd say, "Why? I didn't leave anything there."

Soon after the samples arrived, I got a call. Duff's Smorgasbords was opening in the Carolinas and knew about Casa's meatballs. Smorgasbords were new in the South then, but today, restaurants where numerous dishes are placed on a long table and diners serve themselves are everywhere.

"Be at PYA/Monarch in Columbia, ready to go at 9:00 a.m.," Larry said. PYA/Monarch was the largest distributor in South Carolina. I knew who they were, but I didn't have any friends there—yet.

I drove down early to set up. The sales manager pointed to a spot in the corner of the salesroom, and I soon had my meatballs simmering in a crockpot covered in Joyce's marinara sauce. In the opposite corner was the largest broker in the market. They were Goliath, and I was David. Several people were working at their table, and the PYA/Monarch folks knew them all. The big crowd were all smiling in that corner, and there was just me over in mine.

At a little past 9:00, Sherwood McKenzie, a legend and the head man at PYA, walked in with the Duff's Smorgasbord guy in tow. They headed to the crowded corner. The Duff's guy ate one meatball, then another, making it clear the other broker was about to get the order.

Finally, Duff's came over to sample my Casa meatballs. His face showed no emotion, no preference that I could spot. He just turned and walked back to the other corner. Back and forth. He would ask me a few questions about holding time on a buffet line and under heat lamps, then walk back across the open space.

The paradigm was shifting. Before long, he had settled in with me. Duff's would be using Casa di Bertacchi meatballs. Then, the PYA people came over and asked, "Who are you again? Got a card?"

71

The other broker packed up. Sherwood left the room. The universe had stepped in again, and our meatballs took off like Danish baby back ribs. My choice to let the customer drive demand in search of a fairly priced, quality product was working.

Soon, Casa di Bertacchi was everywhere. From small one-unit sub shops in a strip mall on the outskirts of town, to the small chains like Sub Station II and larger chains like Subway; from Duff's Smorgasbords to all-you-can-eat Chinese buffets; from meat-and-three lunch counters to fancy country clubs, it was the same: everyone wanted the meatball with the funny name. They'd use different sauces, perhaps, add this spice or that. One recipe marinated the precooked meatballs in blackberry jam with blackberry moonshine and brown sugar with lime juice; but inside, where it mattered, the meatball was Casa, and Casa was McIntyre.

McIntyre and Company grew to be more than just two Scotch-Irish lads over the years, and always by following the mission we were later to use in everything we did: "Placing the interest of our Clients and Customers first, maintaining a continuous quest for learning in everything we do, treating all associates with respect and dignity, conducting all activities with the highest standards of integrity, and developing a spirit of teamwork in all areas of activity."

Chapter 14

Embrace the Pain

May 2010

The radiation oncologist Dr. William Warlick was young and to the point as he sat erect in his black leather chair behind his uncluttered desk. The walls of his office were covered in framed diplomas: Medical College of Georgia, class of 1994. Walter Reed Army Medical Center, 1995. University of Utah Hospital, Radiation Oncology, 1998. The credenza behind him displayed a few family photos, but otherwise, the windowless office, with its pale walls, looked like every other medical office Joyce, Laura, and I ever set foot in during that long ordeal.

Holding the PET scan results in one hand as he spoke, he told us my cancer had not spread beyond the tongue, throat, and neck. "Good news," our daughter Laura wrote in her ever-present notebook. "The treatment will be seven weeks of radiation, five days each week. The pain and fatigue will intensify as the treatment progresses, and the throat and tongue will become inflamed. Swallowing and speaking will be affected, but this is usually temporary."

He went on to explain how the giant radiation machine would

be programmed to focus its thirty-five beams, each from a different spot on the large ring spinning around the table, so they penetrated the exact location necessary to destroy each cancerous cell.

Dr. Warlick looked across the desk and said to Joyce, "It's an aggressive treatment plan, but this is serious, and Bruce is otherwise healthy. He should do fine." Then he added, "Remember, we're going for a cure, not remission. So this will be painful."

I heard his word *cure* and forgot the word *pain*.

There were two things Dr. Warlick said I had to do before radiation could begin on June 7. First, I needed to schedule time with the dietitian. Keeping my weight up would be critical; drop too low, and the treatment would be halted. My weight had never been an issue for me. I was still wearing the sport coat I'd bought from Jack Wood thirty years before, but dropping too low and the treatment halted meant they would start with the first treatment all over again, losing ground and perhaps time. So, yes, meeting with the dietitian was important. The second was to have a feeding tube installed before the first treatment, because my throat and tongue would be so swollen from the treatment, I'd not be able to eat normally.

I told Dr. Warlick I would do the two things and that the first treatment date was good, but I'd need to check my calendar about the other dates and times. He leaned across the desk, looked me straight in the eye, and in a firm voice, said, "Be here each morning at ten o'clock sharp. Got it?"

The non-negotiable tone of my young doctor's command was a

giant wakeup call. There was a new world order, and it didn't revolve around me, only my cure.

When I met with the dietitian, she said she'd need to do some research to find a gluten-free nutrition supplement. I'd been diagnosed with celiac disease seven years prior, and it was not something she dealt with every day; however, she was seeing more and more people who were gluten sensitive.

Dr. Gavigan was the gastroenterologist who had diagnosed me with celiac disease in July of 2003, and he did feeding tubes. But after putting me up on the table and poking around, he thought it might be better to schedule general anesthesia to open the cavity and stitch the tube in place. "That way, it won't move around or get dislodged," he said. "Or, if you'd like, I can have one of the younger doctors take a look." I didn't see any harm in a second opinion, so I agreed.

The doctor, younger than our children, walked in. "Let's have a look, shall we?" He poked around, then told the nurse he would need to deaden the area. "We'll go in about here. Can you feel my finger? We'll poke a hole and slide the tube inside, and then you'll be set. Okay?"

"But Dr. Gavigan wasn't sure that would work."

"Well, if it doesn't, you're in a hospital, so we'll fix it, right?"

I unenthusiastically nodded my approval, and he went to work. He numbed the area, then simply poked a hole in my gut. He may have used an ice pick for all I know. Whatever it was, there wasn't any pain, more like something pushing on my stomach but never stopping, continuing inward until the job was complete. I kept my eyes tightly shut.

When I thought it was safe to look, I saw a clear plastic tube, about two feet long, sticking out of my stomach. There was a removable cap on its end and a grommet holding the tube to my bare skin. It all looked official, like it was meant to be there and had been for years.

"That should do it," he said. Simple as that, my percutaneous endoscopic gastrostomy, PEG for short, was in place. The nurse showed me how to coil the long tube and tape it to my stomach to avoid it showing too much under my shirt. Then, after I was dressed, "Maybe just leave it out, like this," she suggested as she pulled my shirttail out. Perhaps she thought I looked too stuffy and needed a more casual style for the days ahead. I'm not sure, but it was easier to manage with the tube coiled on my stomach.

That was it. I was the proud owner of a PEG. I would learn how to use it later. What could go in, what could not. How to keep it clean and all the other things the home health people would explain when it was time for me to put my PEG to work.

Chapter 15

Opportunity Costs Are Expensive

1982

The woman who answered the phones at the Key Man building told me a meat company in Cincinnati had called and wanted me to call back. She handed me a pink "While You Were Out" note with their 800 number written under the name. Having an 800 number in 1981 was a big deal; it meant they were prosperous and should be taken seriously. I returned the call. "Sure, I'll meet the flight, and we can go back to our office," I told the person making the arrangements.

Pierre Frozen Foods was a company who made preformed meat patties. Some had cheese mixed inside, others had spices, onions, and ethnic flavorings. They all had funny names the marketing people made up: Taco Grande, Gold Digger, Pizza Burger, various patty melts, and dippers with special sauce. It would be years before they made a plain frozen hamburger. Let others do that, they reasoned. Frozen hamburger patties were a commodity, and Pierre was "value-added."

Their newest item was a "Rib-B-Que." It had barbecue sauce mixed with pork, and then the mixture was pressed to make ridges on its top. It looked like a small slab of ribs. A Pierre Rib-B-Que with pickles on a bun, and you had a meal. Pierre had a long list of items with nice brochures, not just the red pocket salesman like Rotanelli. Yet Pierre had the same problem as the others: no business in the Carolinas. They would need Don and me to do the pioneering, and pioneer work is lonely, tiring, and often ends with an arrow in your back if the manufacturer goes off with another partner after the hard work is done. Pioneering means you present an item repeatedly and maybe sell something, but maybe not. Either way, it takes time, and time is a finite resource. If it's spent on this, there's none left for that. It's called opportunity cost, and it adds up. If an hour of our time was worth a certain amount, then the results needed to be worth that, plus a little extra for the hour to be profitable. Because every hour spent on Pierre would be an hour we were not spending on Prima, Rotanelli, Casa, and the other products that were now catching on and beginning to pay the bills.

While Stu Warshauer, the Pierre vice president who had flown in for the meeting was talking, I kept having the same thought: *Why should McIntyre and Company take all the risk and Pierre Frozen Foods end up with all the reward?* Steen didn't have any business for his baby back ribs when I found O'Brian's. Angelo's man-o-cot was unknown until two Scotch-Irish lads used the little red salesman. And Larry wasn't selling a single meatball in the Carolinas until Duff's got on board. We had taken the risk, and sure, we got a little, but the manufacturer got more. I'd always heard one hand washes the other, so why not share the wealth?

As politely as possible, I told Stu we would represent them, but only if they put some skin in the game: I asked for money to hire a

78

person—another sales rep.

I waited, holding my breath.

Stu finally spoke. He started by saying he was sorry the regional manager was sick and couldn't be here today, and decisions like this needed to follow the chain of command, and a lot of other words people in high positions use to keep from ever saying anything of value. Then he asked, "Let me get this straight. You find another sales rep to help you and Don, and Pierre picks up the tab for your new hire. Right?"

"That's it," I answered.

Then Stu wandered off into more details—benefits, vacation, sick days, sales reports. Gradually, we worked it out. Stu brought up a car. How would that work? I knew what I was paying for Don's leased Plymouth, so I offered to provide the car if they would add $100 a month for gas and oil.

Silence again.

Finally, Stu said, "Okay." I had no idea what I had done, but it worked. We had a new product line to sell, a free employee with gas and oil, and I was only out the lease payment for a Plymouth Horizon.

The next day I was at my desk, making calls, trying to find someone to hire, when a life insurance salesman knocked on my door. There was no way I wanted life insurance, but he was a pleasant man, older than I, so we talked. As he was leaving, he told me about his son and how he was having trouble finding a good job.

"Tell me more about your son, Mr. Campbell."

I met with Geoff Campbell. He and Don were the same age. Don had a food science degree from NC State; Geoff's degree was in business from Appalachian State in Boone. Geoff had a polite manner that fit what we were doing. Pierre wanted us focused on schools and selling the Rib-B-Que. Geoff was perfect. I brought him on board.

The school women loved him. It took three or four sales calls before he used their first names. They were always Miss or Miz, even after they ordered the Rib-B-Que. He shook hands; they gave hugs. Maybe they secretly hoped their children would grow up like him. I don't know, but it was working.

Geoff's Plymouth Horizon was white. Except it wasn't a Plymouth Horizon, it was a Dodge Omni. The dealer said they were the same, front-wheel-drive subcompact, four-door hatchbacks made by Chrysler. Take the name badge off, and you would never know. The lease payment was the same.

When the Pierre regional manager was in town, he and Geoff would make calls on schools. We sold more and more Rib-B-Ques and Pierre's other items with funny names. Pierre was happy. I was happy. The check for Geoff and his gas and oil came in each month, along with larger and larger commission checks. We were their "Broker of the Year" that first year and in many of the following years.

The Pierre National Account Manager showed the Rib-B-Que to McDonald's, and they also liked it, but renamed it the McRib. We didn't get paid for the McRib, but every time McDonald's featured McRib, our sales on Rib-B-Que skyrocketed.

Dianne Turner joined us. She lived in Raleigh. Now Dianne and Geoff were a team. She had the state's eastern half and down the South Carolina coast, and Geoff had the western half and Upstate. Pierre would have large sales meetings in Cincinnati, and we would drive up for the weekend.

I learned a valuable lesson the day I met Stu Warshauer. Manufacturers' pockets are deeper and their profit margins larger than small companies like mine. If McIntyre and Company was going to do all the work, take all the risks, and take time away from other activities, we deserved a larger slice of the pie. Otherwise, the manufacturer could simply appoint a broker, give them six months or so, and if they weren't happy with the results, move on to the next. Meanwhile, the broker who had "failed" was out the opportunity cost and had financed their own failure. So from then on, if the manufacturer didn't already have a base of business covering our investment, we weren't interested, no matter how rosy the picture they painted might be. It's a simple equation: risk equals reward. The greater the risk, the more the reward, and remember, a reward is like a reinforcement. If something positive, like profit, is added, the reward is the same as positive reinforcement. But if something is taken away, like time, and there is no gain, the reward is negative reinforcement.

Opportunity cost is a concept many don't understand. Its wisdom is grounded in the idea of finite versus infinite. Organizations develop large budgets to attract new customers when half the amount spent on caring for the customers they already have would produce twice the return.

In other words, expense items in a budget are each a cost that can be better measured when spent toward improving the satisfaction of current customers rather than attracting new customers who may or may not be satisfied once attracted.

Chapter 16

Culture Is Not a Slogan

2010

Things were moving nicely with the sale. From conversations with our overlapping clients, it was clear Todd was already making plans for the takeover. There may have been talk among our people, I'm not sure. But I was sure our people would stay in place. And that Todd would make a minimum of two monthly trips to Charlotte and attend any necessary meetings in my place. The combined companies' growth and our profitability would more than cover his investment.

But I was still nervous and kept playing "what if" games in my head. When I couldn't sleep, I'd go upstairs to my office and call Barry. We're the same age, but Barry does something most men our age don't: he plays ice hockey. And the only time his team can get a rink in the D.C. area is in the wee hours of the morning. Hockey gives him a release, what with all the daily compromise and negotiation he does. Aggressive, perhaps, but it works for him. Barry's twenty or thirty years older than his teammates, but no one notices, and no one cares because he can score.

So, Barry was at the office until one or two in the morning, the perfect time to speak to a nervous insomniac and then go off to lace up his skates and play hockey.

Todd visited Charlotte a few times to speak with Kristi and George, our two vice presidents. He seemed to like what he saw and heard, but never said much about the building I had renovated and added so many special features to six years before. Maybe it wasn't important to him, or perhaps everything was just so different from what he knew in Baltimore that he didn't know what to say. Or perhaps he was thinking of changes he would make. Or maybe he was only buying a balance sheet. But no one takes over anything without changing something.

Change takes on different names in any business: restructuring, reengineering, right-sizing, culture shift, total quality management, and strategic vision, but most have little effect. Maybe they lack any sense of urgency, or they don't have complete support from everyone in the organization, or there is a lack of overall vision. Leaders declare victory too soon, or change isn't in the company's culture. But the most significant cause of failure is the top executive's unwillingness to change their personal model or style along with the organization. In other words, they don't walk the walk, they only talk.

Culture is not something created with a few words in a catchy slogan. Culture is rooted deep within the day-to-day things that happen when no one is looking. It's the air the whole organization breathes, not just the purified air of executive conference rooms.

But all of that would be Todd's to learn, or not.

Chapter 17

Did I Spell It Right?

June 2010

Every big story contains countless smaller events, and while it's easy to be swept away by the macro, it's often the micro that holds the most wisdom. So it was with my eventual awareness of the metaphorical meaning of the mask. The hospital called to schedule a fitting for the mask I would need for radiation. It would be molded to fit my face with holes so I could breathe, along with four clamps, two on each side, to keep my head secured to the table. I would be on my back for each twenty-minute treatment, and my head couldn't move as much as a fraction of a millimeter.

When I arrived for the fitting, the technician held a clipboard with a list of rules. "Don't have any dental work done that would change the shape of your face. Don't grow any facial hair. Don't alter your hairstyle other than hair loss. Let us know if you become claustrophobic or anxious. There are drugs for that, or we can show you relaxation techniques." She then gave me a hospital gown and told me to strip down to my underwear, put on the gown, climb up on the table, and lie flat on my back. She excused herself but soon returned, holding a sheet of steaming plastic mesh in her right hand as she positioned me in the center of the table with the other. "This will feel warm, so relax and enjoy," the friendly technician said as she loosely draped the heated mesh over my face and scalp. I could breathe and see okay; I felt like I was getting a high-priced facial in a spa. Next, she gently stretched the mesh to conform to my head, face, and throat and secured the cooling mask to the table. She said she'd be back in fifteen minutes, and I should relax and think about the lovely summer we were having in Charlotte this year while the mesh cooled and hardened.

Well, it hadn't been a lovely summer for me, and I couldn't relax, so I lay on the metal table holding my breath. But that didn't work because I needed to breathe after a minute, and as my breath became more regular, I felt my body relax. Then, suddenly, I seemed to sink two inches into the table as the muscles in my butt cheeks collapsed as if all four tires on my car simultaneously went flat.

Maybe it had only been fifteen minutes, but it seemed like fifteen hours before she returned. And if I could barely hold it together for fifteen minutes for the mask to dry, how would I survive twenty minutes each day for seven weeks? Maybe I would need the drugs, or, better yet, some of her relaxation techniques.

She ran her fingers around the edges and over my face, then used a Sharpie to put a small mark over my right collar bone and a line on the mask directly across from her mark on my skin. Unsnapping the mask, she showed me how the line on the mask would line up with the mark on my neck to assure the mask was positioned correctly each day. "Don't worry, the dot won't come off when you shower," she said. "And if it does fade, I'll darken it."

As I was sitting on the edge of the table, ready to get down, she wrote "McIntyre" across its forehead. "Did I spell it right?" she asked.

I smiled and told her it was fine. I don't remember much about the room, just that it was dark and cold, and although she was friendly, it wasn't the sort of place I'd want to hang out all day.

She said to come back at the same time tomorrow, and Dr. Warlick and his associates would mark my new mask for the best treatment plan assuring that the computer-controlled laser hit each of the cancer spots, avoiding the healthy areas on my head and neck. The next day Dr. Warlick and his staff used a similar marker to put dots and lines on the mask, making it look like a poster of acupuncture points to meridian channels. Or as if some tattoo artist had gotten carried away with his work on a Saturday night.

Later that day, with the computer now programmed, we did a dry run, where they checked where each beam would hit without the radiation turned on.

Everything was perfect, they said, and the mask with my name on its forehead would stay at the Presbyterian Cancer Center for me to use each day for the next seven weeks.

Names on each mask are essential; they assure that each patient gets the mask custom-made for them. The name also lets the technician know who's behind the mask, and while I'm sure they know, even without the name, the writing identifies the person.

I've now had a chance to think about masks and wonder if we all don't wear disguises from time to time. Not a mask with our name written across the forehead, that would make it too easy, but a mask of some sort that hides our deeper identity. I certainly did and still do. I had different clothing for different occasions and even drove different cars to different places. Those "masks" disguise my outside, but there were, and are, masks that also hide my inside. Masks like, "Never let them see you sweat," so you will appear brave and resourceful. Or, "Real men don't cry." What does that mean? Of course men cry. Or how "vulnerability is a weakness." But if vulnerability is about uncertainty, risk, or emotional exposure, it's not a weakness but a strength.

And perhaps when the day comes where the mask comes off for the last time, I can walk away a changed person, free from its protection. Perhaps the mask is like the scene in Charles Dickens's *A Christmas Carol* when Ebenezer Scrooge reads his name on the tombstone in the graveyard and understands that things can change and life can be better if we live without masks, living by the moralizing lessons of past, present, and future.

Chapter 18

The Best Aid for Good Sleep Is Good People

June 2010

It was now time for radiation. Each morning, a bit before ten, I'd pull my black Audi sedan up to the main entrance of Presbyterian, hop out, and toss my keys to the smiling attendant, whose name I used to know but now have sadly forgotten.

"Mornin', Boss. I'll keep it close."

"Thanks!" I said to a smiling face that would continue to brighten my days for the next seven weeks.

I'd walk confidently in the front door, lengthening my stride as I walked down the crowded hallway, past the meditation courtyard and coffee kiosk. I'd inhale, making myself taller, and then slowly exhale, allowing myself to hold onto my newfound height. I'd sweep past the drug store, enter the cancer wing, and finally arrive at the crowded waiting room.

I would look around for anyone I knew, but that was unlikely. Not that people I knew didn't get cancer, just that the people who came to our city hospital to receive care came from fifteen counties in two states.

So, I would look at the mix of people rather than thumb through a magazine. Not staring, just a quick head-to-toe and then move on, later choosing only one to think about, but not stare at.

There was a young woman battling brain cancer with a zig-zag pattern of staples on her shaved head and another woman wearing a loose tank top whose right side of her chest looked like carved-out red scar tissue while the left side looked normal. What were these women thinking? I'm sure they were worried. Others might have problems at work or finances or housing or transportation concerns in addition to their cancer.

I knew each cancer was different, but what were the other differences? What time did they need to be on the road to get here, and when would they be home? What was their life like before the diagnosis, and how had it now changed? How was this affecting their relationships with loved ones? Were they getting support, or did cancer drive a wedge between them? The questions helped me understand that, while we looked different, had different backgrounds and jobs, with various family makeups, the one thing we all had in common was our search for hope.

I sat silently and waited for the nurse to step in and call, "Charles?"

One week of treatment down, six to go. This wasn't too bad. I'd made the right choice; this would be over soon. We'd have a big party, give Todd a set of keys to the building, I'd say my goodbyes, and ride off into the sunset.

Todd had asked to spend even more time with Kristi and George two weeks before, so I agreed to pick him up at the airport that Tuesday and bring him back to the office. I'd told Kristi and George to put it on their calendars so they could get to know the new owner better.

It was a little past noon when Todd walked out of the airport, spotted my car, tossed his briefcase in the back, and got in. I'd had radiation that morning, but the slight redness was on my left, and he was on my right. At first, there was some small talk as I pointed out Charlotte landmarks and told him about the light rail and how convenient it made travel to Uptown, but he quickly turned the conversation to Kristi and George. How long had they been with me? What were their backgrounds and current roles? Todd wanted to know what each did before he spoke to them.

None of his questions surprised me; I would have asked the same. It was common knowledge that the two of them, along with Laura Bates, ran McIntyre*Sales*. I was needed now and then but not often, and it was probably unsolvable if a problem had reached me. I'd worked my way out of a job, and that was the way I wanted it. I'd learned long ago that having good people was the best prescription for a good night's sleep.

As Todd got settled in the conference room, I said I'd tell Kristi and George he was ready, and then, if he didn't mind, I had some phone calls to return.

No one in the office had noticed the redness on my neck from radiation, and if they had, they didn't say anything to me. And as for me being away so much and people like Todd visiting, that was just part of who we had become now that we had grown so large. Everyone had enough to keep them busy without worrying about me.

George drove Kristi and Todd to lunch. I stayed behind. When they finally returned, it was time to head to the airport, so Todd stuck his head in my door to say goodbye, and asked Kristi for a ride to the airport.

When Kristi returned, I walked out my door and down the hall to hers. I went in and closed the door. "So, how did it go? What did y'all talk about?"

I thought she was a bit vague, but she said it went well. Todd had asked about her. Was she happy in her job, and did she plan to stay? Kristi and George had been part of the conversations with Bill Mason, the consultant from Boston, when we decided who to partner with, so she knew her role would change, but no one ever knows how much.

Kristi and I had worked together for years. She had started with no background in the food business and was now known throughout the industry as someone who got things done. I remember our first interview and the two words I wrote in the margin of her resumé: "Hard worker."

Kristi was raised in South Burlington, Vermont, graduated from the University of Vermont, and, like everything else I've learned about Vermonters, was more about performance than flair. Kristi valued people, not by who they were, but by what they got done. She was honest, down-to-earth, and didn't do "spin." It was okay with Kristi to say a glass was half full, just don't say it was full when any fool could see it was empty. She had been incredibly loyal all these years, and now she was being "traded" to Todd. Not even traded, really; more "sold."

Sure, she and George had agreed to the sale. They would be well compensated, and Todd promised lifetime employment contracts, but she had to feel everything was different somehow.

Did George feel the same? George was from Winston-Salem with his MBA from Appalachian State. He'd been a buyer at S & D Coffee before starting with us in sales. He was personable, got along with everyone, and continued to take on more and more responsibility. He, too, was being "sold," and maybe that alone is reason enough to make one wonder who, or what, they should be loyal to.

Chapter 19

Everyone's an Expert

Summer 2010

There was a block of three hours on my calendar with the word CHEMO scrawled across at an angle. There were another two later in the summer. I wasn't looking forward to any of them, except maybe the last, when it would be over.

Dr. Favaro, my medical oncologist, knew my hearing was not good and wanted another test as a baseline. "Cisplatin will only make your hearing worse, Bruce, so get it tested again before we start. That way we'll know how much damage the chemo does."

I'd been wearing small hearing aids for years, although I didn't wear them all the time. I thought my hearing was good enough, and I'd act like I understood when I really didn't. Hearing aids aren't like reading glasses. If you ask, people will repeat what they said, but newspaper print won't get larger just because you squint.

Joyce had said a few years back, "Bruce, you just have to do something about your hearing; you're missing too much of what the kids and I say." I had asked around and was told that if I wanted a good audiologist, I wanted Janne Mack at Randolph Audiology, so I made an appointment.

Janne put me in a sealed room, like a freezer in the back of a restaurant, but this one was carpeted and had a comfortable chair. It was nice, but I still felt locked up. Janne played noises of birds chirping at sunrise, frogs croaking at night, and other sounds, then asked me what they were. She said a series of words, "hot dog, apple pie, baseball," having me repeat each. Then came the beeps, and I had to press a button when I heard one. Sometimes, I pressed the button anyway if I felt it had been too long since the last beep.

When we finished, Janne showed me some graphs with lines that didn't match "normal," whatever normal was, and told me I needed hearing aids. She ordered some little ones she said folks wouldn't notice. When they arrived, Janne showed me how to put the red one in my right ear (it was the worst, she said) and the blue in my left. "You hear better on your left, Bruce." I thanked her and thought how at least getting them in the proper ear would be easy.

Several years later, I needed a checkup, but Janne had left the practice, so I saw Wade Kirkland. He was from Florida and worshipped the Gators; he even had one tattooed on his ankle, but he didn't let it show in the office. He had a good way with patients, especially the older ones, as most of us are. In addition to ears, Wade was an expert on eastern bluebirds and how they were making a comeback in North Carolina, thanks to people like him who built nest boxes and firmly mounted them in sunny, open areas.

I've noticed over the years that when someone is good at their job, they are also good at another. Talent isn't evenly distributed, I'm afraid. And the better I get to know these people, the more of their skills I discover. They are called polymaths, and their knowledge spans many subjects, so they can draw on complex bodies of knowledge to solve specific problems. One such polymath was Leonardo da Vinci. Best known for painting the *Mona Lisa*, he was also an architect, hydraulic engineer, and sculptor. Polymaths like da Vinci take the skills from one trade and put them to work in another. I'm not saying Wade was as good as Leonardo or that being an expert on eastern bluebirds is the same as ushering in the Italian Renaissance, but I am saying Wade was damn good.

Wade showed me new hearing aids that fit behind my ears, not just inside. I thought they were too large, but I liked the little wire that came over the top of my ear. "Wade, I can't wear big things like these behind each ear. People will think I'm deaf."

Wade leaned back in his chair, folded his hands over his stomach the way people often do when they're being thoughtful, and in a sympathetic voice that sounded like my mother when she tried not to hurt my feelings, said, "Bruce, everyone knows you're deaf."

When people with bad eyesight need to read, they put on glasses. If they can't walk, they use a wheelchair. So why hide hearing loss? I was hiding it like I was ashamed of it. And when I did that, I withdrew and avoided groups and crowded rooms. Even a large family meal wasn't fun any longer. I had once been part of the smiles and laughter, but now I was quiet, not keeping up. Wade was right, people did know and I needed to stop hiding it. I bought the larger model that went behind my ears.

But the fatigue of the radiation treatments, unfortunately, made things even worse. I would leave my hearing aids at home some days, which wasn't good. I promised myself that when this was over, I'd keep up with the technology and never be without them again.

I was glad I got the baseline test Dr. Favaro wanted. At least now I knew where I stood. Getting old is lousy enough. No need to be old *and* deaf.

Chapter 20

Cocktails Pack a Wallop

Monday, June 14

I was scheduled for chemo on Monday morning, so Dr. Warlick had moved my radiation to the afternoon for that day. The chemo treatments were not at Presbyterian Hospital but at Oncology Specialists of Charlotte on Randolph Road, across from the Mint Museum.

Dr. Justin Favaro's office looked like Dr. Warlick's, except the diplomas read MD and PhD from the Medical University of South Carolina, training at the University of Texas Southwestern Medical Center, and fellowship training at Duke University Medical Center. His office was not far from the hospital and our home. Nothing in Charlotte is far if you start in the right spot.

There was an entirely different feel to chemotherapy treatments. Radiation was dark, flat on my back with my head clamped to a cold table, and there were eerie sounds as the machine spun around. I was alone. But chemotherapy was light and bright, and I could stretch out in a comfortable recliner with cupholders. There were other people around, each in a recliner like mine. We could talk or not. Flip through magazines or bring a book. Plug in earbuds for music or watch TV.

There were Nabs and soft drinks. Nabs are flavored crackers with a tasty filling, packed six to a package in cellophane. But of course, they have gluten, so I'd pass on the Nabs.

And I could go to the bathroom—if I was careful with the rolling IV pole.

Radiation is faster. Twenty minutes. Chemo is three hours. Although being alone in the dark makes the time seem the other way around.

The other difference is how radiation builds over time, while the cocktails they serve at chemo kick in fast and then taper.

I was already feeling the effects of the chemo cocktail by the afternoon before radiation. It was like I'd been in a fight that didn't end well. I was sick and wanted to throw up but couldn't, even after forcing my fingers down my swelling throat. My head was pounding.

Whatever Dr. Favaro put in my IV that morning was not to my liking, and I wasn't looking forward to another. Yet I still had radiation in the afternoon.

I couldn't wait for bedtime.

Chapter 21

Fishing Poles Make Good Therapy

Summer 2010

Tuesday morning's schedule called for Men's Bible Class, but 7:15 a.m. came and went, and I was still in bed. I was starting to understand how some things on my calendar were more urgent than others. I loved Von Clemans and the wisdom he brought to our group of a dozen or so each Tuesday. We would study a different book of the Bible, with Von helping us understand not only the words but also the people and their ancient culture. So while Men's Bible was important, a few more hours of sleep was urgent. Besides, it was all I could do to make radiation at ten o'clock sharp.

The rest of that week was spent looking forward to Saturday when there would be no treatments, and K.B. and I had plans. Our son was taking me fishing.

K.B. is a far better fisherman than his dad, perhaps more patient, like both sets of grandparents. Plus, he had a new boat he was excited to show me. He planned to pick me up early Saturday morning and then, boat in tow, drive out Highway 16 to Mountain Island Lake.

K.B. and I fished that lake thirty years ago when he was only nine, and we spent the entire morning on the bank of the Catawba River in Gaston County waiting for the fish to come to us. But this Saturday, we'd go to them. Boats, even small ones, are another privilege I hadn't thought about until I did.

It was a beautiful Saturday morning with high scattered clouds and a gentle breeze. By nine, it was already close to 80 degrees. I layered more sunscreen on my white legs. I had on the Chaco sandals I'd worn trout fishing last summer, shorts, and my usual untucked shirt with a blue St. Louis Cardinals cap. K.B. wore camo cargo shorts, a black T-shirt that looked too small (or maybe his deltoids were more pronounced than I remembered), wrap-around sunglasses, and a floppy hat with a string under his chin. He'd packed a cooler with drinks and snacks, but I didn't have any. My throat was already closing down.

I stood in the ankle-deep water at the end of the ramp to help as K.B. backed his fourteen-foot sport-fisherman into the lake, but my help wasn't needed. He had everything under control. He floated the boat off its trailer, got in, lowered the forty-horsepower Yamaha, and maneuvered the boat next to the dock. He motioned me to get in as he parked the car and trailer in the lot.

We caught a few and threw them back. Mostly we talked about his family, how Ellie and James were doing in school, and what he and Mary Beth had planned for next weekend. Along with some talk about his new job, just the kinds of things fathers and sons have always talked about. He never mentioned my cancer. I thought he might, but I'm glad he didn't. Sometimes it's best to take a break.

Chapter 22

Zero-Sum Thinking Only Builds Walls

Summer 2010

There was a problem with the sale. Todd had run some numbers, and the estimated cost of the business—plus the cost of the building—might be more than his banker would go for.

"But the building isn't part of the deal. Todd knows that," I struggled to say in my now fading voice.

"I know," Barry replied, "I think they're trying to get us to come off the price. Let's make it clear that they will lease the building, so it's a deductible business expense. The only thing they're buying is the business. Okay?"

A few days later, Barry called. He had them settled down, but the attorney had reviewed the accounts payable and was concerned about the amount of the rent.

The rent could be reduced, I thought. After all, I owned the LLC that owned the building, and the lease was somewhat skewed in my favor. I'd paid off the loan from the bank, so why not? Why be greedy?

"Let me write up a new lease," Barry said. "I'll lower the rent by

10 percent but keep the original term. The new lease will be fifteen years, not down to the remaining eight like it is now. I'll keep the same language as before. They should be happy with the lower price and not get too caught up in the longer term."

When I built the building and set up the company the business would lease it from, there needed to be a lease. Many leases are triple net, where the tenant pays not just rent and utilities but also promises to pay all the property's expenses, including real estate taxes, building insurance, and maintenance. I then added a fourth "net," which is not generally in a lease. The final net, or quad net, said that even if the building cracked in half, an unusual occurrence to be sure, it would be the tenant who paid to put it back together, not me. Of course, I owned both the company that was the lessee and the company that was the lessor, but that's just business. It's not illegal or tricky, just one of the many things I was learning about how the system favors those "with" more than those "without."

Barry's plan was the perfect win-win.

I'd seen too many deals ruined by zero-sum thinking, where one person needed to win at all costs without giving an inch. I wanted to be fair and knew any good deal had compromise at its core. The best definition of compromise was a deal both sides could live with while neither side was fully happy.

Summer 2010

I wasn't as cheerful pulling into the circle in front of Presbyterian as I was three weeks before. I still acted like I was okay. I chatted with the attendant, but my walk into the hospital was now more a slow shuffle than a confident stride. I had found I needed to leave home five minutes earlier so I wouldn't be late for my ten o'clock sharp. Not that traffic was slow, just my walk.

Some mornings when I checked in, they sent me directly to the radiation waiting room, and other mornings I saw Dr. Warlick. This was a Dr. Warlick morning. His nurse had me step on the scale. "Not good," she said. I was down seven pounds. "Don't get behind the eight ball."

Did she shoot pool growing up? I did, and being behind the eight ball meant I was not in the best position to win.

Dr. Warlick came in, looked at the nurse's number on the chart, and then to me. "I don't like this. You're down too much. Did you see the nutritionist like I told you?"

Yes, I said, and I was doing what she said, mostly, but things didn't taste right, they seemed spicier than usual, and everything was hard to swallow.

No, I hadn't used the PEG tube yet because, well, I just thought I didn't need it yet, but the home health nurse showed me when he visited a while back, and yes, I had the eight-ounce cans he'd brought.

Radiation burns—that's how the bad cells get killed. But it also kills good cells, and the 10,000 taste buds on my tongue were quickly being destroyed. The tissue in my throat was angry, inflamed, and swollen, and the madder it got, the more it puffed up and made it impossible for anything to get by.

Mealtimes were about to change.

Chapter 23

Into the Hundred Acre Wood

Summer 2010

Barry and I talked when I had the strength. He'd sent revisions to the purchase agreement that I would agree with. Todd's lawyer was on board; at least that part was smooth.

But the sale only included intangible assets (existing contracts, customer list, goodwill, things like that), so "cash on hand" and other tangibles were not part of the deal. The furniture, fixtures, and equipment (FF&E), down to each paper clip, needed to be replaced or purchased by Todd. He wouldn't like it, but Barry would talk to Todd's lawyer.

Joyce was now driving me to the hospital for the ten o'clock sharp. With lunch in my small U.S. Foodservice bag, I'd move slowly past the wheelchairs in the lobby, down the hall, and into the radiation waiting room. I was now just another invisible old man making his way down the hall, not the puffed-up artificial bundle of radiance I was a few weeks before.

I passed the intersection where, in early May, I'd unexpectedly run into Dr. Charles Edwards after I'd finished giving the anesthesiologist my list of medications before he put me into a deep sleep for Dr. Harley to examine the lump. Moving slowing forward, I wondered if Dr. Edwards would recognize me today. Chuck was a neighbor from our old street; we often visited, either walking in the neighborhood or at parties. He was a cardiovascular surgeon and had several interns in tow that morning as they moved quickly down the corridor, white coattails trying to keep up. Caregivers walk with a purpose; it's their job, and the old and infirm stand aside.

Chuck had stopped, we had talked, he asked after Joyce and me after Mary, and then he had asked why I was there. He put his hand on the left side of my neck, feeling the lump. "Yes, better get that checked. Who's doing it?" I told him. He nodded, "Harley's a good man; let me know what he finds." With that, he and his students continued their rounds.

But now, dejected, a shadow of my former self, I continued to the radiation waiting room and sat quietly.

"Charles?"

Silently, I followed her to the dressing room like Eeyore, head down, eyes half-closed, trustingly following Christopher Robin into the Hundred Acre Wood on a gray winter day.

She handed me a gown. Barefoot and wearing only the hospital gown over my loose-fitting white boxers, I climbed up on the table as she gave me the special mouthpiece the technician had made to hold my jaw in proper alignment for the powerful beams that needed to hit the same target, again and again, until it was destroyed, then snapped down the "McIntyre" mask.

"All set?" she asked.

I gave her the standard thumbs-up and closed my eyes. It would be over soon, I told myself, remembering to breathe.

When the lights came on, she stepped from behind the partition, unsnapped my mask, and had me spit the mouthpiece into a tissue.

I got dressed, and as I walked into the hall, I heard her say, "Same time tomorrow." I nodded and kept walking. One foot, then the next, bent over as if guided only by my loose-fitting loafers.

I followed each brown shoe past the coffee kiosk, across to the elevators, and then punched three. The infusion center would be my home for the rest of the day. I wasn't even at the halfway point, and already the test showed I needed saline and potassium flowing into my system to replace the hydration being taken away by the radiation. What would it be like at the end?

"It would have been easier if they'd put in a port at the start," the nurse said, searching for a vein.

I'd learned about veins: how they got small, rolled over, blown, and hid when they'd been stuck too many times. The nurses had a rule that they'd step aside and let someone else try if they couldn't get the IV started after three tries. It wasn't long before I knew the name of every nurse in infusion.

After I was hooked up and comfortably settled in the recliner, I opened my yellow bag and had lunch. Always the same: two slices of ham rolled around mozzarella sticks with a mild sauce. A pouch of apple sauce or tapioca pudding, and Gatorade. It's the same convenient gluten-free lunch I'd perfected over my years of helping build Habitat for Humanity homes. But now, my healthy lunch was getting harder to finish, harder to swallow. I was leaving too much in the yellow bag each day. Joyce suggested that if I was going to keep my weight up, I should add a can of nutrition and a syringe with lunch. From then on, I would pour the Carnation Very High Calorie drink into a plastic cup, then fill the syringe, and pump the liquid into my gut. It took four full syringes to finish one can. It had taken me a while to learn the routine, there were messes at first, but everything is easy once you know how. The process was not a pleasant sight, but hospitals don't always do pleasant.

Finishing lunch and relaxing in the recliner as the IV continued to flow into my vein, I often thought about Habitat for Humanity and the lessons I learned volunteering with them. Not just how to set a square and plumb wall, but how to work beside the new homeowner as they carefully hammer each nail.

Last summer, one of my golf buddies asked about my Saturdays and why so many were spent building homes to be given away. I was shocked. Given away? I quickly told my friend how Habitat homeowners must qualify for a mortgage, buy the house, and pay taxes, just like everyone else.

When we reached the next hole, my friend said he didn't know about the homes being sold and was glad I told him. I started to tell him the number of homes built in Charlotte over the years, but then decided to tell him about Judy and Fred. I had gotten to know them the summer before and it was the first home either of their families had ever owned. I told him how proud I was to have been part of their dream. They were happy their two children had a quiet place to do homework. Judy was planning a garden where she would grow tomatoes, onions, and radishes, maybe even some rutabagas for Fred. He liked rutabagas with onions and bacon for supper on a Saturday. They had rescued a puppy, and the family now walked together in the neighborhood park.

When we finished our round, my friend asked if he could join me the next time I went. "Sure," I said. Maybe it was the story of Judy and Fred that got him interested, I don't know. I only know people tire of numbers long before they tire of stories.

I sat with my Blackberry communicating with my unknowing (I hoped) world at work, not making calls because of my croaky voice and sore throat. But also, so that none of the alarms, public address announcements, rattling trolleys, or staff conversations would be heard in the background.

There was no need for my personal life to get mixed into the business, especially not the sale. The balance shifts when one side is injured.

Later that afternoon, IV disconnected, I called Joyce for a ride home.

Chapter 24

The Day the Phone Didn't Ring

Winter 1985

I'd always thought the business would work. I was certain. So I kept acting that way and hoped reality would show up. The most significant step of all is believing what you want is possible. And sometimes that involves making your own luck happen.

A light rain was falling when I headed out Brookshire Boulevard for my morning appointment; it looked like it might turn to snow later in the day. I had given myself extra time because of the weather and was now early, but not by much when I entered the parking lot of Biggers Brothers, Inc., the largest foodservice distributor in the Carolinas. "Better early than late," I said to no one as I looked for a place to park.

With my sample case in one hand, I used the other to negotiate the turnstile with its head-to-toe metal spokes. Over the years, so many feet had walked through the narrow opening they had worn a trench. And now the rain had turned the trench into a donut-shaped lake. Was the turnstile designed to keep people from walking off with a case of rib eyes or a crate of oranges? I wasn't sure, but it was a nuisance if you had anything in your hands.

I walked up the stairs and into the lobby. The receptionist said Tom Parrot, or "Mouse," as everyone called him, was on the phone. She'd let him know I was here when he was free, so I should have a seat. It had taken me weeks to arrange the appointment with the seafood buyer, and I was nervous, so I told her that was fine; I wasn't in a hurry.

It was hard enough to get Mouse on the phone, let alone arrange an appointment. I'd been selling him fish, but not as much as I could or wanted, and while we had met several times, most of our discussions were by phone. I liked face-to-face better.

Should I sit on the leather sofa or on one of the chairs? Either way, I'd sink to the floor in the old, overstuffed furniture. Everything in the lobby was in different shades of brown, even the vinyl floor. Old plaques, a sales award for selling the most frozen peas, and a faded picture of delivery vans hung on the walls in no particular order. None level.

Howard Biggers had passed away, but his brother, George, still came in to pick up his check each week and played golf at the country club the rest of the time.

I chose the only straight-back wooden chair and was thumbing through out-of-date issues of *Frozen Food Age*, when Howard Biggers Jr. walked through. He had on a French-cuffed shirt with an expensive silk tie. Howard Jr. had grown up in the business and now was its president. We had met a few times, but not many; I thought his limp was worse today, perhaps because of the cold rain. The limp was from a car crash when he was young. He and a friend tried to race their cars backward the twenty miles to Davidson. His leg was still in a cast when he married his wife. There were different stories about that race, and although I would have many chances over the years, I never asked which one was true.

"Hello, young man," Mr. Biggers said. "Who you waitin' to see?" If Howard Jr. didn't remember a name, or even if he did, it was easier to say, "young man." Less to remember.

The receptionist answered his question, saying I was there to see Mouse and that she was waiting for him to get off the phone. Before answering machines and voicemail, the only thing to do was wait, then try later. "Go on up, young man. You know where his office is. We can't have good salesmen sitting around. There's no money in that."

"Thanks, Mr. Biggers," I said as I grabbed my sample case, headed up the stairs to the second floor, and walked down the hall past the large corner office with plate-glass windows overlooking the warehouse floor.

Mouse's office was small, with no windows, and if a professional basketball player stood against a wall and stretched out his arms, he could almost touch the corners. The desk came out from the wall, across from the door, at a right angle. Two guest chairs sat in front of his desk, so close a visitor's knees came to their chest. There was room for one vertical file cabinet in the corner, with four drawers. There were shelves on the wall up behind his head.

Mouse motioned for me to sit down while he finished his phone conversation. I slid into the chair next to the wall and waited for him to finish. No sooner had he placed the receiver in the cradle, when it rang again.

Finally, after several minutes, there was a pause in the calls. We said our hellos. I thanked him for taking time to see me and told him how much I appreciated the truckload orders of flounder he placed each week. I asked if he was getting the seafood quotes I was mailing, and he said he was. "Yes, they're right here. Let me get them."

A plan popped into my head as he stood and turned to open the bottom file drawer.

The plain black phone with no buttons, only a dial, sat directly in front of me. I pushed down on the small plastic clip and unplugged the phone.

That was fast, and with time to spare! I leaned back and turned my body to reach for some papers in my case.

"Here they are," he said slowly as he stood and turned to face me. "Oh, and by the way, I like the little mice you put inside each envelope. They're all up there. See?" He pointed to the eleven wooden mice with fake leather ears and tails, not much larger than his thumb. I'd found them when I stopped for gas near Florence one fall evening when I was on my way home after a full day of making sales calls. They were in a big bushel basket marked fifteen cents each or ten for a dollar. I'd given the lady two bucks, so I still had almost half my supply.

I remember thinking how plain my little wood mice looked, arranged in their tight huddle on the shelf surrounded by the more imposing mice of crystal and brass. Were my little mice nervous, like me, or were they carefully planning their next move?

We talked on. Maybe we could go to the International Seafood Show in Boston next year. We'd learn about different species from around the world. We both knew that while folks in the Carolinas were raised on flounder, perch, and catfish, other parts of the world enjoyed orange roughy, Atlantic cod, monkfish, and more. Anyone who could successfully introduce something new was a hero, and we both liked that idea.

Mouse wanted to know more about the Sankyo label flounder I was selling him. Were the flounder really caught on the George's Banks, off Canada, then loaded on large ships and sent through the Panama Channel, across the Pacific to Korea to be processed, then returned to Boston to be sold in the Carolinas? And all for five cents a pound less than Canada's most enormous fish company?

"Yes, I met with Mr. Wong, the plant's owner. We needed an interpreter, but that's how it works. Maybe I can arrange a meeting with him in Boston, and we can all have dinner at Jimmy's Harborside on the pier." I wish I'd cared more about the environment and over-fishing then, but I was a businessman making a nickel a pound on flounder. Money changes our worldview too often, I fear.

Mouse said it was strange the phone hadn't rung. I agreed.

Would I have unplugged the phone when I was calling on Safeway Headquarters? Would I have been that brave? Or was it the relationship I'd developed with Mouse? He bought truckloads of flounder, and I sent little mice in the mail. This was the kind of selling I enjoyed. Transactions follow if relationships are strong.

We went over the sheets he'd pulled from the file. He was happy to see all the different items, saying he'd not had time to study them. He smiled at the little drawings of fish our receptionist Nora Albright put on the weekly mailer. The perch would tell about themselves, where they came from, what kinds of water they favored, and why they were the best, all in little dialogue balloons that let the reader understand fish-talk. They were cute, he said. I thanked him and told him I would be sure to tell Nora when I got back to the office. Nora Albright was the most gifted cartoonist I've ever known.

My time was up. I thanked him again, then stood and reached for the cord.

"Maybe it's this," I said, grinning like Lewis Carroll's Cheshire cat, as I held up the black cord, then plugged in his phone.

It rang immediately.

Mouse answered and began talking, but as he spoke into the mouthpiece, we smiled at each other as he tilted his head to the left, holding the receiver to his shoulder, winked, and gave me a thumbs-up.

All good relationships have some unseen or un-talked-about anchor holding them together. For Mouse and me, it was the day the phone didn't ring.

Chapter 25

My Way

1985–2003

Over the years, more manufacturers were added to our list of Clients, either because they found us or we found them. Each new Client offered us more to sell to even more Customers. This meant I needed more people, both those to sell and those to keep the process flowing. I had built a business, and it was prospering. I was happy—and proud.

Things were looking good at the bank. The prime rate kept falling, yet was still high, and I now understood what Bootie thought I knew from the start: a credit line is like a revolving door, except for money, instead of people. The money goes out, then returns, so it can go out again, spinning around. After the money's outside for a while, it comes back in the same door, bringing extra money, called interest. My line of credit loan gave me more flexibility as I could use the money when needed and repay it when I could. Still, unlike a home loan with a long time to repay and a set interest rate, the interest on my line of credit changed as often as the Fed adjusted the rate banks charged each other for overnight lending. It's complicated, but such is the world of banking when you're on the other side of the revolving door.

Joel Tevebaugh was no longer designing apartment guides but had started his own graphic design firm. We met to discuss our logo. I thought the original looked tired, so I asked Joel for ideas. We talked about designs and agreed on a few points. I wanted to keep "and Company" spelled out and didn't want an ampersand sign or the word *company* abbreviated.

Joel suggested two logos, one formal and one informal. The formal, or traditional logo, would be on one line and look better at the top of our stationery, while the simpler logo would stack the three words and look better as a monogram. The main thing I wanted was a symbol, a simple mark, not words, just something people would see and instantly identify with McIntyre and Company.

McDonald's had golden arches symbolizing stability and consistency. Love 'em or hate 'em, you always know what you're getting at McDonald's. And Nestlé, the world's largest food and beverage producer, had their mother bird feeding her hungry chicks. Procter & Gamble's moon and stars went back to their beginning when the young company shipped soap on river barges and workers put a crude cross-mark on each case, later adding stars.

I had thought about ours for months. Even when I should have been listening to the sermon on Sundays, I would scratch ideas on the back of the bulletin. One Sunday, I hit on the idea of a clover. Not a three-leaf clover like a shamrock, but a clover with four leaves that would stand for faith, hope, love, and luck. I knew how important the first three were, but I also knew we would need the fourth.

Joel agreed, and that clover became our identifying symbol. From then on, the clover was on everything. Even our lapel pins.

We added more rooms at the Key Man Building, but by 1984, it was time to move. Some suggested we find an old house, spruce it up, and turn it into an office. It was a popular idea, and many found it attractive, but I wasn't sure. An old house just didn't look right to me. Houses looked static, and we were on the move.

There was space at 1600 East Morehead Street. More professional than the Key Man Building, and Milton Silver, the building's owner, would make the changes I wanted, so we soon reached an agreement. He added a small dry kitchen with space for freezers to store samples. Plus, he agreed to have his workers expose the brick on the long, windowed wall, then place electrical and phone outlets so desks could be positioned for the open-office environment I wanted. The new carpet and paint he added made everything look fresh, and framing the exposed support poles and covering the new columns with mirrors added the up-to-date look I was after. I was happy with the changes he made.

My desk was the last on the right, no different than the other seven along the wall. We would enlarge that space over the years, but it never had a real kitchen. It would be ten years before we got what we needed. Milton tried to make a kitchen work, but range hoods and other requirements for a commercial kitchen were impractical in his building.

There was space near the airport, off Freedom Drive at 2211 Executive Street. Anne Johnson, the leasing agent, could give us everything we needed. Her contractor, Bill Roper, could do the upfits, and we'd be set. We'd have a full commercial kitchen, a walk-in freezer and cooler, a conference room, storage, a private office (people said I needed that), and customer service and accounting space.

Motorists could see our large sign with its four-leaf clover over the name as they traveled I-85, and not that we were trying to attract them, but it was rewarding for our customers and others to see our name on a modern brick office. The McIntyre name plus "and Company" in large letters on a large building gave me a sense of pride and belonging.

I was certain a business could be built, and I was certain I could build it myself, without an equity partner. If I'd had a theme song (which I didn't), it would have been Frank Sinatra's "My Way." The lyrics are about biting off more than you can chew, eating it up, and spitting it out. About taking the blows and doing it my way.

All brave words, yet there was always more fear than bravado. It's hard not to have some inner nagging fear when you're close to the edge and the ground you think is solid could give way any moment. But I also know it was more fun and cheaper to only build one private office and have one name on the sign.

Chapter 26

Damaged Goods Never Fetch Full Price

May 26, 2010

On Wednesday morning, May 26, I met with Kristi and George. It had been a few weeks since I last updated them on the progress with Todd. I filled in the details of how Todd was worried that maybe he had taken on too much, but how Barry had assured him the sale was only for the business and not the building and how I had reduced the rent by 10 percent. And how Todd now seemed fine.

In previous meetings, we had talked through each detail. Back when we were exploring the idea of their being minority partners in the LLC that would own the building, they learned it would require a second mortgage on their homes. They had met with our accountant to discuss the plan, but neither seemed interested in the idea. They were each getting cash settlements on the stock gifted them over the years, as well as lifetime employment contracts Todd had offered. They both seemed to feel that having Todd own the company was the best and safest choice for them financially.

The lifetime employment contracts were something I hadn't thought of, and those alone were worth their weight in gold in our rapidly changing industry.

They asked how my treatments were going. I had told them, plus Laura Bates, but there was no need for anyone else to know. It was none of their business, and there was plenty for everyone to do without worrying about me. They asked if they were painful and if I was able to sleep at night. I assured them I was okay and that it would all be over and done soon. Just a speed bump, I called it. I hadn't wanted them to worry, so I always made my treatment seem minor.

Laura knew about my cancer, but not the sale, while Kristi and George knew about both. Two weeks later, I would tell Laura about the sale. Maybe she already knew, it's hard to say, but she was worried. I tried to assure her everything would be fine, just as I continued to assure myself.

And the thing I had stressed more than once was the importance of Todd not knowing about my cancer because he certainly wouldn't pay any more; and if anything, he'd insist on paying less.

Chapter 27

Think Beyond Bitter and Sweet

June 2010

My daughter Laura started a CaringBridge website on June 14. The site was organized into sections; the first was "My Story." In it, she explained my cancer and what I was dealing with. The following section was labeled "Journal." There she made daily entries so readers would know what was going on and how I felt. There was a "Guestbook" for people to offer prayers and good wishes, "Tributes" (for contributions to CaringBridge, not me), and then "My Pages." The last section was where Laura put pictures of our family and me.

CaringBridge's free service connects family and friends worldwide to share information, love, and support when facing severe medical conditions. I hadn't known much about their service until I did.

Laura wrote in the My Story section: "When cells change, life changes. My dad will overcome this, but he will be made stronger by you, his friends, from Charlotte to El Salvador to the ends of the earth. Whether you've hammered nails in a Habitat home together, shared endless hours fishing, traveled around the globe, worked food shows, sold groceries, sweated over car engines, served communion, or played MPCC's course millions of times. Or enjoyed ice cream with Salvadoran sisters and brothers; my dad extends a linked arm to you. Join him with locked elbows as he embarks on the journey to his cure."

As followers joined, the site caught on, and guestbook entries appeared daily.

A few weeks later, Laura posted a short text message I'd sent her.

Sent: Jul 3, 2010, 8:41 a.m. "Not to be too gross, but I am sitting on the terrace looking out at a beautiful Saturday morning, pumping breakfast into a tube inserted in my stomach while I run my fingers through my hair, having it come out in clumps."

Even with so many followers, no one at work had said anything to me. Kristi, George, and Laura were holding up their end of the bargain.

Tuesday, July 6, 2010

My second chemo came on July 6. It was scheduled for four hours in the morning. When I arrived, I was told Dr. Favaro was on vacation and that I would be seeing Dr. Geoffrey Chapman, one of the partners. After checking the blood work, Dr. Chapman said my white blood cell count was low, but we could go ahead with the chemo anyway. He would add additional potassium to the list of things to be pumped into my system each day at Presbyterian's Infusion Center. From then on, usually in the morning, I would cut up a ripe banana and put it in the blender with a can of Carnation before pumping the mixture into my stomach with the syringe. I hoped the banana would not only add potassium but brighten the look of the dishwater-colored meal, but all I got was the same liquid in a lighter shade.

The four 8-ounce cans of Carnation VHC (Very High Calorie) gave me 2,240 calories and 90 grams of protein daily.

That afternoon I met with Dr. Warlick at Presbyterian before radiation. "You're not going to El Salvador in September, but you probably know that," he said. He was right, of course. I had told my radiation oncologist earlier about our church's work in El Salvador with Habitat for Humanity and my planned return trip in September. Yet, he had only nodded and said, "Right." in a way that really meant, "We'll see about that." So, yes, I knew it, but I hadn't let myself say it out loud.

I barely had enough energy to make it to the teak bench in our own backyard on July 4, just two days before. And, after Joyce helped me light one of the sparklers she had bought for our small celebration, I was too weak to hold it, let alone stick it in the ground. So, if I couldn't walk in my backyard and hold a sparkler, how could I change planes in Atlanta, let alone keep up in El Salvador?

Warlick continued, "And not to give you too much bad news all at once, but the treatments from here on only intensify. That's how radiation works. It builds on itself. Your pain level is high now but will grow higher from here on out. It will level off in the last two or three days, but from here on, buckle up."

I knew about multiplier factors and how increasing one area would help others. And I knew the best results came from not just leaving the investment alone but adding to it regularly. So, the success of regular radiation treatments was just compound interest. Why didn't he say so?

"Okay, but when can I eat? When can I have, like, a steak?"

"Aim for Christmas," Dr. Warlick said. "And as for its taste? I just can't say. Everything will taste different. Some of the things you liked before could taste awful from now on. It will change over time; eventually your taste buds will grow back and may be the same, but maybe not. And these changes may go on for the rest of your life."

I just nodded and headed off to the radiation waiting room, too weak to say more and my mind unable to take in any more information. Christmas was still half a year away, and that was only a goal, not a guarantee. The doctors said we were going for a cure, but that wasn't guaranteed either, was it? I hadn't done any planning since that day on the flight to Baltimore months before. I'd just set those aside and said I'd get back to them when this was finished, but I was beginning to think this story might now have a different ending.

I went straight to bed when we finally got home. The second chemotherapy and the twentieth radiation had taken their toll. I was nauseated and had been a nervous wreck about it when I was locked on the table under my mask for the entire radiation treatment. What if I choked to death on my own vomit? I kept envisioning what a horrible ending that would be.

While I was in bed, Joyce went to St. Francis Animal Hospital to pick up Caroline. She had needed her gallbladder removed, along with a piece of wood she had eaten, and had a bad reaction to the Cipro they had given her. Like me, she had been hooked to an IV for fluids and antibiotics. And she hadn't eaten for three days. But now, her vet said she was ready to come home. Joyce was excited to pick her up, and I realized how much my wife was going through. Adding Caroline to her already high level of caring for me was exhausting.

Caring for a sick or injured loved one can be the most challenging job any of us will ever do. Especially if the weight of caregiving is simply added onto an already heavy load. Joyce was already doing the housework, shopping, cooking, laundry, transport, and had more recently taken over paying the household bills. Paying the bills was easy now, I jokingly said, now that we had money. It's paying the bills without money that's hard. She was rolling the large trash buckets to the curb each week, plus cleaning up the yard after Caroline went out every day. She helped me get dressed when I was too weak, put a cold washcloth on my head when I had a fever, and mixed the various prescription medicines into my syringe each time I pumped in a meal. All the things one does when they are a live-in nurse.

Every doctor visit resulted in new prescriptions, and each needed to be compounded into a liquid so it could go in through the feeding tube. The only pharmacy doing that at the time was Giant Genie, and their store was on South Boulevard, a little over ten minutes away. More people were calling and leaving a message when we were out. People were stopping by to deliver food. But only Joyce could eat any of it, because now the only thing that went in my gut was Carnation. When she could find a few minutes, she'd get on the internet and search for answers—searching for hope, perhaps. She was suddenly on call 24-7.

Dr. Lacouture, my primary care doc, came by one morning with a copy of Dr. David Servan-Schreiber's book, *Anticancer, A New Way of Life*. The book is a moving story, "of one doctor's inner and outer search for wellness and a radical exposition of the roles that lifestyle, environment, and trauma play in our health." Unfortunately, Joyce had driven me to radiation and then stopped by the grocery before coming home, so we missed him, but he left Dr. Servan-Schreiber's book on the front porch with a nice note. Dr. Lacouture had become more than just my doctor, he was a friend. He had managed each step along the way of diagnosing my celiac disease and found me the best doctor in town for the lump on my neck.

Maybe Joyce would get depressed sometimes, but she never talked about it if she did. Depression among caregivers is common, often exacerbated by not eating right, not exercising, and not getting enough sleep. But who could sleep with their partner up every hour coughing and gagging?

And then there was the simple fact of me being the center of attention. It wasn't that Joyce wanted some sort of medal, just that she was always on the sideline. Care for the caregiver is as important as care for the sick, but it's hard to say that to a loving caregiver—it sounds selfish.

Our daughter Laura and daughter-in-law Mary Beth helped, but I don't think Joyce ever took an entire day off. I often thought that if CaringBridge wanted to add another service, it should be for the caregiver. They needed prayers and support as much as the sick, I reasoned, perhaps even more. The new site would let the caregiver tell how they're doing and share what new coping skills they've learned. And above all, let people pray for them as much as the sick. There are websites like this today; I only wish they'd been around then.

As for the CaringBridge site Laura created for me, its readership was growing, and the comments from friends gave me strength when anxiety kept me awake. After tossing and turning, covers untucked, I'd read the comments. Each had its way of bringing light into my darkness, but none was as bright as the unexpected entry from Jerusalem.

We'd traveled to the Holy Land with Marion and Von Clemens, along with a small group from our church, in 2007. Saad Shaar, an Arabic Palestinian Christian living in Jerusalem, had been our guide. Saad showed our group around Jerusalem and the Sea of Galilee, and the spot where Jesus fed 5,000 with two fish and five loaves of bread. We spent time in the West Bank, swam in the Dead Sea, and rode the tour bus a short distance from Bethlehem into The Wilderness to a deep gorge named Wadi Qelt—The Valley of The Shadow of Death.

There were only a dozen on the trip, and even with the bus's microphone, it was easier for me to understand Saad when we sat up front. I watched his lips, but Joyce noticed his runny nose and swollen eyes. A dry climate is best for some allergy sufferers, but others find the dryness worsens things. Saad looked miserable and must have felt worse.

Joyce opened a small zippered compartment inside her bag and pulled out a sleeve of red pills. She popped two out and handed them to Saad. Joyce was a prepared mom who always had Band-Aids in her purse when the kids were little, and when we went camping Joyce was the one who would remember to bring toothpaste, toilet paper, and paper towels. The Boy Scouts claim "Be Prepared" as their motto, but moms invented it.

"Take these. You'll feel better." Maybe Saad had taken Sudafed before, or perhaps he just trusted her face; either way, he was soon better.

She'd give him two reds each morning and later in the afternoon, and he'd look after us each day. Special treatment? One hand washes the other, even in The Holy Land, or is kindness universal?

Near The Tree of Zacchaeus in Jericho, while the group was sitting down for a Western lunch, Saad invited Joyce and me to join him, along with the other guides and bus drivers, at a table in the kitchen. The round table was set with small bowls of olives and falafels made with chickpeas, hummus, a flatbread pizza-looking dish called manakeesh (the crust probably had gluten, I feared, so I passed), and grilled halloumi, or goat cheese. There were bowls of ful medames made with fava beans, vegetable oil, and cumin. All this, and more, plus a tangy fattoush salad comprised of lettuce, fried squares of pita, diced tomatoes, cucumbers and onion, garlic, lemon, olive oil, and mint.

There was a large carafe of water in the center of the table for our small glasses that reminded me of the brightly colored glasses Mom used when I was growing up. Hers came from the corner grocer with jelly inside, but the glass remained when the jelly ran out. At the end of the meal, everyone leaned back in their straight wood chairs, none of which matched, with small cups of Arabic coffee, like Western coffee but with cardamom, and talked about the day. Joyce and I couldn't understand the talk, but the food was incredible, and the people were welcoming and seemed to genuinely want us included.

I'm sorry my friends from Charlotte didn't get to enjoy the flavors and spend time with the people of that ancient land who value generosity and hospitality and who take time to linger with unannounced guests over food and life stories, savoring the flavor in both.

I learned a lot on that trip. Lessons from Saad, the places we visited, the people we met, and from my Charlotte friends. I learned to slow down and pay attention, to smell not just the food but everything else in the day, to take it all in, and to add salt when needed, but only a pinch. To think beyond bitter and sweet to the hundreds of other flavors life brings. To try new things, like swimming in the Dead Sea, but remembering to keep my eyes closed against the water that's eight times saltier than the ocean at Myrtle Beach. To be brave and walk the Ramparts Walk around Jerusalem's Old City, but to be mindful of its narrow and uneven ancient walkway that changes elevation and stops and starts for no reason, all the while trying to envision the culture of Jesus's day.

I've been savoring my life ever since and using cardamom to trigger my awareness. And if we ever have coffee, don't be surprised if I bring my own because cardamom is not a spice you'll find on the counter in our fast-paced Western world.

Saad helped us pick out oriental rugs on the Mount of Olives and lifted Joyce on her first-ever camel ride, and we formed a friendship that lasted over the years. We stayed in touch by email, occasional phone calls, and later FaceBook. So I guess I shouldn't have been surprised when Saad found the CaringBridge site and wrote a note. *"Dear Bruce, I am very sorry to learn about your cancer. You are like family to me, and I think highly of you and Joyce. I will pray for you and light a candle in Bethlehem and at the Holy Sepulcher for your recovery. I think of you often and lovingly and hope we will meet again. Your friend, Saad."*

Saad's prayers may have been in his native Aramaic. Did that make them easier for God to understand? Did the location of the candles matter? I didn't say any of that in my reply. I only thanked him as best I could and said, "We will meet again, I pray. Your friend, Bruce."

As a Christmas present, Laura had the CaringBridge entries and comments bound with a photo Jeff Lohr, my friend from Habitat for Humanity, sent Laura for its cover. The picture shows an open boat on a beach with a gentle sea in the background. Jeff captioned the image, "Get in the boat. Go out onto the water. There will be a storm. You will not die."

Rev. Dr. Steve Eason had used similar words from Mark's Gospel for a sermon he delivered at Myers Park Presbyterian Church, titled "Jesus in the Storm." Jeff had taken the photo of the open boat in El Salvador, but it could have been taken anywhere. His wife, Margie, had used the image and caption on her cancer journal, and they wanted it on mine.

Chapter 28

Loads Are Lighter When the Lifting Is Shared

July 9, 2010

J oyce watched me struggling to get out of her car at the hospital and said, "You can't walk, can you? I'll have them put you in a wheelchair."

On my way to radiation, I told the volunteer pushing my chair I wanted to see Dr. Warlick. He rolled me into the doctor's waiting area, but Dr. Warlick wasn't there. Would I like to see his partner, Dr. McGinnis?

Moving one of the visitor's chairs aside, the blue-coated volunteer locked the chair's wheels in front of Dr. McGinnis's desk. As I waited, I thought about how I hadn't put a bite of food or a drop of water in my mouth for weeks. How I hadn't spoken above a whisper for days and then only rarely. How my throat was making large clumps of mucus and I kept coughing up stringy globs, and my throat muscles had atrophied so much that when I swallowed, it felt like I was strangling.

Dr. Scott McGinnis soon appeared. He was as professional as Warlick, maybe a little more casual, but still with the starched needle-point dress shirt, carefully knotted regimental tie with its diagonal striped colors, and freshly laundered white coat boasting half the letters of the alphabet behind his name. His relaxed demeanor may have come from living in the South and attending the Medical College of Georgia and the University of Alabama, where he had graduated eighteen years before.

"I want to quit," I struggled to say.

"Why?"

I gave him my reasons as best I could in my croaky voice. I bent closer in the locked wheelchair, resting my arms on his desk: I was tired; it was too much, not how I thought it would be. I was sure the radiation and chemo had done their job, so why didn't we just stop? Then they could do a PET scan in a few weeks and see what was there. I'd pay for everything if insurance wouldn't.

He listened patiently and nodded from time to time. Maybe he understood, I thought; perhaps I was making headway.

"Is that it?" he asked politely.

"Yes."

His once-pleasant Georgia voice now took on a stern, authoritative tone. "Then let me have the nurse roll you to radiation, you get on the table, and we get on with your treatment. This protocol is predetermined, and it doesn't make deals."

So I climbed on the table for the twenty-fourth time, held the stick in my mouth, and let the technician snap down the thermoplastic mask that would keep me in perfect alignment to be blasted with thirty-five radiation beams for twenty minutes.

I was quiet the rest of the day. I'd used what little energy I had to talk to the doctor, but that hadn't worked. I worried: would I survive?

Joyce picked me up after infusion, then home for a four-o'clock conference call from our living room. Steve Wade, my CPA, and Barry had talked a few days before. I was glad everyone on my team knew all the players and often asked each other questions and compared notes. Steve had been my accountant for years and had all the numbers. Barry knew the legal landscape.

So along with Tom Shaw at Republic Bank and my financial planner Joe Gordon managing financial planning for the company and our family, I had a great team, all with permission to share when it helped the cause. In other words, I never wanted one hand not knowing what the other was doing. Some people gave one advisor one slant and presented a different view to others, but I never saw any advantage when the end goal was to provide me with the best overall advice. Better to have everyone moving in the same direction, I reasoned.

Steve would moderate the call with Todd in Baltimore, and Steve and me in Charlotte.

Steve pulled into the driveway a little before four. Joyce showed him into the living room and got him a glass of Perrier, no ice. Then she came to our bedroom. "Steve's here. It's time for your call."

We had traded emails, but it had been a month or more since we last met in person. I could tell by the look on his face that he was shocked by my appearance, but he didn't say anything. He must've thought when I was ready to say more, I would.

I'd been careful where I shared my diagnosis. Barry knew. Kristi, George, and Laura, but I hadn't told Steve everything, only that I had some medical problems affecting my voice. And, of course, Todd was to be the last to learn that anything was wrong.

My short nap had done me good. I still had no voice, but I wasn't as weak. I sat on the sofa; Steve was on the yellow loveseat by the dining room wall, and Joyce was in one of the blue chairs. I had already placed a fresh legal pad with several pens on the sofa where I intended to sit.

The plan was for Steve to do the talking, telling Todd I would join shortly. "Tell him I've been detained but that I called to say I'd be along soon," I wrote on the pad Joyce handed him. I hoped he could read what I'd scratched. Besides, it was too painful to speak, and when I did, my voice was so soft you could barely make out what I said.

Once Todd was on the line, Steve explained how I would be joining shortly, but that as most of this call was about accounting, he had the numbers in front of him and could fax Todd anything he needed. Barry had coached Steve well. They had anticipated everything Todd wanted and how to best position each answer. Once Todd asked if I was there yet, but mostly he seemed fine with what Steve was telling him. If Steve was ever unsure, he'd write out his question, and I'd scrawl my answer on the pad.

After about half an hour, as the call was winding down, Steve risked saying he thought he heard a car pull into the driveway. Did we need to keep talking? It wasn't much of a risk as Todd had said he had a hard stop at four thirty.

"No, I've got what I need. Thanks," Todd said.

That was that. As Dr. McGinnis had reiterated that morning, I had no say in my treatment, and now I had disengaged from the sale. I was no longer calling the shots.

Loads are lighter when the lifting is shared.

Chapter 29

Dark Night of the Soul

July 9, 2010

I tried to go to bed early that night, but I spent most of the time doubled over the bathroom basin, coughing and gagging, waiting for some unnamed and unrecognizable internal organ to land in the sink. I'd bang my fist on the counter and scream at the face in the mirror, but the hard counter hurt my fist, and there was no sound to my cry. It was all a bad dream, like I was watching a black-and-white silent movie of a tortured face in a desilvered mirror. But I didn't recognize the film or the face and thought whoever or whatever it was, I didn't want to watch any more.

I was powerless and hopeless. Was this the dark night of the soul people talk about? Was this the time everything I knew no longer made sense? Would suffering show me the way?

Is it strength that gives hope, or hope that gives strength? It was dark, and I was lost, so I went back to bed, hoping I didn't wake Joyce; she needed sleep.

Chapter 30

Birthdays and Bubblegum

July 14, 2010

I woke to children rushing into the room that morning. Laura and Mary Beth had arranged to bring the grandchildren to visit and give me my birthday surprise. They'd painted a T-shirt with the message: "Get Well Granddaddy" along with their handprints on the front. Then on the back, the shirt said, "Behind You. Liz, Ellie, Kenny, James."

The entire scene was priceless. I wanted them to stay, for us to go to the shop, measure them on the door frame, and marvel at how each had grown. To get out projects from their cubbies, to relive the days we had spent together doing this or that, but their mothers said they needed to be going, and besides, I still needed to pump my breakfast, shower, and tape down my tube to make it to my ten o'clock sharp.

I'd cut my hair short, military short—what there was of it—so it was easy to comb, and I didn't need to shave now that my beard had stopped growing; but still, everything had been moving in slow motion since this nightmare began.

On the next Dr. Warlick morning, he asked again if I'd seen a dentist. Was everything sound? "You're going to lose any teeth that aren't strong," had been his words. Radiation is powerful; if your teeth aren't strong, they won't survive.

If there was one thing I was sure of, it was my teeth. In fact, the first person who looked at the lump, other than Joyce, was our son-in-law, Kenneth Corsig, DMD, MHS at CharlottePerio. Joyce had called Ken and asked if he would look at the lump when I first felt it.

Laura and Ken lived only a mile away. They had bought our former home on Hertford Road and moved in the same day we moved out in 2004. Their children, Elizabeth and Kenny, wanted to grow up in their mother's house, so how could Joyce and I say no? Ken had gotten me in to see Dr. Crowley, the oral surgeon, the next day and had followed my treatment ever since. I think, in some way, Ken felt he should have noticed the cancer. Still, as Dr. Harley had explained to him more than once, "Ken, you would need to climb down his throat to find it, and even then, you would have needed a magnifying glass; so no, in no way could you have spotted your father-in-law's cancer." But from then on, Ken had taken multiple X-rays and scrutinized each tooth to be sure they were strong.

"Do you chew gum, like bubblegum? Bazooka or Dubble Bubble?" Dr. Warlick asked.

I knew them, of course, but where was he going? Did he see a sugar build-up in my blood work or something on my teeth?

"Sure, well, I don't anymore, but I did when I was young. Why?"

"Buy some Dubble Bubble. Most stores have it. Then chew a piece or two on your way to the hospital, so it's soft, then before you get on the table, pack it tightly around your teeth, especially the ones in back with the gold crowns," he said.

Was this in a medical journal he'd read? I had no idea, but that afternoon, when Joyce and I were at the grocery store in Park Road Shopping Center, a friend from church saw me pushing the cart, or actually, using the cart for support, and asked how I was doing. She and her husband, an architectural photographer, sat in the pew behind us each Sunday and had been on our trip to The Holy Land in 2007. Rebecca had been following my story on CaringBridge and asked how I was holding up. Then she politely asked if I needed help finding anything, so I told her I was looking for bubblegum. She didn't look puzzled but merely said, "Follow me; I'll show you."

We went to the candy aisle, and she picked out a large bag, but cautioned, "You realize there are six grams of sugar in each piece, so I'd go light on this stuff if I were you." I dropped the bag in the cart, hugged her, and went on my way.

From then on, I kept the gum in Joyce's car, put two pieces in my mouth on the way to the hospital, packed them in place before getting on the table, then spat them out, along with the stick, before climbing down.

Getting the gum ready was the hard part. My weeks of only pumping meals meant my jaws were no longer strong enough to chew, even gum. But slowly, I managed.

I must have been quite a sight, being wheeled to the cancer wing with my cheek bulging out with what might have been a wad of chewing tobacco, looking all the while like I was ready to spit.

After packing the Dubble Bubble around the crowns and putting the locking stick in place, I was ready for the mask. My taste buds were gone, but the sweet smell of the sugar-loaded gum lingered inside the mask. Instead of my usual panic, there was a euphoric intoxication for the next twenty minutes.

Now, at night, instead of coughing up extended slimy globs of yellow mucus, the globs were pink.

Chapter 31

Details

July 2010

Barry said he learned Todd's bank wanted his vice presidents to cosign the note. Todd's attorney told Barry they were not overjoyed but had signed anyway. Another step forward.

Then Barry told me about another conversation with Todd's lawyer. "Remember, this sale only includes intangible assets, not the tangible ones of cash or furniture, fixtures, and equipment. So Todd will need to buy a lot of stuff or lease the FF&E from Bruce. That's the deal. Remember?"

Todd's lawyer must have forgotten that part.

Chapter 32

Room 304

July 16, 2010

I didn't make it home Friday evening; the dehydration and a fever were enough for the doctors to want more fluids, potassium, and antibiotics pumped in through the IVs than I was getting in my afternoon infusion sessions. So they found me a room in the old part of the hospital.

From my window in room 304, I could look through a large magnolia tree over the former home of department store founder William Henry Belk, built in 1920, and down Elizabeth Avenue, all the way to the Uptown skyline. Closer to the hospital, on the right, was a red brick building with a faded sign advertising, "Anderson's World's Best Pecan Pie." The restaurant had closed a few years back, and its absence made me sad, not because of the pie, but because so many landmarks I had loved for over thirty years were disappearing. The Copal Grill, where I tried to sell premade coleslaw to a Greek owner boning out a side of beef, to The Epicurean, with their biscuits people would buy on Saturday and serve on Sunday when the family gathered after church. The Coffee Cup, clearly the most diverse restaurant in Charlotte, where everyone freely gathered, to The Chateau with its piano bar. All were gone now.

How many lives were gone with them, and what about their stories, were they gone as well? Were the stories buried with the people, or were they still being told? Around tables at family gatherings, perhaps, or were they written down? Or maybe the African proverb was true: "When an old man dies, a library burns to the ground."

If everything happened as planned, my company was about to end; and just like so many signs around town, ours would come down. A sign thousands saw when they rode the light rail. And what about the people within our building—would they be okay? Todd said so, but how did I know?

On Saturday, our daughter, a lactation consultant at Presbyterian, was teaching her regular class to expectant mothers on breastfeeding. A few of the husbands would attend, but not many. Laura brought her daughter, eleven-year-old Elizabeth. They wanted to visit me before going to the hospital's classroom.

They were in my room when Dr. Favaro came in. Pushing the mobile X-ray machine to the corner, he said he had just come from looking at the film, and there was no sign of pneumonia. Then he stood by my bed and said, "This entire treatment plan is painful to watch, but it's expected. The chemotherapy and radiation build over time, taking their toll. It's harsh, and I wish we could prepare patients and families for the difficulty. But it's not until the final weeks that reality sets in, and everyone understands the intensity." His words were helpful, but I didn't feel any better.

The room was quiet when he left. Laura stared out the window.

Was she looking at the skyline and the faded Anderson's sign, or was she worried there might be an empty chair at Thanksgiving?

Elizabeth's jaw fell open as her big eyes darted between her mother and me. She was looking for answers from the adults in the room, but there were none, only questions. Nothing was clear to any of us. Maybe I'd make it, but what if I didn't?

I lay back in the bed, my Macy's parade helium balloon now deflated, yet still tethered, but not by wires held by guiding hands. Now I was attached to tubes that went from dwindling bags of fluid into my crumpled body. My face was as blank as my daughter's, my white skin barely covered by the thin hospital gown. I was praying this would all be over soon—one way or another.

Laura came over to the bed and hugged me, saying she loved me and that I was in her prayers. Elizabeth put on her big-girl face and added, "I can't wait to visit the shop, Granddaddy; I want you to measure me. I think I've grown."

I couldn't wait either.

I was still in the hospital on Sunday morning when The Open Championship from the Old Course in St. Andrews came on the TV. I remembered when I played that famous public course in Scotland, tourists and locals all mixed together. When I asked my caddie if I could get to a particular hole using my six iron, the Scot answered in a serious yet calm voice, drawing out each syllable, "Eventually."

Our foursome had paused for the traditional photo on the footbridge spanning the narrow creek on the last hole, and I'd reached over to put my hand on my playing partner's arm and suggested we enjoy the moment, walk slowly, so we could remember. Because it's more than a game, isn't it? It's about trusting others and being honest even when no one is looking. It's about being outdoors, not just on bright sunny days but also on cold rainy days in places like Scotland. It's about playing the Old Course at St Andrew's, where people had played the same course with the same fairways, bunkers, and greens since 1764, a dozen years before America was even a country.

Maybe I'd watch highlights when I got home. But for now, I just closed my eyes and tried to rest.

Chapter 33

There Is a Yes If You Keep Looking

Spring 2001

Our vacations had come a long way from the $4 campsites at Cape Point on the Outer Banks. Now, rather than a payphone on a pole two campsites over, we had a phone in our room.

Camping was something we had begun when we lived in Winston-Salem. It was a family activity, and we enjoyed it. Our first camping trip was to the Outer Banks, and the weather forecast each day was the same. "Today will be another bright and sunny day for Dare County with clear blue skies, light to moderate winds with cumulus clouds building offshore in the late afternoon. No rain in sight."

We returned often. Bought more equipment to go with our green four-man tent. A dining fly, plastic water jugs, and a camp stove that could use kerosene if we ran out of white gas.

Our favorite spot was Cape Hatteras, where we could walk to the lighthouse and The Point.

Then, after we moved to Charlotte and I started the business, the $4 per night price tag kept drawing us back. There were various ranger programs all day, and then each evening, as the sun settled over Pamlico Sound, one of the rangers would give a talk by a bonfire in a small cut-out amphitheater tucked back in the dunes.

We would throw a cast net in the sound to catch bait, surf-fish for spots, crockers, flounder, and the occasional blue, then clean our catch at the wooden fish station before putting our iron skillet on the camp stove. I tried to make a pot of coquina stew once, but the little clams were so tiny and the meat so hard to find that all we could taste were the bits of carrot and onion I had used in the salted water.

Our favorite campsite was A-7, near the campground entrance by the ranger gate post and the tall flag pole, across from the restrooms and cold showers, and next to a payphone mounted on a concrete pillar. With no cell phones back then, pay phones were my office.

We'd bring a cooler full of Danish baby back ribs, Casa meat-balls, Pierre Rib-B-Ques, and anything else we were selling at the time. Buy milk and eggs from Conner's Supermarket in Buxton, and enjoy our week together, always remembering to pick up ice when we were near a store.

Laura wanted to grow up to be a ranger with the Park Service. K.B. wasn't sure; maybe he'd work at Natural Art Surf Shop.

Once I arranged a sales call while we were there. I managed to knot my tie while getting dressed in the tent, then drove to see the Dare County Foodservice Director. Joyce and the children walked to the beach while I drove the fifty-three miles to Manteo.

Joyce and I were in Scottsdale vacationing at the Camelback Inn in the spring of 2001. There were only two of us, and we weren't under a green dining fly eating Rib-B-Ques or frying flounder on a camp stove. Instead, we sat down to meals from Scottsdale's finest chefs under cantilever umbrellas on the patio. Then, after dinner, we would walk around the immaculate grounds and listen to the mellow Native American flute music from speakers disguised as rocks in the spa's desert landscaping. Later we would sit and talk on our balcony, admiring the view of the top of Camelback Mountain as the sun's soft yellow light slowly crept up the side until it was gone for the day. We'd come a long way from our tent vacations.

I called the office each morning. On Wednesday, I learned Eric Chapman, the head of foodservice at Rogers-American, had left to start his own business. Many of their manufacturers were going with him, but not all.

Smucker's, the jam and jelly people, were not; they would be interviewing for a new broker. I got the name and number of the regional manager quickly enough, but when I reached him, he said, "Sorry, our calendar is full."

That just wouldn't do. We were the best choice, and Smucker's didn't even have time to give us an interview? No way!

I started making calls until I found a broker who represented them and had a list of the others around the country who also sold Smucker's. He faxed the list to the front desk of the hotel. I didn't know four of the names on the list, but I knew the rest. My years in national trade associations and time spent on advisory boards had introduced me to most of the major agencies around the country, and it was time to cash in.

I stayed on the phone that day and the next while Joyce went to the pool.

Herb Ring was the vice president of sales, and every Smucker's broker I had reached in the past days called him on our behalf. "McIntyre is your only choice, Herb. You'll love Bruce and his team," they said.

On Friday, Keith Harkins, the regional manager, called. "Something has opened up at the end of our day. Can we meet at four o'clock on Tuesday?"

"Perfect," I said. My campaign had worked. Visibility and exposure, or what some call "connections," might be the most misunderstood privilege of all.

Our team nailed it that day. Everything about the interview came off as planned. You could read the outcome on their faces as they left our office.

We were now selling J.M. Smucker Company's fruit spreads, peanut butter, ice cream toppings, condensed milk, and Folgers coffee.

We won contests, Broker of the Year, and other awards. Herb never regretted his decision, and I never forgot the lesson of not taking no when there's a yes if you keep looking.

Chapter 34

It's Good to Be King

Perhaps it's because I was born in July and am comfortable as a homebody. The zodiac sign for people like me is the crab, and like all crabs, we're more comfortable in our shell—or office. Or maybe it was my faith. The Presbyterian religion grew from the Calvinist tradition, and there isn't a neater and more orderly group anywhere than we "frozen chosen." Appearance is essential every day, not just on Sunday.

And if it's not those, then it's just the simple notion that it's not enough to do the job well but to do it in an environment that reflects both the performer and the performance.

So it only follows that I must have subconsciously felt that having the right office would help us sell more groceries.

1989

We'd been in business almost twenty years, and things were going well. The bills were being paid, there was enough money to meet payroll, and we put a little aside each month. Plus, I was managing the credit line the way Bootie had intended. Life was good.

Joyce and I often took a walk after dinner and would visit with our neighbors Tommie and Tom Shaw, who lived on Norton Road around the corner. Tom was the senior vice president of Republic Bank and Trust. His bank was building a new office on South Kings Drive, and Tom invited me to stop by and look at what they had planned for the convenient yet oddly pie-shaped site.

When we met in his small office in the triple-wide mobile trailer the bank had put in the corner of the construction site, I was fascinated by his unusual organizational style. Tom didn't seem to like file cabinets. Maybe he thought he'd forget about something if the file was put away, so he kept everything in view. And, while other bankers dressed for meetings in board rooms, Tom dressed for work, and his work was wherever he was needed. It might be on an assembly line floor, in the mud at a job site, or in a new restaurant's kitchen. And his red suspenders did the job just fine, so why change because the pictures in *Banker's Quarterly* only showed alligator leather belts on bankers these days? Plus, his black Weejuns went on faster than Bootie's cap-toe six-eyelet lace-ups.

As I no longer had a relationship at BB&T, it was an easy decision to move my banking over to Tom. An outside service had begun managing our payroll, so paychecks were automatically deposited in whatever bank our people chose. I only needed a relationship with a banker who could give me an answer without waiting days for a committee to meet.

When it came time for my company to stop paying rent and own our own building, I invited Tom to look at a site I had chosen around the corner from our Executive Street location and across from the Freedom Drive Post Office. As we stood in the middle of the vacant two acres of overgrown weeds, Tom said, "It looks good to me. It's away from the noise of I-85 and close to the airport. You'll want to be sure the ground can support the building you want to build, but make the owner an offer, and I'll draw up the papers." And with that, I became a landowner without a single meeting being called to order. That's why, to this day, if you ask me where I banked, I wouldn't say Republic, I'd say Tom Shaw.

I hired an architect, and the process began. We soon decided a LEED-certified building (Leadership in Energy and Environmental Design) would be good and we'd have the first in Charlotte.

Integra Realty Resources had studied the vacant lot before its purchase, so when we were ready to start construction, I invited Fitzhugh Stout, the owner of Integra, along with Tom, to review the plans. It was exciting to think about being the first in Charlotte to care enough about energy conservation to build a LEED-certified building.

When Fitzhugh and Tom arrived, I had the scale model the architect had built positioned in the center of the conference table. The model was impressive with fake trees and grass, little people walking in the front door, trucks backed into the loading dock, and cars plugged into electric charging stations, even when electric cars were still years away.

Fitzhugh examined the model, played with the little cars, and then looked at the plans. He asked if there was a private phone he could use. I suggested my office, and when Fitzhugh returned, he gave us his thoughts.

Before Tom or I even asked, Fitzhugh said, "Or, you could do the same thing with an older building, repurpose it. Call it up-cycled. Whatever the term, you could get more square footage in an old warehouse, put in new windows and doors, plumbing, heating and air, the works, and still be under what you will spend here."

Tom looked at me; I smiled and thanked Fitzhugh for his work. I knew his bill wouldn't be cheap, but his advice was worth every penny. I later learned his call had been to an associate studying the increasing value of buildings in the older neighborhoods of our city and that locations closer to town were where people wanted to be.

I started looking at old warehouses. The architect was disappointed, and I understood, but he would find other clients.

At the time, I was losing weight. Maybe all of this had been too stressful. Perhaps not think about it so much, try to relax. Eat better, I told myself.

I would drive each block of the older neighborhoods looking for a possible site. I was interested in 1610 North Tryon Street; the building was solid but larger than we needed. The location, near the Amtrak station and backing up to eighteen railroad tracks, was somewhat off-putting, but the views of Uptown were spectacular. Extravaganza, the event venue and production company, ended up in that location.

Then I focused on 2161 Hawkins Street. It was an out-of-business auto repair shop, and the building would need to be razed to the ground before we could start. The land alone was more than I wanted to pay, so I decided to pass. That location would become Sycamore Brewery and is now about to become a twenty-four-story luxury apartment building.

So, Fitzhugh and his associate were right. Older neighborhoods with close-in locations were where people wanted to be.

Eventually, I found a 20,120-square-foot abandoned sheet metal shop on Old Pineville Road and Southside Drive. It had been vacant for years, with broken windows and homeless living inside. There was a textile warehouse behind it, with 500-pound bales of cotton sitting on the covered dock next to a rail siding that crossed Old Pineville Road, allowing freight cars to reach the textile warehouse and the abandoned sheet metal shop.

A previous owner had bricked in the loading dock of the sheet metal shop and covered the railroad tracks with asphalt, which now had weeds growing through the many cracks. There was a rusty concertina razor wire fence, protecting what I don't know. But from everything I could tell, the building was solid, just in awful repair.

Curtis Rudolph, a Myers Park Country Club friend, had the listing. He thought he might have the plans somewhere; he'd look. And yes, he'd open it up so I could see more, walk around inside, and take pictures.

On the second visit, I took my banker Tom. He could see the possibilities and how the large sections, with their solid walls, could be used for various functions. There could be offices up front, a warehouse in the middle, and a large meeting room and kitchen in the back. Even the two old metal fire doors could divide the kitchen from the meeting room. It was unusual for a banker to get this excited, I thought. But Tom Shaw was clearly not the usual banker. I had walked away for a moment, and when I returned, Tom was examining the piles of heavy metal shelving pipes used when the building was a warehouse for beauty supplies.

"Look at all of these, Bruce. These alone are worth at least $35K." I know Curtis heard Tom's comment, because that number came up when we settled on the final price.

We'd need to get Fitzhugh's company involved. When the report came back, full of images taken from more critical angles than I had snapped, it listed a few things that needed to be addressed. There was asbestos in the back area we planned to use as a kitchen. The asbestos also covered pipes. There had been motor oil poured down a drain in the back, probably from changing the oil in a truck, but that didn't matter because we'd be putting in all new underground drains along with water and gas lines anyway. Then, last on the list, five abandoned fuel oil tanks would need to come out and the soil around them tested after removal.

"All in all, an excellent building for sixty years of age," said Fitzhugh. "The classic bowed truss roof is solid and shows no signs of leaking."

Curtis got the owner to agree to the repairs and complete everything before we closed.

Work began.

The five oil tanks proved a more significant challenge than even Randy Buell, a long-time oil tank removal expert, could quickly complete. He kept going deeper and still couldn't collect a clean sample. Getting the necessary No Further Action letter from the Environmental Protection Agency wasn't going to be easy—or cheap.

So far, Curtis had been able to get the seller to pay, but finally, Curtis stopped getting the okays. "Bruce, the building's owner will pay up to $27,500 for Randy and the asbestos removal, then you're on your own for the rest. He said you could take it or leave it; he doesn't care."

I stewed over that. How long could it go on? How big could the bill be? Randy wasn't any help. I'd yell up to him as he sat on his giant yellow backhoe; he'd yell down and keep working. "We'll get clean dirt when we get it, and not before." Or something like that. What else could he say? Growing piles of contaminated soil dotted the now damaged asphalt parking lot, making it look like a battlefield.

Finally, Randy had the samples he wanted. The EPA sent the No Further Action letter. Done and done.

With more stress came more weight loss. My energy was gone after lunch. Eventually, Dr. Lacouture got worried, and after scheduling various tests and procedures, referred me to Dr. Gavigan, a gastroenterologist. Dr. Gavigan soon diagnosed celiac disease. Like so many little fingers, my tiny villi soaking up the nutrients from food got slicked down and stuck to the wall of my small intestine. No matter how much I ate, the nutrients just passed through. I learned proteins for energy and calcium for bone health were the first to slide by.

"It's a serious autoimmune disorder for which the only treatment is lifelong abstinence from gluten," Dr. Gavigan said.

I was gluten-free from then on. Not because I wanted to be, or because of some new diet fad, but because those were the doctor's orders, and they didn't expire until I did.

My energy returned when the gluten disappeared, and my weight quickly rebounded.

With the No Further Action letter in hand, it was now time to get estimates on the repairs and modification to the building. Bill Roper had done the two remodels on Executive Street; we got along, and I liked his work.

Bill and I walked every inch of the space, inside and out. He didn't think we needed an architect; we could do it ourselves. "I've worked with you, Bruce; you already know what you want. Why pay someone to put it on paper and make little cut-outs when you see it so clearly?"

Bill returned with his estimates; I added those to the cost of the building and arranged an appointment with Tom.

Yes, Republic Bank and Trust would do the deal.

It was all that simple, perhaps because the one thing I had learned over the years was how all bankers hated surprises. More than anything else, if you want to stay on a banker's good side, never, never surprise them. So whether the news is good or bad, the first person to know is the banker; and for me, that banker was Tom.

The building would be owned by Executive Street Properties, an LLC separate from the corporation. The bank would make the seven-figure amount available with nothing down, paying out the money as needed, with interest starting only when the money was used. And the rate was below prime, not the two points above I'd started with twenty years before or even the prime rate Tom had given me when I switched banks.

I drew up a fifteen-year lease for the company to sign. The lease went up three percent each year, or an amount equal to the

Consumer Price Index, whichever was greater.

I signed the lease as president of McIntyre*Sales* and again as the managing partner of Executive Street Properties, LLC. Joyce signed as secretary/treasurer of both. The monthly rent checks would cover the loan, plus a bit extra.

We were still writing a rent check, but the check was payable to Executive Street Properties, and that was me, the landlord. And the new signs said McIntyre*Sales*.

It's good to be king, I thought. I learned so much being a business owner. That's how it is, I guess. You start doing something and gather so much more along the way.

Chapter 35

There's Gold on the Internet

July 2010

I wasn't going to the office at all now, what with spending each day at the hospital. Everyone seemed fine with emails and texts. Todd and I already had the signed Agreement in Principal and much of the work between the lawyers was complete. From what I could tell, Todd had told most, if not all, of his manufacturers, so everything seemed like a fait accompli. But nothing is ever done, till it's done.

When I needed to talk with Kristi or George, I'd make the call from my car. That way, if I sounded terrible, I could blame it on the phone. Of course, they knew about my cancer; I just didn't want them to think I was so sick I could barely talk. From my conversations with Barry, I could tell that any frustrations the two of them had came from not knowing the exact amount of their share when the sale finally closed. But as Barry had explained, until we knew the total number, there was no way of calculating their portion.

I wished they had trusted Barry more and knew how hard he had worked to get the maximum out of Todd, but I'd known Barry for years, and they had only met him a few months before. Maybe they were regretting the sale in the first place. Perhaps they now felt they could run it on their own. I don't know. Either way, their lives were changing, and that's never easy.

There would be no third chemotherapy treatment. The Cisplatin and other platinum chemotherapy drugs in the cocktail flowing through my system could damage the cochlea, and my hearing was bad enough already. Dr. Favaro assured me the first two treatments had done the job, so why do a third and risk a significant loss that would be permanent? Poor hearing may be one of the most debilitating conditions I can think of. People notice if you use a white cane, and if you're on crutches or in a wheelchair—it's obvious. But with hearing loss, people think you're either not listening, ignoring them, stupid, or all three. So if Dr. Favaro was satisfied, I was okay with skipping the last chemo.

Joyce had been scouring the internet for anything and everything she could learn about my treatments. There's a lot out there, much of it scary, wrong, or both, but every so often, you strike gold.

George Karl, the NBA coach of the Denver Nuggets, had a similar cancer to mine, or as similar as can be when the subject is cancer.

In an interview, he said he used a mucus eliminator machine, which was like a vacuum cleaner you stick down your throat to suck out the mucus. The tube empties into a glass bowl. Just plug it in, switch it on, and suck away slime.

My doctors said it wasn't in the protocol but did some research and came back with an all-clear. The home health person delivered the machine and taught me how to use it. I'd switch it on and work its tube around the inside of my mouth, then down my swollen throat. It made the usual sucking sounds as it moved about, then a loud "slurp" when it finally pulled a glob loose from where it had been hanging on. Once done, I rinsed my mouth with a saltwater mouth-wash and cleaned the glass bowl.

The scene reminded me of the old Steve McQueen movie where *The Blob* was taking over the city, consuming everything in its path. But, armed with my trusty machine, I was the hero, sucking up the giant globs of mucus before they harmed anyone.

Laura wrote on CaringBridge: "The finish line is in sight. It's been grueling. No coasting in here. No gloating at the competition, no showboating. It's a steadfast, humble, one-foot-in-front-of-the-other, dogged determination that will win this race. We are told that the radiation beams are more focused and intensified in these last few doses. My dad's spirits are good, but his body is tired. His tempera-ture creeps up and then hovers at a low grade. His voice comes and goes. His throat hurts, and his neck is burned . . . considering the physical strain his body is under, he looks good. He is slightly leaner and pale, and his hair is much thinner."

Laura was only being kind, I felt. My spirits may have seemed fine to her and those around me, but everything about me was chang-ing, and I didn't know if that was fine. Maybe my hair would grow back, or perhaps it wouldn't. Maybe I could return to having meals with my family or need to eat alone—using my tube. And would my heart and head return to normal, or is normal just another question groping for answers?

"The paperwork is finished," Barry's email said. Then he added a P.S. "Todd will lease the FF&E, so you should do an inventory when you're able, then we'll calculate its value and write a five-year lease."

Wednesday, July 28, 2010, would be my last treatment. Ten o'clock sharp.

Chapter 36

Culture Is on Display When the Boss Is Away

February 2004

Newspapers were a big deal at the start of the twenty-first century, and everyone read the *Charlotte Observer*. It was something one did if one wanted to be a part of the capital of the New South. But sadly, the *Observer*'s circulation has declined in recent years, and the shortfall in revenue means less money for journalists giving readers the stories they want. It's a vicious cycle in every industry. I'm not sure where it stops until it hits an unknown bottom and may, just may, start to rebound like the small towns around the country where red-and-white striped poles offering "two barbers—no waiting" have been replaced with Aveda salons owned by the hippest women in town. And the only bank is now a French restaurant with the wine cellar and best table in the open vault. And a coffee kiosk smack-dab in the middle of the main street where only pedestrians and bicycles are now allowed. Local journalism will return someday, not in newsprint spread open on the kitchen table, but as hand-held web journalism.

The Business section was the first part of the paper I opened each morning. So, my heart skipped a beat that Sunday morning on February 29, 2004, when I opened the *Charlotte Observer* and saw the feature story with both a picture of my building and me.

"When Bruce McIntyre's wife Joyce saw the south Charlotte building he'd selected for his food brokerage's new home, she asked only one question: 'Are you out of your mind?'"

Doug Smith, the business editor, continued, "Now completed, visitors see an old warehouse from the street but are greeted by modern design, ambient lighting, new plumbing, HVAC, electrical, and energy-efficient windows once inside. It's no longer an abandoned sheet metal shop but a modern functioning workplace."

With the rise of the internet, we needed a domain name for our website and email. The name I wanted was taken, so I searched for another. McIntyreSales was available, so I registered it as ours. The more I thought about the name, the more I liked it. McIntyre and Company could be anything from a municipal bond trader to a small engine repair shop, but McIntyreSales at least said we were about "sales." With both words put together, the way domain names need to be, I wanted some separation, which was accomplished by putting *Sales* in italics. That way, the two words were different. Then I added a tagline, "Expect Results," and our new name was complete. Of course, I kept the four-leaf clover, and when the signs went up on Southside Drive, there we were—McIntyre*Sales*.

170

Of course, I couldn't see into the future when I bought the old building, to the day when Old Mecklenburg Brewery, GoodRoad CiderWorks, Sugar Creek Brewing, and Great Wagon Road would be our neighbors. Nor could I see that Yoga-on-Tap would be a few hundred yards down the street, all with the historic Queen's Park Cinema sign towering overhead, between the Scaleybark and Wood-lawn stations on the light rail. But I did know that Doug Smith's article meant we had arrived. We were now an official part of the city and a player in our rapidly growing foodservice industry, where in the same year, Johnson & Wales, the most prominent foodser-vice educator in the world, combined their Charleston and Norfolk campuses in Charlotte.

February 2006

The parking spaces near the front door of our building were marked for visitors. Two were handicap spots, but the others were for guests. So I was curious when I pulled in that afternoon and noticed a car in one of the visitor spots. Could I have forgotten an appointment?

As I walked through the front door, Glenda, our receptionist, tilted her head toward my office, then followed me in, closing the door behind her.

Without even a hello, Glenda whispered, "He came in about an hour ago and said he knew it was unusual, but he would like to visit with some of our people, anyone who could spare a few minutes. He didn't tell me his name, but he said he didn't think you would mind."

Then she added, "I put him in the small conference room off customer service, not the big one. I hope I did the right thing?"

171

I knew Glenda well enough that, no doubt, it was fine. But who was he, and what did he want?

"Hi, I'm Bruce McIntyre. Can I join you?"

"Sure. I'm Brian Lamontagne with Nestlé. You've got a nice place here. Grab a chair and join us if you have time." The scene was surreal as the "us" Brian was referring to were my people, not his.

Resisting the urge to speak, I listened as he asked how objectives were set and how people knew what to sell. He said there were no right or wrong answers; they were all just opinions. Stacey Garrison was there, and he asked her some things about customer service and what she thought was important. Debbie Etters, the senior customer service specialist, told him we didn't just solve problems, we fixed the process. If a mistake or a problem arose, it was usually caused by a fault in our system. "Fix the process, and the problems disappear," Debbie said.

Then Candy Jaroszynski jumped in, "Hey, we make mistakes, everyone does, but that's when we shine if we treat the mistake like an opportunity. We fix the mistake quickly and fairly, so our once unhappy customer is soon the happiest of all."

One of the newer salespeople told Brian about something George Howard taught him when he first started. It was the story of how Biggers Brothers had asked for our help. Biggers had a branch in Knoxville that was stuck with over two hundred cases of frozen artisan bread, baguettes, sourdoughs, and boules. The branch had been opened in preparation for the World's Fair, but neither the branch nor the fair did as well as anyone hoped. The broker who sold them the bread had tried, perhaps, but it wouldn't sell. So, the vice president of purchasing in Charlotte asked for help. Bruce told him,

"Sure," so the bread was transferred to Charlotte. We went to work and had the bread sold in no time. The bread's manufacturer had already paid the commission to the Knoxville broker, so there wasn't anything in it for us except the goodwill of helping a customer out of a jam. But that vice president of purchasing never forgot, and George wanted everyone at McIntyre*Sales* to learn the simple lesson, "Take care of your customers, and your customers will take care of you."

Soon the impromptu meeting was over. Brian said he needed to go. "Have you got another minute?" I asked.

Brian stepped outside into the afternoon sun and said he didn't want to start rumors; he just wanted to see what was available. He said he'd heard good things about our company before today, and they were all confirmed with this visit.

"We'll talk more," Brian said as he slid behind the wheel of his car.

My head was spinning. I went back inside, sat at my desk, turned the chair around, and stared out the window. Nestlé was one of the most sought-after manufacturers in the country. Every item they offered did well. Their Stouffer entrees, packed in 96-ounce pans, were featured daily in most college and university dining rooms and hospitals, where they could go straight from the oven to the serving line. Vegetarian lasagna was famous with co-eds, along with Lean Cuisine. Minor's Bases were the first choice of every chef in the country. Nescafe coffee and tea were everywhere, and Nescafe liquid coffee concentrate was beginning to replace Douwe Egberts in large-volume operators. And to my delight, they had Häagen-Dazs and Edy's Ice Cream.

Nestlé always took multiple booths at food shows, and people would be three and four rows deep in front of their booth to sample all the items the chefs prepared. Their chefs often wore a microphone and talked to the crowd as they effortlessly prepared culinary delights, then asked people to try a bite. There were always eager volunteers.

I called the group that had spoken with Brian back into the conference room. "What did he say? What did he ask? How did you answer?" I wanted to recreate the entire scene.

They told me he wanted to know how we were organized, how we introduced new products, and if we focused more on the customer, the end-user, or were controlled by the large distributors. All the questions that would be asked in a formal interview, but different.

Brian was smart. This wouldn't be the first time I saw him go at things differently. He was a chef by training but a businessman at heart; he'd gather information and then decide. He had gotten better answers by arriving unannounced and meeting with a small group. He'd not given us time for preparation, so the answers were more honest. Plus, he'd talked to the people doing the work, not those at the top who only thought they knew what went on.

It was like someone dropping in, unannounced, on a Saturday morning to join you for coffee when you were still wearing your flannel pajamas, and the place was a mess from Friday night. Nothing had been fancied up, nothing hidden from view.

I thought about Brian and his unorthodox approach. Was he being rude or just using a variation on a selling skill I'd learned years before? Large corporations spend millions on high-priced think tanks to invent words to train salespeople in a week-long seminar at a fancy Florida resort when the busy schedule never lets anyone see the sun or walk on the beach. In one of those darkened rooms, I learned the concept of "selling in-depth."

It's a simple idea. You get the information you need not from the person buying the product or service but from everyone else. Buyers are trained to say no. They are the roadblocks keeping warehouses from being clogged with products that don't sell and systems overloaded with dysfunctional software. So, good salespeople look for the bridges that can connect them to the information they need to correctly position the reticent buyer.

And while Brian wasn't trying to sell us anything, he was asking questions, gathering information to make a better choice, and the best answers come directly from the people who would be doing the work—for Nestlé.

Soon Nestlé scheduled an interview with the usual top people, but it all seemed anticlimactic. Chef Brian had learned our culture, so anything said now only confirmed or canceled impressions already made.

Culture is not what the boss says or what happens when people are looking; culture is in the day-to-day when the boss is away. That's when you see the organization on full display.

We became the Nestlé sales agent for North and South Carolina, and the large Nestlé booth with chefs wearing pressed whites and tall hats was part of McIntyre*Sales*, with the three- and four-deep rows of people circling everything we did.

Thinking more about Brian and how he went about making his decision was not so different from how other Clients had made theirs. Like Brian, they may not have walked into the office unannounced, but they asked around. They watched us at food shows and saw which brokers used chairs in their booths and which did not. We never allowed chairs in our booth; the customers were on their feet, and we should be as well. And we never let people just walk by; we spoke to them. And, if there was a manufacturer without a broker, we were eager to help. Maybe we'd offer to fill in if they needed a restroom break or help them carry their stuff to the car when the show was over. You never know when a manufacturer might decide their fixed cost model would be better off with the variable cost of a broker. Rickitt & Colman, Chandler Barbecue, Larry's Sausage, and Adluh Flour all employed their own salespeople until they found us.

Everyone in an industry like ours knows everyone, and they talk more than people think. And they either say good things, or they don't.

Chapter 37

Positioning

2010

The new home for our business on Southside Drive had become our best asset. Our best foot forward, our better side in any portrait. It was easy to get to from anywhere, and once in the neighborhood, our McIntyre*Sales* black metal sign with the familiar green four-leaf clover was hard to miss. It looked like any other red brick bowed truss fifties building from the outside, but when you stepped in, the magic began.

The front door opened into a small yet tasteful waiting room with four guest chairs and a modern reception station under another McIntyre*Sales* logo. Glenda, our director of first impressions, would greet you and say we had been expecting you and were excited to have you with us today. She would ask you to make yourself at home in my office and offer to get you something to drink. Then she'd say I was probably in the back, helping George Rhinehardt, the warehouse manager, unpack samples and that she'd let me know you were here.

I'd appear in rolled-up shirtsleeves with my tie loosened, maybe sit in a side chair but never behind my desk. I might point out the poster from thirty years before and laugh about how, back then, I saw the food business as centered on me. And now, if I redid the poster, it would be centered on the customer.

Then I would say we'd meet in the conference room, but there was time to walk around first. As I unrolled my sleeves and buttoned each cuff, we'd start down the hall, the conference room with its double doors swung wide on the left with all the trophies and plaques naming us the best at this or that plainly in view. There were offices on the right and another small private conference room on the left, yet another straight ahead. Perhaps we had more conference rooms than most brokers because conference rooms are the best place to meet for a fair exchange of ideas. They are not "your place" or "my place." They're a "third place."

Kristi's office was the last on the right, then left at the computer room with its glass door letting visitors see all the wires and blinking lights.

We would step outside onto the double-loading docks, and I'd show them the prewired gas generator available for power if we needed phones, computers, and lights in a storm. During Hurricane Hugo in '89, power was out for weeks, and most businesses came to a halt. But with our generator, we could power what we needed, and even if our people couldn't make it to work, our new technology let phone calls automatically transfer to their homes. With our associate's home computer connected to our system, the caller thought we were business as usual.

They could see down the extended storage area that had once been an outdoor dock with its rail spur ending at our docks. The cracked asphalt, railroad tracks, and rusty fence had been replaced by crape myrtles and grass, courtesy of the City of Charlotte because when the light rail was built, the city needed a place to store construction equipment, and I had worked out a deal. The city could use the space for storage if they improved it when finished.

The large cotton bales were still on the neighbor's dock, but it had been years since I'd seen a rail car. Cotton had given way to microbrewers by now.

Back inside, the double stainless-steel sink and counter from the old Executive Street office had been repurposed to clean food show equipment as it returned.

We'd walk further inside, under a sizable double-pitched skylight directly above customer service. The natural light from the skylight, uplighting from the top of the binder bins, and carefully positioned workstations gave the space a comfortable feel, unlike most hectic call centers. We'd stop and visit a customer service specialist who would explain how they were organized, not by manufacturer, as were our competitors, but by distributor. Doing this meant a caller never needed to be transferred from one person to another. One call did it all.

Then, a visit with Gayle McKenzie, who managed deduction resolution. Gail would stand, smile, and offer a firm handshake in a way that let the guest know she was friendly and no-nonsense at the same time. She would explain how any invoice not paid in full meant the transaction wasn't complete, and as we were paid only on a completed transaction, we needed everything closed. Dragging it out was painful and costly for everyone. Gayle had been Mr. Biggers's secretary years ago, and she knew everyone, and everyone knew her. She could dig inside any problem and get to the answer, the resolution. Think of it as forensic science: not for evidence of a crime, but for the chain of events in a business transaction. Our competitors let salespeople try to resolve these problems, but that didn't work. The salesperson had often been the problem's cause by misquoting a price or some other mistake, so it was better to hand the deduction over to an expert who knew where to look. Yet another example of shifting the paradigm by letting people do what they do best.

Kristi's marketing team was next. Her five people had their own space, usually more creatively cluttered than the others. It might be the middle of summer, but John Brandtner would have a small aluminum Christmas tree in his corner with a vintage color wheel slowly revolving its red, blue, green, and yellow light on the sparkling icicle tinseled tree. When Kristi suggested something unusual for a presentation or meeting, the idea usually began with John. It is easier to turn down creativity than crank it up. And never shut it off entirely. Lauren Murray might be working on an Otis Spunkmeyer brochure, moving words and images around. She'd explain how salespeople told her what they wanted to accomplish, like selling more cookies to retirement homes, and she'd design the best tool for the best results. She'd also explain how Kristi would need to approve the final design and language before it was printed. That way, everything McIntyre*Sales* did had a consistent look and feel. Kristi stayed in contact with her marketing counterparts at the manufacturer to be sure we were using the words they wanted and the latest logo or design. Keeping "on message" was essential, Lauren would say. It was the same with any communication; other than interoffice memos, we wanted everything our Clients and Customers saw to be in optimistic yet straightforward "McIntyre-speak," as Kristi once called it. We didn't like each department writing in a different voice, using different typestyles, as though each department spoke a different language and rarely spoke to each other.

Around the corner, then out through the double glass doors from the air-conditioned office into the warehouse.

Concrete floors, a high bow truss wooden roof with three skylights, sprinkler system painted red. There were four-high racks with pallets stamped with our McIntyre*Sales* brand facing out. A large, noisy fan in the roof pulled hot air out while it sucked outside air in from the louvers in the long hall. The best we could do was have the temperature inside match the outdoors, and that's just what warehouses were in the South until SYSCO opened in Columbia. They air-conditioned everything, justifying the extra cost by attracting the best workers.

Rhinehardt would meet us, interrupting his sample unpacking or some other chore. I'd joke about how George Rhinehardt and I had an agreement: I ran the front, and he ran the rest.

We had used the walk-in cooler and freezer from the old office, plus added a new freezer more than six times the size of the one we brought with us. The new freezer was not only large enough to walk in, you could use a pallet jack or drive the forklift in if you wanted. It was huge.

The short hall between the freezers led to the covered dock we now called the bowling alley. Rhinehardt would point out the blue plastic storage bins with hinged lids we used as food show kits to store the items a Client needed for shows, like unique cutting boards, knives, mixing bowls, decorations, and whatever else our Client wanted in their booth. When the kits came back from a show, Rhinehardt would inventory the contents, clean everything and have them ready for the next show. He would zip-tie the lid and put the kit back in its spot. If the tie was in place, the equipment was ready for the next show, but if broken, the kit stayed until the contents were correct. This avoided the heated discussions when everyone was anxious in the final minutes of setting up for a show.

Then, back into the warehouse, where the racks my banker Tom Shaw had liked when he first saw the place had proven to be perfect. They gave us four-high shelves for pallets accessed with the forklift, moving up and down the five rows. Use the forklift to set the whole pallet down, get what is needed, and put the pallet back. Safer than using the fourteen-foot ladder or the rolling stairs. And, yes, both Rhinehardt and I are OSHA-compliant certified forklift operators.

Rhinehardt would point to a spot he'd picked for the prospective Client's samples. The location could be the warehouse, the cooler, or the freezer. And if they were a large client like Nestlé, they'd need a spot in all three. Rhinehardt would explain PAR levels—Periodic Automatic Replenishment—and how he would inventory the samples regularly, making sure what was needed was on hand. With over thirty Clients, each with dozens, even hundreds of different items, just keeping the samples organized could have been a full-time job. If the prospective Client had not started taking notes, this was when they usually began. We were answering questions they didn't even know they had. Everything was setting the stage.

Next, back into air conditioning as we walked under a large American flag hanging at the end of the warehouse, through another set of double glass doors into The Clover Café. With the remaining two pebbled chicken-wire glass skylights, this room could host a sit-down dinner for 150 guests using the dinnerware, flatware, and stemware Oneida gave us when they appointed us to represent them in the Carolinas. Oneida gave us our choice of patterns, and we chose an all-white sculpted design highlighted by our black-on-black checked table linen. That much dinnerware required multiple large rolling Cambro storage containers, another equipment manufacturer we had begun working with.

We held various events, including our annual Atlantic Coast Conference Final Four party. Customers watched the games on our giant screen while our chefs—in tall, pleated cylindrical-shaped white hats, white double-breasted jackets with knotted cloth buttons boasting the McIntyre*Sales* logo and their name and kitchen hierarchy embroidered on the chest—stationed themselves behind the Oneida silver chaffers, carving stations, and draped tables, preparing tapas plates for our guest. The whole scene rivaled the finest private clubs in the country.

Chef Charles usually wore his black loose-fitting pants with red chili peppers that he got when he started his career in New Orleans. Others wore their favorites.

The Clover Café staged new product launches, hosted distributor meetings, and provided the perfect venue for our neighbors to offer craft beer tastings. We could have quite a party with our five in-house executive chefs, all using only the products we sold.

Or, if the giant café needed to be more intimate, our rolling screen dividers could break the room into smaller sections or pull everything in tight for a small group around the open presentation kitchen. The presentation kitchen had all the usual equipment: two side-by-side convection ovens, a six-burner range with an oven below, a chargrill, a flat grill, and fryers, and everything on quick-release gas fittings so various pieces of equipment could quickly be added. If we needed to use an impinger conveyor belt pizza oven, we'd unhook one of the convection ovens and roll the special pizza oven into the spot. All under a twenty-seven-foot range hood that cost more than the yellow Plymouth all those years ago.

Piedmont Natural Gas was just around the corner on Yancey Road and had an even larger all-gas kitchen than ours. PNG used theirs to demonstrate the benefits of gas appliances over their electric competitors, mainly that gas costs less and that a gas flame is hot the moment you turn on the burner without waiting for it to warm up. We often swapped equipment or hosted overflow meetings when theirs was booked. Chef Aidan Waite, from Ipswich, England, was the Piedmont Natural Gas executive chef but spent almost as much time in our kitchen as theirs.

Two angled walls in each corner were designed for projecting a giant image of one of our chefs at work in the presentation kitchen from a camera high in the bowed ceiling aimed at the workstation. A large projection screen could also be lowered by pushing a button. A professional audio-video firm had wired the building from front to back. Screens, projectors, microphones—everything was state of the art.

Red metal fire doors led into the prep kitchen, held open by a weighted pulley system with lead fuses that would allow the doors to slam shut when melted by the flames of a fire. This design was typical in old buildings, and the fire marshal said, "If you're going to keep 'em, they gotta work." Finding the lead fuses wasn't easy, but the red doors added the perfect "pop" to the room when we had our white china on black covered tables with yellow chairs and the green four-leaf clover of The Clover Café sign above—all in a space that was still a warehouse with a concrete floor.

We'd go into the prep kitchen through the open fire doors and see the stainless-steel tables, overhead racks for utensils, reach-in coolers, freezers, and a Bunn commercial coffee and iced tea maker for the 150 guests. Two gravity-fed #10 can racks. A steamer, a ten-quart Hobart mixer, and a Hobart slicer. A fully vented dishwasher with the necessary racks, an Ecolab EPA-approved washing and sanitizing system, a three-hole sink, and a white Maytag washer and dryer set for our linens.

This room always held the biggest surprise for me. Either it would be empty, and I'd explain its use, or one of our chefs would be preparing for a presentation. Our chefs were not *cheffy* chefs, only there to make things look nice; ours were selling chefs, meaning they had customers to call on and sell to. Many of the larger operators and chains liked being called on by an executive chef; it was the prestige, perhaps. But also because more restaurants, hotels, private clubs, and up-scale retirement communities were finding it better to have their chefs out of the kitchen where they could visit tables, answering questions about ingredients or allergens, rather than being stuck in the kitchen preparing recipes seven days a week. So, our chefs could work with their chefs to find better, more consistent choices for the guests to rave about, freeing the chef to be seen by the patrons.

Besides, if a country club really wanted everything done in-house and from scratch, as they claimed, they would need to convert the entire 18-hole golf course into a farm and raise their own pigs and chickens, stock the ponds, grow their own grain, and all the others things necessary for an authentic farm-to-fork experience.

Don't get me wrong; farm-to-fork, as the idea of buying local food from local farms, is terrific as long as guests are okay not having lettuce or strawberries year-round. Otherwise, many products need to be trucked in. And as for making everything from scratch in the kitchen, sometimes that's fine, but at others it's foolish. The concept called "foodservice math" says it costs less to pay more. And as crazy as that sounds, let me give you an example.

A restaurant can buy large shrimp that average twenty-one to twenty-five shrimp per pound. The shrimp will have been frozen just as they were pulled up from the ocean's floor, so the complete shellfish with head, shell, legs, little claws, and tail fins for swimming are all still in place, along with a sizeable digestive vein that runs the entire length of the shrimp. Depending on color and origin, the restaurant will pay around $9 to $10 for a pound of these shrimp.

But now, the shrimp must be headed, peeled, deveined, and cooked, and when all the steps are complete, our shrimp will have lost half their weight. So, the shrimp have doubled in price, and the restaurant still hasn't paid the employee for all the work. Plus, the restaurant doesn't want just anyone doing all of this, because if they mess up a few or accidentally pull off the swimmerets for the ones going in the shrimp cocktail, that makes the remaining shrimp even more costly.

Alternatively, the restaurant can pay about $23 a pound for a processing plant to perfectly prepare the shrimp and not need someone standing for hours doing the tedious work. You can see how it costs less to pay more.

We could also talk about cookies. I can't begin to count the number of tastings we won with our Otis Spunkmeyer cookies. The country club's pastry chef could labor for over half a day to bake cookies from scratch, whereas we would pop our frozen Otis cookies in the preheated oven for under fifteen minutes. Both batches would come out of the oven piping hot, but the Otis cookies would cost no more, often less, and as I said, were judged to be the best.

While using phrases like "from scratch" and "in house" may conjure images at their best and most satisfying, it's not always practical or even the tastiest. But it's hard to explain that to someone with an ego, especially with the ego of someone making hundreds of thousands of dollars each year from the illusion they've painted for naive patrons and unaware upper management.

So we stuck to the people who would listen because, after all, we weren't paid on conversations, only sales.

With the various backgrounds of our chefs, we could match them to the operator's needs. Chef Sian Doran was from London, living in Winston-Salem on a green card. Chef Charles Deal lived in Wilmington, North Carolina. He was from Slidell, Louisiana, graduated from Johnson and Wales in Charleston, and had worked in the best kitchens in New Orleans. Chef Ed Sautro from Levy Restaurants in Chicago worked in Raleigh. Chef Tim Zehnal was from Pennsylvania, and Chef Brian Palombo was from The Bald Head Island Country Club, where he had served as executive chef before moving to Charlotte. Chef Brian from Bald Head was particularly knowledgeable about cheese. He could tell you which side of the hill the cows grazed on from his first bite. If it was imported, he knew about it, and we sold it.

In the prep kitchen, we might find a gathering of distributor sales representatives in the glass-walled Product Knowledge classroom, where a group could meet at one end of the kitchen as they evaluated menu ideas. Or we might come upon one of our sales associates meeting with an operator who had stopped by to pick up a sample for a menu review meeting their restaurant chain was holding on Monday.

Whatever we found, I'd let them explain why they were there and the value of our facility. Better to let others do the talking, sometimes. Plus, it gave me a break.

Everyone said the health department would give us a perfect score, but since we never charged, we were never inspected.

Back through the warehouse and into the front office with the mail room on the right. The giant copy machine would be spitting out the color Otis Spunkmeyer brochures Lauren had created and Kristi had approved, and I would offer the prospective client one as a sample. I'd then point out the literature storage area where we kept fact sheets on everything we sold. There wasn't a single product that we didn't know the exact nutrition breakdown and ingredients of, and those were more and more in demand as restaurants found their customers now cared about what they were eating. Then past the small customer service conference room, and finally up front to the main conference room.

We had made a giant circle with a few detours as we toured what many said was the finest facility of its kind anywhere. It was quite a building, and every bit of our tour was scripted, except what we might find in the prep kitchen. But isn't that what it's about? There is no better one-word definition of sales than the word *positioning*. And scripting lets the process move the buyer to a position of needing what the salesperson is offering. In other words, the want becomes the need.

By the time we were back in the main conference room, most questions had been answered, and the buyer, or the prospective client, was positioned to need what we offered.

We had the usual PowerPoint presentation ready if needed. One of the managers would give a short overview, but the purpose of each word—each image—was to help the audience progress through the message. We would plan each image as if it were a traffic sign directing the conversation to a successful conclusion.

There was one thing I'd saved for last. Maybe I had alluded to our "Carolina 500" on our tour but never explained it in detail. The name sounded like a NASCAR event, but it was our proprietary database of the top 500 operator customers in the market. They were restaurants, chains, hotels, hospitals, schools, universities, and anyone else serving food away from home. They had been chosen, not by size but by influence. These 500 operator customers knew how to speak up and get what they wanted. Our tag line said, "Expect Results," and these 500 guaranteed delivery.

We could sort the data by type, size, location, preferred distributor, menu rotations, and day-parts (that's foodservice speak for breakfast, lunch, or dinner. Easier to say *day-part*, I guess). We even had birthdays for decision makers and would send a card.

We could do a query asking for the restaurants in the Triad who bought from SYSCO and served breakfast, then, with the mapping software we had developed, plot our sales rep's route, much as UPS and others do today. When this select group was presented with a new item, demand swelled. SYSCO needed to stock the item because that's what so many wanted. It wasn't McIntyre*Sales* forcing something on them, only that so many of SYSCO's customers wanted the item available. Subtle perhaps, but essential to the relationship we needed to maintain.

Yes, the *Observer* had been right in the story about our building: " . . . visitors saw an old warehouse from the street, but once inside, they were greeted by modern design, ambient lighting, new plumbing, HVAC, electrical, and energy-efficient windows. It was no longer an abandoned sheet metal shop but now a modern functioning workplace."

McIntyre*Sales* had come a long way from the two Scotch-Irish lads selling Italian man-a-cot to Greek restaurant owners.

So that is what Todd wanted to buy. Not the impressive building, as he would lease that, but a business and reputation built over thirty years by people putting their drops in the bucket of our success. People like Kristi and George, Glenda and Rheinhardt, marketing people, sales professionals, chefs, K-12 school specialists, nutrition specialists, beverage specialists, customer service, and accounting. All understanding that nothing happens until something gets sold.

Chapter 38

clang, Clang, CLANG, Went the Bell

July 28, 2010

Number 35 of 35, my final treatment. I climbed out of the wheel-chair, with help, and onto the cold table.

I gave the wad of Dubble Bubble a few last chews as best I could, packed it in place, then positioned the mouthpiece just so. My last chance at perfect, I thought.

The tech matched the faded dot on my skin to the line on the mask, then snapped it in place for the final time. Next, she stepped behind her protective wall. The light-gray targeted radiation machine began its slow build to a whirling muffled aggravation which I tried to ignore. I repeated to myself:

Yea, though I walk through the valley of the shadow of death, I will fear no evil: for thou art with me; thy rod and thy staff they comfort me... Thou preparest a table before me in the presence of mine enemies: thou anointest my head with oil; my cup runneth over... Surely good-ness and mercy shall follow me all the days of my life: and I will dwell in the house of the Lord forever.

Again, from the top.

Charles Bruce McIntyre

The Lord is my shepherd; I shall not want... He maketh me to lie down in green pastures: he leadeth me beside the still waters. He restoreth my soul: he leadeth me in the paths of righteousness for his name's sake. Yea, though I walk... I drifted off and lost my place. Started over. *Again,* I told myself. I knew the words; I'd been reciting them all my life. They were in there; I just needed to get them out.

Finally, the machine began to slow, and the rumbling noise receded: "That's it!" she said as the lights came on.

"Hurry, unsnap the mask!" I wanted to yell. The confinement of having my head strapped to a place I didn't want to be had been terrifying these past seven weeks. What if she forgot? Had a heart attack before she reached me? What if I was there for hours, yelling for help, and no one came?

Finally, I was free. I spit the bubble gum and mouthpiece into the tissue I'd kept in my clenched fist as she rolled me to my right and swung my winter-white legs off the metal table, my bare feet hanging limply above the tile floor. With help, I slid, ever so thankfully, into the waiting wheelchair.

A group in maroon scrubs had gathered in the hallway as she rolled me out. Locking my chair, the tech helped me reach up, her hand over mine, as together we took hold of the knotted lanyard to give the brass ship's bell mounted on the wall a swift strike.

"Clang" reverberated softly but loud enough for the entire wing to hear. "Again," I demanded. Then I asked, "One more time?" Everyone laughed. I tried to find a smile but choked up, my hands rising out of my lap to hide the tears of relief streaming down my face.

It was over.

"Want to keep your mask?" one person asked.

192

"Why would I?"

"Some people like them. Souvenir, I guess."

"No, I don't think so. I won't have any trouble remembering." And besides, I didn't plan to be wearing as many masks as before.

They did give me a "Certificate of Completion." A blue-coated volunteer rolled me out. I was a different man than the one who had jauntily strode in the door seven weeks before. I was tired and weak, skinnier and with less hair on my head, but humbled in ways that would take years to understand and even longer to explain.

Now to make it upstairs to infusion. My hemoglobin should have been between 14 and 18 grams per deciliter. Instead, it was 8.5. Rather than a magnum of sparkling Chardonnay (which my swollen throat couldn't swallow anyway), it would be two units of blood as my celebratory toast.

It was a big week: I finished radiation Wednesday, and on Thursday, a FedEx envelope arrived at the front door from Barry with the paperwork to be signed for the sale, along with a return envelope. I signed the papers, and Joyce stuffed them in the envelope and took everything to the nearest FedEx drop-off box. The sale was now complete. Todd's wire transfer would hit my bank Friday morning. I sat on the dark terrace, exhausted, slowly pumping a midnight snack, thinking about how it was time to start rebuilding what the treatments had torn down.

Chapter 39

Zen, Baby

Joyce and I had started Pilates in 2009 when our friend, Sabrina Berry, began teaching at the Iron Butterfly. Sabrina was also our granddaughter's ballet teacher, so we had known her for years. Once the treatment plan was determined, I wanted to maintain whatever strength and flexibility I could, so I'm sure I was the only student who climbed on her reformer to do "serve-a-tray" and "draw-a-sword" with a feeding tube sticking out of his belly.

July 30, 2010

I spent Friday trying to relax around the house. I took a nap in the morning and another after pumping lunch. I was gathering my energy for that evening. I planned to shower after dinner, tape down my tube, and put on some clothes I'd found in the back of my closet from when I was so thin with celiac. I'd bought them in the boy's department at Belk, but they were nice enough and as stylish as men my age ever look.

"Zen, Baby," choreographed by Sabrina Berry, would premiere in Booth Theatre that night at eight. The performance was by the

North Carolina Dance Theater's (now Charlotte Ballet) advanced-level modern students, and I'd been looking forward to this evening since I learned about it a few weeks back.

Sabrina, a Juilliard School BFA in dance, had choreographed the performance in tribute to me and my fight, and wrote in the program: "I am hoping it will capture a very focused push through something heavy and that it can be a tribalist stirring of healing energy to send his way."

Zen, Baby would be my coming out party, my reveal. I knew many who planned to attend, but not all. And, of course, there would be the usual eclectic balletomane. Or ballet enthusiasts if you prefer.

I wondered, as I began to drift off in another nap, would the applause at the end bring Sabrina to the stage? Would someone hand her a large bouquet as she bowed to the audience with the back of her free hand, lithely sweeping the foam-backed flooring, then straighten, motioning me to join her? All done in the fluent way ballet dancers have of looking aesthetically graceful while performing the most demanding of feats.

We planned to leave the house at seven to be early and get good seats. I was doing okay, not great, but okay when I stepped through the bedroom door. Then suddenly, an imaginary giant hand shoved me back across the bed.

"You ready?" Joyce called from the hallway.

"I can't," I whispered, too weak to say more.

I tried again, but there was no way I could even explain how I felt. I rolled to my side and lay facing the window.

By eight, I was still fully dressed, but sound asleep.

The next day I learned the performance had been a huge success, a sellout.

Sabrina wrote on CaringBridge how beautifully everything went and how much positive energy each dancer sent me. James Ferguson, the dancer who played me, wrote how he had wanted us to meet before the program began, wanting to capture my spirit for his performance, but that Sabrina had coached him well. James hoped I could feel the flow he was sending.

Several friends from the Urban Ministry Center where I volunteered were in the audience and made CaringBridge entries.

Disappointed, oppressed, crestfallen, and sad. I stewed all weekend. I planned to call Sabrina on Monday, hoping she would understand. I had been so looking forward to the evening, the celebration. It would have been my return to the living, like Jesus raising Lazarus from the dead (not really, but that's how I felt).

Laura wrote on CaringBridge, " . . . in the piece, I saw portrayals of my father's journey, including diagnosis, shock and horror, treatment and effects, and the beginning of recovery. Dancers represented my dad, mom, doctors, and Dad's friends. The dance was beautiful and strong. The dancers projected a focused, intense energy, courage, determination, and the essence of a community who lifts each other up when fatigue overcomes."

And I missed it.

The group went to El Salvador without me in September and brought back a poster from the ice cream shop we always visited. Yolanda, the shop's owner, had given the group a giant poster showing all the various La Neveria ice cream novelties, and everyone had written, "Get well soon," on the sign, even Yolanda.

Would ice cream taste good melted and pumped in through a tube? No, I'd tried that with coffee, and it's the taste buds that do the tasting, and they're not deep in your gut. So I'd need to wait until my fried buds grew new tasters. And that would take time.

Chapter 40

A Farewell and a Beginning

The first day of August was the day Todd took over the company. Did he have a big meeting, then bring the different teams together? I'm sure Kristi and George were helpful, but what did everyone say, what did they ask, what did they think?

"The king is dead, long live the king" is the only expression that comes to mind. I was gone, and Todd was now in my place. There's no contradiction in that idea, business is business, and loyalty should follow the name on the bottom of the paycheck.

In ways, I would have liked to have been there, but it was right for Todd to be the main event. It was his time to take center stage. He was the consolidator, and the consolidations would only continue. His turn was now, but in time it would be someone else. Everyone thinks their industry is different, but from automobiles to airlines, bookstores to barbershops, on and on, there is never much left of small businesses after consolidation begins.

I would have liked to go in and say goodbye to a few people, maybe late some afternoon, but no one asked, and I was too weak to have accepted even if they did. I stayed in touch with Laura Bates, who helped wrap up some details for the company. I kept the McIntyre*Sales* bank accounts open, and Laura paid the final bills. We would meet somewhere away from the office, and I would sign the checks, but she was never eager to talk about how things were going, so I stopped asking and slowly drifted away. It was over.

August 1

August 1 is the day my ancient Celt ancestors called Quarter Day, the day equally between the summer solstice and the autumn equinox, and the time of year crops begin to ripen as much by night as by day. I wondered if the darkness could be as crucial to my healing as the light. I wasn't sure, but I sat on the terrace, pumping in nutrition, surrounded by darkness. I thought, *Be still, breathe, think, listen. Listen to my mind while listening to my heart. Those two are equals, the mind and the spirit, the darkness and light.*

The Celts in my family came from Scotland and Ireland, but also from the Netherlands and Western Europe. They didn't bring much with them because they didn't have much. But then, it's not the "haves" who bring; the haves only stay and take.

The one thing my ancestors knew was that there was land here in America, open land and plenty of it, with no stone walls, no landed gentry, and no rules. Just pick a spot and make a life. And if that spot was taken, move further west. The Celts, and all the others who came with them, understood that America offered hope and that alone was worth the risk.

And that's what my ancient Celt relatives kept close, that feeling of hope. And it's the same feeling I was sitting in the darkness with on Quarter Day all these years later, waiting for the arrival of the sun and the arrival of hope.

A Farewell and a Beginning

It was as though I was in a battle to add more years to my life; at least, that was my hope. And each time I looked further into the future, I also looked further into the past. For the first time in years, I thought about how it all began, about my parents and the lessons they taught me.

1941

My parents were in their mid-thirties when they had me. I was the only child of Helen Lorene Kaltreider McIntyre and Kenneth Brown McIntyre. Mother, three months older than Dad, was born on December 16, 1905, in Pinson, ninety miles northeast of Memphis, the youngest of Mattie and Daniel Kaltreider's three girls.

Daniel Kaltreider had a farm, and my mom rode her horse to a one-room school each day, where the horse waited outside until lunchtime when she gave him the apple she had packed. At Christmas, she and her older sisters got oranges and nuts in their stockings, and maybe a bolt of cloth from the store to make dresses.

My dad was from Eden, just outside Sparta, Illinois, but he always claimed Sparta as home. On March 19, 1906, he was born the second child of Eliza Jane Adams McIntyre and Martin Steele McIntyre.

My grandfather Martin was a coal miner, and Dad knew that was not the life he wanted for himself, so when he graduated from grammar school, he headed west, aiming to look for gold. After six months in San Francisco, where he acquired a large heart tattoo with a dagger thrust through its center and a banner across the middle with a blank spot for a name on his left upper arm, he went north to Seattle.

Out of money, he saw a hand-painted sign advertising for men to build telephone offices. Phones were new then, and he didn't know much about them. "Apply Within," the sign said.

It wasn't gold, and he hadn't made it to Alaska, but it was a job.

After that first year, homesickness set in, and he was ready to go back east, or at least as far east as Illinois.

His boss said he was sorry to see my dad go, but did he have a job waiting for him when he got home?

The boss had an idea. Western Electric, the company he worked for, needed telephone offices everywhere, not just in Seattle, so why not let Western Electric give him work back east, plus pay his way across the country? Relocation, they called it, and it would be the first of many paid moves for my dad.

Western Electric was the only company my dad ever worked for.

His work was now in St. Louis, and he drove his maroon Ford convertible the fifty miles to Sparta on weekends.

Meanwhile, my mom was now living in town after her mother had died of pneumonia. Her dad had remarried, and his new wife said farming was too much work, so they'd bought a general store. Edith and Ethel, Mom's two older sisters, were off on their own by now, so Mom did what she could to pitch in at the store, kept the books, and helped behind the counter on weekends.

Her father's store had caskets on the third floor and two carriages for funerals: one white, even the horses, and the other all black. Mother mostly drove the white carriage, but sometimes she would drive the black rig if the hired hand missed work.

The only picture I ever saw of Daniel Kaltreider's new wife, my mother's stepmother, showed a tall, tight-lipped, straight-backed woman in all black, standing alone in front of a wood-frame house in need of paint. The woman looked like she might break if you bent her wrong. Mother wrote on the back, "Miss Alice, my stepmother who my father married when I was about twelve years of age." They didn't get along.

Mother was visiting her sister, Ethel, in Memphis when she learned that American Telephone and Telegraph needed operators to work the switchboards in Western Electric's new offices. This was her chance to get away from her stepmother. The man at the interview said she had her choice of two spots, Hendersonville, North Carolina, or a new development in Florida called Miami Beach. She knew about mountains, being from Tennessee, but not about beaches or oceans, so she chose the second.

She lived in a dormitory over the drug store on Miami Beach with six other girls on Collins Avenue. She plugged cables into the holes on the switchboard all day while the real-estate men, in their fancy cars, drove their clients up and down the empty beach that stretched forever, selling every square foot of sandy land they could see.

She and her roommates probably made footprints in the sand until the waves washed most away, returning the beach to its pristine condition. I wondered if she still carried memories of those days or if time, like the waves, had washed them away.

I wondered, late at night as I sat on the terrace or under the giant oak on the bench: Would time take away my memories of cancer like the waves took away her footprints? Or is it possible for some memories, like some footprints, to remain?

Maybe Mother got homesick too, like Dad. But rather than return to the general store in Pinson, she got a transfer to St. Louis. She was doing the same job as before, bored maybe, and often gazed at a shiny maroon Ford convertible parked in the same spot each day. It looked like a fun car—top down, warm spring days—she wondered who owned it.

You can probably finish the story on your own, but that's how they met, and on my mother's twenty-third birthday, December 16, 1928, they married.

New telephone offices were springing up everywhere back then, so they packed what little they owned in the convertible every six or nine months and moved to the next job and their next furnished apartment.

Dad was good at what he did and wanted to do more, but needed more schooling. Telephone equipment was complicated enough in the beginning, but now it was growing more so. He needed training.

Correspondence school was the answer since they never stayed in one place very long. The school mailed the assignments to Dad's new address, and he returned the work quickly. It took a long time, but eventually, he earned his Electrical Engineering degree, with straight As on every report card.

Now he was a supervisor, telling others how to build the offices, and Mom and Dad didn't need to move so often. He could sit behind a desk. They started buying their own furniture, fishing on week-ends, and driving to Florida for vacation.

They visited Miami Beach a few times; I'm sure Mom showed Dad where she and her dorm mates took picnics when they went to the beach.

A Farewell and a Beginning

On Friday, October 18, 1940, Dad went deep-sea fishing with four other men. Maybe friends, but probably average guys who signed up for the adventure. In a photograph taken when they returned to the dock, they look proud standing next to the sailfish each caught that fall day. Dad's fish was six foot ten inches long and weighed forty-two pounds. Dad is easy to spot in the group of men; he has the broadest smile. The certificate lists his address as Vinita Park, Missouri, not far from where I went to school many years later.

With a swagger in Dad's step, no doubt, Mom and Dad returned to the hotel where they were staying for a quiet evening. I was born in St. Louis on July 14, 1941, nine months and four days after my dad landed that prize sailfish.

I'm happy my mother saved the photo along with the certificate. And I'm glad she let me figure it out on my own. Sometimes that's best.

Chapter 41

The Curious Red-Headed Boy

August 2010

I greeted another day and another pumped meal on the dark terrace—the way all mornings seemed to start now. Sitting there was like watching a slow-motion montage of pages being repeatedly torn off a calendar and then flying away in the breeze, but there wasn't a button to speed up the video, so all I could do was be patient as I sat looking at the dark golf course and waiting for the sun to reach the tops of the trees.

Overlooking a private golf course is like overlooking a vast ocean. It's fantastic by day, but a giant nothing at night. Just darkness, a vast void. "Pump in the nutrition; it will be morning soon," I said to myself.

Be still, breathe, think, and listen. Listening and doing it fully and well is the greatest gift you will ever give yourself or anyone else.

My mother only had one name for me when I was born: Charles. When Dad and his friends visited the hospital, they goggled at the cute little baby and called the new arrival everything but Charles. There was Charlie, of course, and Chuck, Chip, Chaz, and Chad. That wouldn't do. I needed a name that wasn't so common without all the different ways to say the same thing. She thought and thought until she came up with Bruce. Charles Bruce McIntyre, that's who I'd be.

And that's all fine, but people get called by their first name, not the one in the middle, so I was in kindergarten before I learned about my "Charles" name. I'd been there three days, and the teacher kept marking Charles absent until she asked, "Who are you?"

To this day, if asked to give my name for something like a carry-out order in a restaurant or coffee shop, I say, "Carlos." It's easy to remember, like Puny Mann, and in no way do I look like a Carlos.

August and September were spent in bed or on the terrace. Or in the blue chair in front of the TV if my Cardinals were playing. Watching a baseball game on television was a nice treat, especially in the early afternoon in the middle of a work week. Before, I was always too busy to keep up with the standings, let alone watch a game.

Frankly, I felt guilty. I knew everyone at the company was busy, restaurants were crowded, and the hospital was always full. Maybe the woman who molded my mask months ago was right when she talked about relaxation being a cure for anxiety. Perhaps I had finally learned to slow down and no longer needed to check every box on my long to-do list.

So, I leaned back in my blue leather recliner and watched the game. I had my favorites; we all do, I guess. Mine were guys like

Yadier Molina, Matt Holliday, and Chris Carpenter. But my most favorite of all was David Freese. Yet, after the 2013 season, he was traded to the Angels. But that's baseball. That's business. That's life. Not like when I was young, and guys like Stan Musial spent their entire career in the same town with the same team. Or my dad, who spent his entire career with the same company.

Four meals a day was my pattern, my necessity, each the same. Mary Holland, the licensed dietitian at Presbyterian Hospital, with her master's in public health, researched and found a fortified meal supplement that would do the job. Four each day gave me over 2,200 calories and 90 grams of protein. Yet even with that much protein, I felt like it was winter, despite the swampy heat of our Carolina summers. Not that I needed a sweater, but my energy was moving inward, to my core. Like I was resting up for something, hibernating, perhaps. For me, sitting for hours on our terrace was becoming a time for contemplation and the restoration my body needed. Adding another Carnation might help. That would make almost 2,800 calories, and I doubted I'd get fat.

I was still returning to Presbyterian Hospital for IVs—I needed more hydration and could only make myself pump in so much water. The mechanical suction pump from the home health people was still collecting mucus; I still had as much, maybe more, but the process had become more routine. Do anything often enough, and it becomes a habit, I guess.

Ken gave me soft disposable red toothbrushes from his CharlottePerio office, and a simple mouthwash solution of baking soda and saltwater helped remove the layer of scum that continued to coat the inside of my mouth. The homemade mouthwash burned some, but not bad. Any medicine, even a pain reliever like Tylenol, needed to be liquid and go in the tube. Just staying clean and fed was a full-time job. *Be still, breathe, think, listen.*

When I was only about one or two, my dad was transferred to the AT&T home office at 195 Broadway in New York City. It's just across Sixth Avenue from where the original World Trade Center would be built in 1973. That was during World War II, and they said his job was essential—part of the war effort—so we'd be there for a while. Mom and Dad found a small house in Kearny, a suburb of Newark, on a little patch of land, and Dad rode the train to work every day. Mom and I stayed home and played in the yard. I remember stomping tin cans flat and putting them in a gunny sack. All part of the war effort, like rationing books, coupons for gas and food, and us needing to live in New Jersey.

Mother was able to buy a few things while we were there. On a shopping trip where people set up stuff for sale on the sidewalk, we'd call it a pop-up today, she bought a small picture that was made from different colors of felt cutouts. The boy, about my age back then, is holding a baby chicken, studying it closely as the mother hen stares up at her young chick in his hand. He's got a straw hat pushed back on his head and a casually sewn patch on the left knee of his gray overalls. His red hair comes down on his forehead from under the hat as he examines the baby in his hand.

I called the picture "The Curious Red-Headed Boy." He was with me until I went to college and out into the world, but his curious spirit stayed with me. And when my mother moved to Charlotte in 1984, she brought the picture along.

Today, as I write this story, he is standing watch from his spot over my study window, still looking, still curious. I wonder if he is curious only because he is young, or could it be curiosity keeping him that way? Whatever the answer, he's not changed. His hair is still red, while mine has turned gray.

Chapter 42

Cancer-free

September 28, 2010

"One hundred percent cancer-free," Dr. Harley said after reading the PET scan on that last Tuesday in September. It had been 140 days since May 13 when he stood at the foot of my bed in the recovery room to tell me I had cancer, and now it was over.

Joyce hugged him, careful not to let tears fall on his starched white coat. I reached out for his hand, but he pulled me into the hug with Joyce. Maybe he didn't care as much about his white coat as we thought.

Waves of emotion began to hit me. Relief and gratitude were first. It had been a long journey, and now I was free. I would have shouted if my voice were stronger. I had always been the loudest voice in the audience when our grandchildren performed. My *"Brava!"* or *"Bravo!"* was perfectly timed for the moment so it could be heard over the others and they would know it was me. But now, it was all I could do to whisper a faint, "Thank you."

The waves of emotion kept coming, more serene, peaceful some-how. I was rid of my cancer. Its weight removed, I could stand taller, all the things I had prayed for since I first feared the worst. I was fortunate. Others were not so lucky. I thought about them and their pain when the results were not like mine. The shattered hopes.

I was grateful for all the care I had received, each trained professional, every gentle hand, and so many drops in the bucket. The prayers from so many, the angels who guided my way.

Joyce suggested we celebrate with a nice dinner. I agreed, and even though I still had the feeding tube in place, I could eat more on my own these days. She suggested a few places, but I insisted on the Golden Corral on South Boulevard.

Golden Corral ran commercials during baseball games, and my dry mouth would start to water when I saw their ads. Plate after plate of mouth-watering food you could enjoy until you could barely make it out the door. That's the celebration I wanted.

Laura and her children, Elizabeth and Kenny, were able to join us, and the five of us sat at Golden Corral as I slowly worked my way through another slice of prime rib and more mashed potatoes.

I was now strong enough to go back to Pilates. Sabrina had opened a studio in the Dilworth Artisan Station. Sandvi Studio was on the second floor, looking up at Charlotte's skyline.

When Joyce and I first visited, Joyce reminded me to thank Sabrina again for the coffee table books she had sent as a get well gift. I had written her a note, but it never hurts to say something like that again.

Sabrina had no way of knowing the significance of the two books she had chosen: *Scotland, Where Golf is Great* with its connection to my past, and *Sacred Places* with its connection to my family's future.

Scotland, Where Golf is Great contains a section devoted to Loch Lomond and Ayrshire, Kintyre, and the Isles, where my dad's people were from before crossing the twelve miles of Irish Sea to the Antrim coast of Northern Ireland.

The other, *Sacred Places*, includes the pilgrimage of Camino de Santiago in Spain. Our oldest granddaughter and Sabrina's pupil would walk that sacred journey years later, perhaps searching for purpose and meaning in her life.

It felt good to be out in the world again as Sabrina began our "duet." She put Joyce on the tall reformer and me on the shorter one, nearer the hardwood floor, in case I lost my balance. Sabrina kept one hand near my waist when I was on the reformer, knowing my body was weak. She worked out a series of exercises I could do; not much to begin with, but adding more each week. It takes hundreds of baby steps to get to a giant leap, but I was getting stronger. It was fun getting back to serve-a-tray and draw-a-sword. Hard work, but fun.

The artists were just arriving when we left Sabrina and the Dilworth Artisan Station. Their doors were open, and the unmistakable aroma of linseed oil and turpentine assured me my sense of smell was returning.

After Sabrina's, we would go to Toast, a restaurant on Park Road, where I would order a stack of gluten-free pancakes along with two eggs over easy. Lots of butter, maple syrup, and coffee. The eggs came on a separate plate, but I slid them on top of the pancakes like I'd seen Grandpa do when I was little. Then I lifted each pancake with my fork to get plenty of butter and syrup on each, stacked the whole thing up, then put the remaining syrup on top. Salt and pepper the eggs, pick up my knife and fork and cut one slice at a time like I was serving slices of a tall layer cake at a party.

Joyce patiently waited as I chewed each bite. Eating was slower now, and many said that was good, so I was doing okay. She had long since finished her regular pancakes and coffee.

My taste buds were gone for so long, but now they were returning. Maybe my new taste buds taught me the enjoyment of simple things—like hot pancakes with melting butter and warm, comforting syrup. Perhaps the simple things I discovered by accident brought more joy than my eternal search for something I might never find.

I was reading more, but not the business books I'd favored earlier in life; these were books that spoke to me where I was now. Barbara Taylor Brown's *Learning to Walk in the Dark* was a gift from Michelle Thomas-Bush at church. Taylor Brown challenged me to think of darkness differently, guiding me spiritually in ways I could see and not. Tan Twan Eng's *The Gift of Rain* and *The Garden of Evening Mists* are Malaysian novels with a deep understanding of nature and its powerful yet silent effect on healing, both in remembering and forgetting.

And I read *The Shipping News* by Annie Proulx, set in harsh Newfoundland, the most easterly province of Canada, a place I had visited and would, in time, return, but as Marcel Proust said, with "new eyes."

Poco a poco, my friends in El Salvador would say as we worked together building Habitat for Humanity homes. Little by little, I was finding my way back to normal. Things can be better that way. Baby steps rather than one giant leap were how a new spirituality entered my life, and I liked that approach.

Enlightenment can be like darkness giving way to the dawn, *poco a poco*. Wait until the sun crosses the horizon to step outside, and you miss the best part. The drama comes before the main event.

I'm absorbed into daily rhythms without my calendar controlling the cycle, more like gentle tugs of the universe than the ticking hands of a clock. I wear a sweater when I'm cold— take it off when I'm not. I'm not controlled by the seasons but by an inner sense of well-being.

In the same way, I think about my healing not as a pattern I control but as nature knowing when it's ready. I can take more steps each day and try harder, but is it my extra effort or the universe opening the door?

Poco a poco. Absorption isn't static, it's a process, and if I'm part of nature, part of the universe, then I play by her rules.

Chapter 43

Alternatives

2011

I was driving again, not far, but back on my own. I began acupuncture with Amy Rhodes a few months after my last treatment. Her sessions helped open my throat and made swallowing easier. I went to the Buddy Kemp House, a support center for cancer patients and their families, trying to process what the disease had done to their lives and to meet other people who were going through similar struggles. I developed a Tai Chi routine with my instructor Mike Gentile, who I met at the Cornwell Center. It's part of Myers Park Baptist Church, offering fitness and wellness classes, art, pottery, kids camps, and after-school programs. They provide an unmatched setting and a wide range of programming to develop the mind, body, and spirit.

I'd practice Tai Chi each morning as the sun moved down a single tree in our backyard. I envisioned myself as fluid as the tree in the lightly stirring morning air. I began yoga with Mary Lou Buck and started passage meditation after reading books by Eknath Easwaran of the Blue Mountain Center of Meditation. I started deep-tissue massage with Sara Vavra to realign the deeper layers of the connective tissue in my neck and throat.

I was exploring alternative ways of healing, and each was exciting. There's much to learn from other cultures, when we are willing to explore. Maybe that's the key because if readiness is essential for learning, then openness is essential for readiness. If my mind is closed, there's no sense even talking about things. But there are more healing ideas when I'm open, and maybe the only difference between a conservative and a progressive is that the conservative hasn't been open to a new idea in twenty years. Or, as Voltaire said, "Uncertainty is an uncomfortable position. But certainty is an absurd one."

I talked to others about their experience, their journey, what had helped, and what had not. No two cancers are alike, just as no two people are alike, so I listened. Many, like me, were finding help in alternative ways.

Now, when I talk with people just beginning treatment, I am careful not to give advice, but only tell my story and what worked for me.

After about five weeks, I began eating small bites of solid food. Only scrambled eggs and grits at first, then I tried applesauce and flan (not as fancy as it sounds—just milk, eggs, and sugar, and you buy it premade in the store). But nothing tasted right, or not like I remembered. Maybe I couldn't taste at all, plus the doctors had said some tastes might never return, so this was how it was going to be, I guessed. Still, eating was slow. My throat was still swollen, and just the simple act of chewing wore me out.

Chapter 44

Work on It for a While, and Then I'll Be Along

Circa 1950

The relocations continued as I grew up. My mother counted thirteen different grade schools, and while I can't name them all, I do remember my third-grade year being divided between Little Rock, Wichita, and St. Louis.

Being an only child with no brothers or sisters and parents older than most kids my age had meant I learned to play by myself, to make up games, and even rules. Things other kids did with playmates, I did alone. I had books like Tom Sawyer and Huck Finn, but the large blue books called *My Book House* were my favorites. They held popular children's literature that Olive Beaupre Miller edited to equip children for life. She presented the stories as the child was ready to understand their meaning. Again, you might say: readiness is essential for learning. There was Shakespeare, Wordsworth, Dickens, and others, along with countless colored illustrations, all laid out in a natural progression as I matured. The volumes had stories like "Little Black Sambo" and "The Tar Baby," but Ms. Miller would later take those out as "distorted." I'm not sure I read every story in each book, but I read many and marveled at each drawing.

My parents felt Scouting was necessary for any boy's upbringing, so I started as a Cub. Mom was our den mother and always had projects waiting when our den met. One was a plaque cut from a sheet of plywood with a jigsaw; she told us to be careful with the saw. After drilling three holes to mount the Wolf, Bear, and Lion heads we cast from white plaster in rubber molds, we shellacked the plaque.

We couldn't finish the project in one meeting, so she sent the boys home with their unfinished work and told them to bring it back next week. I asked Mom if she'd help me with mine. I'd get a jump on the others before we next met.

"Sure," she said, "but I've got a better idea. Why don't you work on it for a while, and then I'll be along?" I got each animal's color right, then painted their red tongues and white teeth, but there were still bare spots where I didn't get the glue even before I sprinkled on the fuzzy fake fur.

That scene repeated itself often as I got older. It was always the same when I was working on something, whether it was Mom or Dad saying, "Work on it for a while, and then I'll be along."

I knew they were busy. Mom had laundry, cleaning, meals, and dishes to keep her on her feet all day. After dinner, Dad would spread work papers out on the dining room table, maybe have another cup of coffee, and then, with an ashtray nearby, work at the table until way past my bedtime. I'd come into the dining room and tell him good night and then, the following morning, see his coffee cup in the kitchen sink, the work papers neatly stacked, and the ashtray over-flowing with crushed cigarette butts.

So, I followed their advice and began work. And now I see how those words shaped who I am today because what has always been true is no matter the project, maybe help comes, or maybe it doesn't, but either way, there was a start, and nothing ends without having started.

The camp box was the same way. I needed a project to earn my Carpentry Merit Badge as a Boy Scout. The manual said I needed a scale drawing with measurements before I began and that the plans were to be submitted with the finished project when it was reviewed by the counselor. All these extra steps were required for the Scout projects when all I really wanted to do was hammer and saw. But again, that's part of the learning, isn't it?

"Can you help me get started?" I asked.

"Why don't you work on it for a while, then I'll be along," Dad said.

I'm not sure the box ever had an official name. It was about thirty inches long and eighteen inches square, front to back and top to bottom. It was like a small trunk with a lid that opened with hinges and a hasp with a wooden peg I'd carved to hold it shut. The peg was attached to the box with a short length of chain, so it wouldn't get lost. The camp box was solid, and the spots where I'd used my dad's crosscut saw, never the rip saw, were even. The Merit Badge coun-selor was happy with the drawing and the box and signed off on my badge. I was proud, and Mom and Dad said, "Good job."

That box eventually got painted green and brightly colored shelving paper made the inside look better. It went on camping trips to hold cooking utensils and later to hold sand stakes when we were at the Outer Banks, where the short stakes that came with the tent wouldn't hold in the wind. So, yes, you could call it a camp box.

I have fond memories of those evenings in the dark basement, working alone at my father's workbench with the only light flickering down from the fluorescent strip mounted to the wooden joists above. I felt so grown up, even though I needed to stand on a stool to reach the bench, and it got wobbly when I used the vise bolted onto its surface. I needed to climb half onto the bench to reach most of his tools.

Chapter 45

Jobs Matter, Especially When Young

2011

I was making progress, but slower than I would have liked. I was used to getting things done—and quickly. But healing from something like cancer takes time, even when you're lucky. I was missing the routine of work, I guess. Work was part of my life; it was who I was.

1952

There were always after-school jobs. My first was when we were living in Little Rock. I was ten years old and wanted a new baseball glove, but Mom and Dad said the glove I had was fine and that if I really needed a new one so bad, I would need to get a job and pay for it myself. So, I wrote a note and left it on the kitchen table, and walked the six blocks from our home on South Pine Street to Weber's Root Beer Stand, a drive-in with carhops across from the Arkansas State Hospital.

Mr. Weber was my Little League coach and seemed to understand, so he paid me twenty cents an hour to wash mugs and stack them in the freezer. Mr. Weber would fill a frosted mug with root beer, sometimes adding soft-serve ice cream, and hand the icy cold mug with a straw sticking out its top through the window to a carhop, who put it on a metal tray and then ran to the customer's car and hung it on their door. We also sold hot dogs from a case that kept the buns moist and the dogs hot, and for five cents extra, Mr. Weber would add an ounce of chili.

Mother kept the note I had written that day and later wrote at the top, "March 24, 1952. Age 10 years, 9 months." And on its back, "Bruce's first job." Joyce had the note framed a few years ago. I'm glad she did. The framed reminder is on my shelf and I look at it often.

And believe me, there's nothing quite as good as a Coney-dog on a moist bun with a tall frosted mug of root beer by its side.

Kenter's Clothing was in the center of the two blocks of Overland we called downtown. Kenter's was on Lackland, near the F.W. Woolworths. We were back in St. Louis County, and I was in junior high when I sold men's clothing for Mr. Kenter after school some weekdays and all day on Saturdays. I had people try on shoes and step on the machine that X-rayed their toes to see if they fit. That was easy enough, but I was nervous the first time I had an older man try on a suit and then stand in front of the three-way mirror to mark where the tailor should cut. Would I be able to draw the lines right? Did I know how to mark where to take the trousers in at the waist?

When the man left, I told Mr. Kenter I thought I'd marked the left leg too short, but he said he'd take a look and not to worry, suggesting I go for an early lunch. So, I went to Woolworths for a hot open-faced turkey sandwich with mashed potatoes, extra gravy, green beans, and a Coke. I tucked a napkin in my shirt collar; I'd seen men do that, so it must be what you did when you wore a tie and ate in public. I was glad I had come early; the lunch counter had people behind every stool when I was ready to leave.

When I returned to the store, Mr. Kenter said he'd looked at the white chalk marks on the suit, and everything seemed fine. "We'll know when he comes in next Saturday, okay?"

The man brought his wife that afternoon. He tried on his new suit and stepped in front of the mirror. The wife, a stern woman with her hair pinned up and glasses with no rims, had on a wrap-around dress with large flowers that looked like our living room sofa and mid-heel leather oxford lace-up pumps. She looked at her husband in his new suit from every angle, having him turn this way, then that. After far too long, and without any change of expression, she said she liked it, the color looked good on him, and the fit was perfect.

I breathed a sigh of relief, but still thought the left leg was too short.

I paid $95 cash for my first car with the money I'd earned at Kenter's. A 1950 Chevrolet convertible that was black until I painted it blue. When I worked on my car after dinner, it was the same. "Dad, I've got the manifold on with the two new carburetors, but it's idling rough. There's a main jet adjustment screw at the base of each bowl, but I'm not sure which way to turn them. Can you help?"

"Why don't you work on it for a while, then I'll be along."

Chapter 46

From a Cat Named Iggy to the Night Sky

2011

$\mathbf{M}$emories continued to flood my mind as I sat, pumping, thinking, getting stronger. More scrambled eggs, grits, and then gluten-free toast. Friends would stop by for a visit and said I was looking better, but I wasn't sure. I was in a different place somehow, not like before. Without an office to go to, and even the ten o'clock sharp now gone, my mind had shifted into a different gear, slowing down, relaxing, and wandering. It wasn't my usual pattern of focus and control. Even my once crowded calendar now only showed an occasional doctor's appointment to look forward to.

I reflected more on my childhood, events with my mom and dad, where we had lived, and the dogs. Did we always have a dog? I don't remember a dog in New Jersey, only a cat.

1943

One spring Saturday, my mother fixed a backyard picnic for the four of us (counting Iggy). After lunch, Dad and I tossed a bean bag back and forth. "You gotta start 'em young if they're gonna grow up to play ball," my dad may have said. My toss back to him went astray and landed in Mom's roses. A thorn scratched my cheek as I went in after my bean bag, and Mom wanted Dad to take me to the doctor to have it stitched up. But Dad said, "Only girls get stitches, Helen. Bruce is a boy."

Over forty years later, those words would come back to me when I offered to have the scar on our son's chest reduced from an operation to repair a defective heart valve when he was born. "No need, Dad," my son said. "Besides, chicks dig scars." Sometimes sons, more than fathers, know best.

So, Mom doctored the scratch, which was deeper than Dad thought, as best she could with dark-red Mercurochrome and gauze pads. Then, as it began to scab over, she used carbolated jelly or "black salve," as she called it, to lessen the scar, not knowing that years later, the FDA would remove both products from the shelves because of their harmful ingredients. It is, after all, a "learn as you go" world, and who knows what poisons we will find on today's shelves.

The neighbors were sure Iggy, our fiery cat, had scratched me, but try as she might, Mom never convinced them. She said sometimes neighbors prefer to believe what they think happened rather than listen to what she saw.

By the time our children were born, the scar had vanished. Scars of all types build character—if we are patient enough to let them.

But we had a dog everywhere else.

I have a picture of my dad and me in front of our '48 Chrysler with Brownie, a Cocker Spaniel mix, beside me. I proudly held a long stringer of crappie over my head, the tail of the fish at the bottom of the metal stringer touching the ground. We had gone fishing at Lakeside Club that day in one of the metal boats they kept at the dock. My dad mounted his one-horsepower outboard motor on the back of the boat and searched for the perfect crappie hole while Brownie and I sat up front.

Boys had cigar boxes for their treasures back then. But girls, I was told, kept diaries with a key that opened the lock, then wrote stories about each day. The treasures in my cigar box had stories too, but I don't remember most of them because they're not written down. There would be a lesson there if only I'd learned it.

You can't tell your mind to slow down, I don't think. You can't shift to a different gear. Change needs to happen gradually, like wind settling or water becoming still. You don't just snap your fingers. But when the leaves stop blowing, you can see each of them better, like you see deeper in still water than in choppy.

So, I rested and let my mind go where it wanted. I sat on the terrace, looked at the stars, and marveled at their arrangement. Were the stars scattered about, or were they each carefully placed by a mind that understood math far better than even Dr. Warlick when he calculated where the radiation beams should land on my neck? It must have taken eons to do all the calculations holding those stars in place. It's the details that matter. When I look at Orion, The Hunter; Taurus, The Bull; and even the Big Dipper, I want them to look the same each night, be in a spot I can find, and not need to hunt the entire sky to find them and then have them not look the same because they are only some stylized *en plein air* version of themselves. I like continuity and the neat and orderly arrangement of things.

But when I relax, really relax, I don't see the constellations or even each star, only the darkness between them. The darkness is older and wiser. The stars are only distractions; the real wisdom lies deep beyond, in the dark.

Chapter 47

Prairie Dogs Are Tough

In the summer of 1954, I was standing in front of St. Louis's Union Railroad Station, wearing my Boy Scout uniform with an overloaded backpack hoisted on my shoulders, and headed west to Philmont Scout Ranch in New Mexico. My parents had encouraged me to sign up, and I was both excited about the adventure and nervous.

Philmont is 140,000 acres of wilderness in the Sangre de Cristo Mountains, and I was to be with a dozen or so other boys I had not yet met for two weeks of high-adventure Scouting. I was thirteen years old and alone when I stepped on the train, but as I walked through the cars, I soon spotted a group wearing uniforms and joined my new friends.

Once out on the trail, we would walk each morning, take a break for lunch, then walk some more until we made camp for the night. Food would have been dropped off at the site for us to each prepare our meal, so I'd unpack my mess kit and go to work. The skillet's handle held everything together with its wing nut clamp over the lid. There was a small pot with a lid and a metal cup inside. I had a small leather case with my knife, spoon, and fork on my belt. Everything I'd need to prepare my meals during the two weeks of trekking.

After dinner, the leader asked us to sort through the various items we had carried on our backs all day and decide what we needed and what could be left behind. He spread blankets labeled with our names so we could put anything we weren't using on our blankets to be boxed up and ready when we went home. My blanket said, "Charles," my name for two weeks. I was able to see more scenery when my back straightened with the lighter load. It's okay to have what you need, just don't take more.

I carried half a pup tent in my pack; another boy had the other. We buttoned them together each night and found two sticks for poles and rocks to hold down the sides. There wasn't a floor or any front or back. Just something over our heads if it rained.

We were each put out on our own for two days with nothing but a scout knife, some stick matches in a waterproof case, and a wool blanket. If my new friends were anywhere near, I couldn't see or hear them. I was to build a fire to keep warm and eat berries or anything else I could find. I tried to catch fish in a stream, but they were too fast. I threw a rock at a prairie dog, hit him in the head, and skinned him like I'd seen my dad do when we hunted squirrels with a rifle. I put a stick through him and roasted him on the fire. I don't know how hungry you need to be for a prairie dog to taste good, but I wasn't that hungry.

When I got home, I told the other boys in my troop how much fun we had and that they should go next time. I'm unsure if any ever went; either their parents wouldn't let them or couldn't afford it. Everyone spends their money differently, I guess, but for me, I'd rather have fewer things and more memories than the other way around.

I learned a lot from my years in Scouting, not just how to survive in the wilderness but how to build fires and how different fires have different uses. How big council fires light up the night, but small teepee fires keep you warm. I learned how to tie knots and that each had its purpose. I can still tie a bowline and a bowline-on-a-bight, but I use the first one more than the second. Square knots are secure, but granny knots are a waste. I learned basic first aid, and most of all, I learned leadership and how to work as a team. I could dig a latrine and cover it up. And I also learned there were some who only knew how to complain that we needed more toilets without the slightest idea of how to build their own.

I completed the Eagle Award requirements a year later, and Mom and Dad were there to pin it on. I was fourteen. Now my son is an Eagle, along with both grandsons. Once an Eagle, always an Eagle has become something our family says often.

Chapter 48

Be Still. Listen.

2011

My walks in the yard were longer now; I was getting stronger. My stops at the bench were more to enjoy the sun on my pale skin than to rest. Joyce was now fixing us scrambled eggs and grits, and we would sit together, eating, talking, me savoring the tastes that once were so familiar. One morning, I tried a splash of Frank's Original Red Hot on my eggs, but that didn't work. Frank's, a brand McIntyre*Sales* made famous in the Carolinas, was more about flavor than heat, but it was still too hot for my tender mouth.

My mind and heart continued to savor the images I pulled up from my past. My mother always wanted me to play in the band, so I started with the clarinet, but reading music was a problem, so the teacher moved me to drums. I played the snare drum in the marching band and, later, timpani for the concert band and orchestra. The timpani were my favorite. I could stand behind the three large copper tubs and show off, and since I was the only one playing the timpani, no one knew if I was right or wrong until it was obvious. I called it improvising, and that was fine until Mr. Rose, without missing a beat, or even lowering his baton, turned his head and lifted his left eyebrow.

The entire Ritenour High School music department was only Mr. Rose, and I made As in all of his classes.

Westminster College is a small Presbyterian school in the middle of Missouri, about twenty miles south of Columbia and the big university. Back then, it was all male. Winston Churchill spoke at Westminster College in March 1946 when he said an iron curtain had descended across Eastern Europe. That was thirteen years before I arrived, and the Cold War he described was just beginning.

My parents may have thought a small all-male college education would keep my mind on my studies, forgetting there was an all-girls school a few blocks away. And that because we were Presbyterian, and Presbyterians valued education, and with a name like Westminster—connecting to the Westminster Confession of Faith and not the Palace of Westminster—they must have thought Westminster College was where I belonged.

But I'm not sure I was thinking about all that back then. I just knew there were two choices. Either you graduated from high school, got hired someplace like McDonnell Douglas Aircraft near the airport, and were lucky enough to work on F-4 Phantom II fighter jets, or you went to a college like Westminster, got your degree, and then supervised the people who built the fighter jets. Being the boss sounded like the better choice.

I had been baptized at Westminster Presbyterian Church in Sparta, Illinois, my dad's hometown. The church was on West Broadway Street, just a block over from my grandparents' home. Caledonia Cemetery nearby is where all the McIntyres and Adamses (my paternal grandmother's side) are buried. The church in Sparta had moved into the city from Eden, where my dad was born. Rev. Samuel Wylie and other Wylies settled in Eden in the early 1820s when they moved north from Chester, South Carolina.

"Reverend Wylie collected a congregation for his Associate Reformed church and held services in a house down where the graveyard was afterward made," says my research from the history of Township 5 Range 5. The first wagon shop was established by W.R. Brown (my father's middle name) in 1839, and for many years the shops in Eden supplied wagons, carriages, and plows for much of Illinois and the surrounding states.

That church had been a stop on the Underground Railroad in the Civil War. There were many McIntyres; most had moved to Illinois from Ireland and Scotland, and some had moved north from the Carolinas when the war broke out.

The ones from the Carolinas could have come from around Charlotte, where, during the American Revolution in the fall of 1780, General Cornwallis sent 450 of his men with sixty wagons out Beattie's Ford Road toward the Hopewell Presbyterian Church to forage for supplies. As the Redcoats loaded their wagons with bags of oats and corn at McIntyre Farm, they accidentally knocked over a hornet's nest and found themselves under attack by the swarming hornets. The fourteen Patriots and the angry hornets fought so hard against General Cornwallis's Redcoats that he called Charlotte a "hornet's nest of rebellion." Today, you see the hornet's nest on police cars as part of the Mecklenburg County seal.

Reverend Wylie's church playing a role in the Civil War, Wylie being the name of a nearby lake, and McIntyre Farm helping turn the tide in the American Revolution are all stories I'd like to explore someday when I have time.

My dad got sick when I was away at college. I didn't know how sick, and they may have kept it from me, not wanting me to worry, but he had a heart attack and couldn't go to work. He recovered at home, on the living room sofa, on Addie Avenue in Overland, not far from his younger brother Thurlo, where my cousin Tim lives to this day.

It was the same sofa and living room where my grandfather Martin had recovered from having his right leg amputated.

My grandfather retired from the coal mines and had been working maintenance some at the dress factory. He also worked part time as a deputy sheriff in Randolph County, Illinois. One evening, after supper, he got a call on the telephone in the parlor about trouble at the frozen custard stand, so he put his Colt .38 police special on his belt and headed over.

The boys were there, making trouble, like the call said. Grandpa only wanted to fire a shot in the air to scare them, but when he pulled out his pistol, it went off, sending a bullet through his right foot. Too embarrassed to tell my grandmother Eliza Jane when he got home, Grandpa bandaged his foot as best he could, hid the ruined shoe in the back of the tall wardrobe where he kept his fiddle and mandolin, and went to bed.

Several days later, green streaks headed up toward his knee, so he told Grandma, and she called the doctor, and Grandpa ended up in an ambulance headed to St. Louis to have his leg amputated above the knee.

He recovered on our living room sofa, or enough to go back to Sparta, but once there, he soon was on a bed they rented and put in the parlor so he could have callers.

I was alone with Grandpa when he took my hand and said, "Take good care of yourself, Bruce." Then he closed his eyes. It seemed like a long time before the others returned from Aunt Pet's house, where they had been using the phone to call his daughter Gladys in Seattle to tell her of her father's rapidly failing condition.

When they finally walked into the parlor, I said, "I think Grandpa is dead." The rest is a blur. Grandpa was eighty. I was thirteen.

My dad made it back to work some after the first heart attack, but mostly he was home. He was coughing more, and the doctors were worried. He went to Saint John's hospital between my sophomore and junior year for what they said would be an exploratory operation to see what was wrong. He was in room 316 when I visited the

241

evening before surgery. He was in good spirits and told me everything would be fine and not to worry. But I did worry more than I knew all those years when he was sick, and the worry showed in my grades at college. How could I study when I was worried about him? I would read a page or two in a textbook and then realize I had no idea what I had just read.

When the doctors opened his chest, cancer was everywhere. They said they needed to decide whether to sew him up, hope he lived for a few weeks, or try to get it all and save his life. I'll never forget the hospital and room—John 3:16.

The death certificate listed hemorrhage as the cause, but the killer was cancer.

Hindsight being what it is, I wonder if my dad had celiac disease long before his heart attack and cancer. Back then, adults weren't thought to get celiac, only babies got that, and the doctors called it "failure to thrive." But now, with better technology and ways to look closer at the gut, numbers are increasing. Celiac is a hereditary disease passed from one generation to another. Sometimes, it skips a generation or two, but it's somewhere. I now see all the signs of it having affected my father. My dad was skinny, not as strong as his brother, and often seemed tired; there were bouts of diarrhea with frequent trips to the bathroom. I wonder if things would have been different if doctors had known what they know now back then. But I'm sure there are countless medical stories like my dad's. Dr. Favaro has told me more than once how things change daily in the complex world of medical research. My celiac diagnosis came almost forty years after my dad's death.

With untreated celiac, everything atrophies, even organs like the heart and lungs, and that weakness gives the bad guys, like cancer, a way inside.

I had just turned twenty when my dad died. He was fifty-five. My father was buried in Sparta, in a plot near his father. Grandma would join Grandpa in 1964. My mother, Helen, lived until 2004, then joined my dad. She was twenty-three years single, thirty-two years married, and forty-four years a widow. All are in Caledonia Cemetery near the tall trees.

When I'm still and listen to the memories in my head, when I'm not in charge of my own thoughts, my mind relaxes. When my thoughts improve, I get closer to what I need to hear. My mind reminds me how I was raised, about the experiences, and all the things I usually push aside when I'm too busy. Then, after my mind tells me, my heart helps me understand.

Looking out at the stars, sitting on the terrace, pumping in nutrition, I knew I was simply one of the billions of people on earth, connected to this place, to Joyce and my family. I was complete. I didn't need to do anything but be in this moment. And there was a satisfaction, a grace, in that.

Be still. Listen.

Chapter 49

780 Miles to Houston

1961

Two weeks after Dad's death, Mom and I drove from St. Louis to Houston to visit her sister, Edith. We were gone for ten days, driving a 1959 blue Volkswagen Dad had bought to save on gas, which had risen to over thirty cents a gallon.

"Three hundred twenty-seven miles to Houston," Mom read on a sign after we got through Little Rock.

"Howard Johnson's twelve miles on the left."

She read the signs, not offering an opinion or suggestion, just stating a fact. Then talked about how lonely her father must have been after her mother died and how soon he married Miss Alice. How, of all women, could he pick her?

Her mind and heart were in a tug-a-war for control.

"One hundred twenty-four miles to Houston."

We opened the cloth sunroof near the Gulf, let the salt breeze fill the car, and mess up our hair. We drove on the beach, stopped, and got our feet wet in the surf. I found a starfish washed up on the sand and threw it back in the water.

There aren't any pictures from that trip. Maybe we forgot to bring a camera or weren't in the mood. It would be nice to look back at a woman in her mid-fifties with her son, who had just turned twenty, walking along a deserted beach. I'm sorry we're not able to look back at that scene, to see my mother with as much of her life ahead as behind. Better yet, to be able to read her thoughts. Was she thinking about Dad and her life now that he was gone? Or was she thinking about me and how I had needed her when I was young but had been turning to him more as I got older? Or was she thinking about how happy the three of us had been, and now it was over?

It's impossible to know, and even the best photographer with the best camera could never give us those answers.

Maybe that would have been the time to ask Mom about Dad's tattoo. What was the blank space in the center for? Could it have been for a name? But it never came up.

What I now know, or think I know, is that my mother just needed to talk, which was her way of thinking it through. She wasn't looking for answers from me; she would find those on her own. But for now, she just needed to let her mind wander, much like mine was doing after selling my business and making it through grueling cancer treatments. Being able to talk and have someone listen, truly listen, is a gift and a way of having answers appear when they are ready. I went back to college in the fall of 1961. I had gained a blue VW but lost a dad.

Mom got a job at the bank to help pay my tuition. Web Naunheim, the president of her single-office bank on Woodson Road in Overland, had her answer the phones and manage the safe-deposit boxes.

The bank was close enough so she could walk back and forth from home and even let Brownie out at lunch.

After ten years, she retired, and Web threw a party, made a speech, and gave her a pension—$30 a month. Even after the Bank of Overland merged with First National Charter, the checks continued. Then Boatmen's, then Nations Bank, more acquisitions and mergers than I can count, until her death and the last check in 2004 from Bank of America in Charlotte to my mother's home address, also in Charlotte. Almost four hundred checks arrived on the first of each month for over thirty-three years, all for answering the phones and letting customers use their safe-deposit boxes.

Meanwhile, I worked in the college dining hall during my first year. Usually, I just checked names off a list as students came through; missing too many meals meant you would get a visit by the nurse. Now and then, I'd be given other jobs in the kitchen—slicing sheet cakes and plating each square or getting the sheet pans of cold Jell-O from the cooler and cutting it into little cubes and piling the cubes in parfait dishes. Slater Foodservice Management, my employer, was the largest provider of meals in the country back then. The following year Slater was acquired by Automated Retailers of America, a vending company that today is the giant Aramark Corporation, providing everything from food to uniforms to facility maintenance for schools, hospitals, business and industry, prisons, and even ballparks.

After that first year, I only worked summers. Better to keep my mind on my studies, my mother thought. One summer job was with a catering company in Clayton, a nearby suburb. They mainly did wedding receptions and special events.

One Saturday afternoon, there was a large, high-profile wedding with a sit-down dinner where round tables were set up on the expansive Forrest Park grass terraces in front of the St. Louis Art Museum. I was pushing a rolling rack of plated chicken cordon bleu down the ramp from the truck and up behind some trees on the newly cut lawn when I hit a bump, and to my horror, the cart toppled. Plates of chicken and vegetables went flying in every direction in what, in my mind, looked like slow motion. I panicked, but a quick survey showed no plates broken, only terrible disarray. We only had the correct number of entrees for the meal, so I scrambled on hands and knees out of sight of the guests, using my shirt sleeve to brush off each plate. Then, with my bare hands, I carefully arranged the chicken and vegetables, righted the fallen cart, and put things back together as best I could.

Everything was fine until one well-dressed woman carefully eyed her plate. Then, she lowered her tortoiseshell half-frame glasses and asked about the green sprinkles.

"Seasoning," I said with confidence. "The chef must have thought the chicken needed parsley." She seemed satisfied.

Whew. I sighed in relief, took a few deep breaths, and moved on.

Chapter 50

Mudsills Are Heroes

2011–2012

Before cancer derailed my schedule, volunteering with the Urban Ministry Center and Habitat for Humanity had become a routine. A routine I now wanted to return to as quickly as possible. I wasn't strong enough to build houses yet, but certainly I could manage a few hours of listening to another person's story at the Urban Ministry Center.

Volunteering was a way I saw of being part of the community. Some call it giving back, but to me, the better word is *belonging*.

The old scrap of legal pad was still on the workbench in the shop. I'd sketched out my plans on the flight to Baltimore before the cancer was even diagnosed, and now it was time to bring them to life.

It was time to head back to 945 North College Street.

It was Joyce who had introduced me to the Urban Ministry Center, where she volunteered at the front desk for years. The "neighbors"

would ask if they had mail, and she'd check the slot, then give them a ticket for a place in line if they needed to wash out what few pieces of extra clothing they had in their black plastic bag or take a shower. She always seemed so satisfied when she got home that I asked if I could try. I didn't want to horn in, but maybe I would enjoy it too. So I started and had been volunteering each Wednesday until I needed to stop because of my treatments.

Returning after those long months of treatment, I parked near the recently painted retaining wall, picking a spot away from the red mulberry tree where the birds nested and ate berries. The wall was covered in street art, becoming more common in Charlotte, and the fresh montage on the wall looked like something Maud Lewis, the impoverished folk artist from Nova Scotia, would have done. There were Maud's brilliant signature primary colors, connecting the homeless to Charlotte and Charlotte to them. The scene would make the perfect Christmas card, I thought. It felt good to be back.

Walking toward the new building across from the old railroad station, I recognized many in the courtyard. But many of the faces were new, some forced into homelessness through no fault of their own because they got laid off, missed a rent payment or two, used their last bit of savings for food, then the landlord padlocked their place. The next thing they knew, they were living on the streets. But these are the situationally homeless. Their condition is temporary; they'll bounce back. The situationally homeless can survive. It's the others I worried about. The people like Chilly Willy who hadn't known a home—other than a camp in the woods or under a viaduct—for years. Homelessness is chronic for them. They may crash on a friend's couch for a week or two, but soon, they're back on the streets. They are the ones I pray for; they'll die on our streets if something isn't done. But things are being done, and people do care; and if you want to learn how much, read *The Hundred Story Home* by Kathy Izard. In her book, you'll learn how you can help change the world and change yourself.

My old volunteer friends Penny and Cathy were there, along with David Beers. He was counseling both mornings and afternoons on Wednesdays now. David taught me the ropes when I started.

Officer Michael was standing directly across from the front desk, at the bottom of the stairs leading to the second floor. He was in the perfect spot to see everything happening in a room where so many different cultures collide. His dark-blue CMPD uniform, Glock service pistol, and tall, muscular frame sent a message of security to a few of us. Yet, to most, his presence only added to the anxiety in their disadvantaged lives. "Hey, Bruce. We been missin' you. Welcome back," Michael said, still focusing his eyes on the room.

Barbara, the new volunteer coordinator, didn't waste any time putting me to work. "You can't have forgotten too much, Bruce. Use the Blue Book or see me if you have any questions. I've put you in room three, okay? Oh, and welcome back." With that, I was ready for whatever the afternoon brought. Neighbors come in all shapes and sizes, and the problems they bring a volunteer counselor are just as varied.

"Neighbors" was the term the Urban Ministry Center had used since it began in 1994. Dale Mullennix, the founder and executive director, used the word to remind the city's privileged how, while the homeless didn't look like the people from their neighborhoods on their tree-lined streets, they were still, as Christ taught, our neighbors.

My first neighbor was a routine visit. He needed an ID. A valid North Carolina ID, a form of identification in place of a driver's license, is essential for the homeless who are forever losing their wallet or pocketbook, often having it snatched while sleeping under a viaduct. And using 945 North College Street as an address gave you a place to receive mail and means you are a Mecklenburg County resident and eligible for county services.

I carefully walked him through each step.

He needed a document with his full name and date of birth. A birth certificate was best, or sealed school records would work, and if you went to school in Charlotte, those records were on file in the Bob Walton building on East Stonewall Street. But don't break the seal after they give you the envelope. The secure seal shows you didn't tamper with anything, like the dates. One document with his full name and Social Security number. A Social Security card was perfect, even if badly worn, and you can get a new one, but that's a different procedure at another agency, so we could talk about that another time. Two documents showing his current address. If you use the address of Urban Ministry, your mail comes here. And if you are not a citizen or have changed your name, we'll need to talk more.

Then he could ride the van to the DMV on Thursday. "No, I can't give you a bus pass to the DMV. That's what the van is for."

Sound complicated? It is. Having permanent housing for neighbors keeps their wallets from being stolen and a whole list of other things. Permanent supportive housing doesn't cost taxpayer money; it saves money. And I can prove it to you with pencil and paper if you like.

My neighbor said he'd gather the documents he needed and be

on the van tomorrow or Thursday week. I wished him luck.

My next neighbor's requests for help weren't as easy. She talked about wanting a job and then switched to needing bus passes. Next, she said she was hungry, so I explained how she could get food at several places with a referral from us to Loaves and Fishes if she hadn't gotten any other referrals from other agencies or us in the last thirty days. None of this seemed to be what she wanted; she wouldn't stay on one subject long enough for me to understand.

"Well, thanks," she said as she stood to leave, then turned, adding, "Oh yeah. I need an abortion."

"Better sit back down, uh . . . " I stumbled for her name, quickly looking at the file, "Sally. Give me a minute; I'll be right back."

I stepped around the corner to Ashley's office. She would know what to do. Her small office's closet had overflowed years ago; chairs were piled with shoes, jackets, hoodies, you name it. If a neighbor needed it, Ashley had it, no doubt.

"Close the door, Bruce. Have a seat." I removed several sneakers and two pairs of jeans from a chair and sat down.

"You sure know how to pick 'em. I remember that first day eight years ago when you met with a woman who needed colonoscopy bags." We both laughed, not that colonoscopy bags are funny, but how out of place I was talking with a homeless woman in that condition.

"It's a tricky subject," she said about the abortion request. "We get funding from organizations who approve of abortion, but some do not, and they wouldn't want their money used that way. The best I can do is give you a phone number, and you have your person call that organization."

I headed back to room three.

"So, I guess you've decided not to keep the baby? What does the father think?"

"Who knows?"

"You mean you haven't asked?

"I would if I knew who to ask."

I gave Sally the small slip of paper with the handwritten phone number on it, then told her the front desk kept condoms in a drawer for those wise enough to use them.

The next few visits were routine—most wanted bus passes.

Bus passes seem easy, but they're another tricky subject; bus passes are like cash. They have a street value. A ten-ride pass can fetch up to twenty bucks or four nickel bags of weed. If someone was starting a job, I could verify with a phone call, then a ten-ride would get them back and forth to work until they got their first paycheck. Otherwise, well, they were tricky.

"How'd it go?" Joyce asked when I got home.

"Fine; they all asked about you," I said. "They said to say hello and come back whenever you wanted."

One thing and another had caused her to stop volunteering regularly, and soon the volunteer coordinator needed to put someone else in her spot.

I stuck my head in Megan's office the following week to ask about someone who needed housing. He got a small government check each month, but it wasn't enough, and Megan, who worked for the county, and had an office at the Urban Ministry Center, knew the ropes. Soon he was under a roof.

People like Barbara, Ashley, Megan, and other social workers are unsung heroes in our community. They navigate systems controlled by bureaucrats whose life mission seems to be making things complicated. Maybe it has to be that way, but without an advanced degree in gobbledygook, there's no way to make it through the first few paragraphs of any regulation, let alone read the entire fifteen pages. Social workers make things simple for us, which may be their most incredible gift. Yet, to some who may not be cognizant or recognize social workers' essential roles, these public servants seem like mudsills, when to our marginalized neighbors, they are heroes.

Chapter 51

This Killin' Time Is Killin' Me

2012

I'd spotted Chilly Willy a few times off and on after my return to the Urban Ministry Center, but this Wednesday he looked different, more relaxed. His clothes were cleaner, his hair not so tangled but still in dreadlocks. I didn't know who was doing his barberin' these days, but they were better than his last. The smell was gone, along with the dirt under his fingernails. His skin was clear, but the Harley Davidson tattoo was still there, squarely in the middle of his forehead. I sat next to him in the courtyard, leaned over, and said, "Hi Chilly, remember me?"

After an extra-long minute, he turned to face me and replied, "Maybe, but I'm not Chilly anymore. I'm Larry Major."

It turned out the folks at Moore Place had gotten him off the streets and into a small furnished room with people around to help keep him clean and sober. There were good days and bad, of course, but like so many others, sobriety was something Larry had needed for years.

We didn't talk much that day, but later, if I saw him walking between the Urban Ministry Center and Moore Place, I'd pull over, and we'd go to the convenience store to buy cigarettes. He'd ask the cashier for two packs of Marlboros in the crush-proof box, and I'd slide the money under the thick, bulletproof plexiglass shields some neighborhoods deal with while others do not.

I knew smoking wasn't good for you, but it's common among the addicted. One addiction is replaced by another. So, I'd rather it be a box of Marlboros than a few hydromorphone tablets washed down by glug after glug of Thunderbird.

Back in the truck, Larry lit up. I asked him to put down his window. He fumbled around until I pointed to the handle, and he cranked it down. "I remember windows like these," he said. I chuckled, and said, "We all do, Larry, except my grandkids; they're still trying to figure them out."

He always buckled his seatbelt since that first time he'd told me how seatbelts were a restriction on his freedom, and I'd simply said how that might have been true for Chilly, but he was Larry now.

He liked the long handle on the gear shift coming up from the floor and the short one to put the truck in four-wheel drive. He'd reach over to touch the gear shift with his tattooed fingers.

Larry told me he'd always wanted an old truck, but his wouldn't be white; it'd be red. Not a bright shiny red, but a red that looked old, like it'd been left in the sun so long it'd turned a dull orangey color, like over-ripe yams pulled out of the ground and left in the field. And how he'd keep his guitar on the seat next to him, and how he'd park down by the railroad track, put the tailgate down, and sit for a spell, strumming and singing, "This killin' time is killin' me."

"Oh, and mine'd be a Ford; what kind's this 'un?" he asked.

"It's a Ford, Larry, can't you tell?"

"Sure, man, I knew that."

The Urban Ministry Center opened Moore Place, where Larry lived, in early 2012. They called it Housing First, and many didn't understand the simple idea. The old way said to quit doing drugs and drinking alcohol, and then there could be help. It was like saying to a wood-burning stove: give me some heat, then I'll give you some wood. When we should have been putting the wood in all along. Having a place of his own let Larry get clean and sober, off and on, for the first time in years.

Tragically, Larry was struck by a car on a Thursday night in October. He'd been drinking and stumbled out in the street from between two parked cars. It was dark, and the driver couldn't stop in time. Larry, a legend, lay dead in the street. The service was at a church on East 36th Street in NoDa. Larry was fifty-eight. The sanctuary was packed.

Chapter 52

Feeding Tubes and Plastic Trash Bags

2011

Dr. Favaro said he was happy my weight had increased, then asked if I was still using my tube. I told him I was, but didn't need to all the time. "Buy a scale, Bruce, and keep track. If you can add weight without using the feeding tube, it'll be time for your PEG to come out. But we don't want it out too soon, or you'll end up with another scar in your belly, and that'll be even harder to explain when you make up stories about how it all happened." We laughed.

When the time finally came that everyone felt the tube could come out and I could maintain my weight, I made an appointment with Dr. Wallace, the surgeon I'd seen in the hospital six months before. His office was in Matthews. Joyce and I were early and waited until the nurse stuck her head in the lobby to call, "Charles."

We went in, and he asked how I was doing, while motioning me up on the table. No need to undress, he said, just unbutton your shirt.

While his new nurse was turned, getting something from a cabinet, he double wrapped the tube around his right hand, braced his left hand on my hip, then, with his right elbow angled toward the examining light, gave the tube a quick yank, like he was pulling the starter rope on a lawnmower.

Suddenly, there was a loud noise, like a cork coming out of a bottle—but louder.

Joyce jumped, the new nurse whirled around with a shocked look, knocking a metal container of cotton balls to the floor, and there the tube was, hanging limp in his hand. He looked at it closely, like someone admiring a turnip they had just pulled from their garden, then tossed it in the red trash can with the biohazard symbol printed on its side.

I didn't feel a thing, I was just startled by the noise. I'll never forget that sound, though. Like a cork, but also like having the lid on a jar of preserves finally open after you've struggled for so long.

That was it. The shellshocked nurse put ointment on the hole and covered it with an adhesive bandage. Then he said to call if he could ever do anything for me. "Oh, and watch for any infection. You'll feel sore for a few days, and some yellowy stuff may ooze out, but no worries. Call if the pain gets too bad, and I'll write you a script for something, okay?"

There would be a scar, and maybe if it were in a different place, stitches would have helped, and perhaps a plastic surgeon could do something with it now, but why bother? It's a memory.

Joyce and I left his office and the tube behind.

I returned to Men's Bible Class just as Von began the Gospel of Mark, using *Say To This Mountain* by Ched Myers. We started exploring the connections between Mark's discipleship and the demands on our lives today.

I wondered about when Christ did return, would He be white, black, or brown? There weren't any white people like me in the Bible that I could remember. And when He came, would He be born to parents in one of the tony neighborhoods or a woman at the Center of Hope on Spratt Street?

And could He be a She?

My work continued at the URB, as many called the Urban Ministry Center, because it was easier to say the first three letters of "urban." I never liked the nickname much, like I don't like "Pres" or "Presby" when the word is "Presbyterian." To me, both my religion and my hospital are "Presbyterian." It had taken me years to learn how to spell the word derived from the Greek word "presbyter," or a body of people of equal rank.

The one thing I heard from each neighbor I talked to was how much they needed a job, but the recession of '08 had brought dark days to Charlotte, and the once towering building cranes had moved on, taking the jobs with them. Day labor had been the answer for our neighbors, but now there were few openings, applications for anything available were handled online by a computer, which the homeless don't have, and interviews were rarely in person. Our folks were discouraged.

Some advised we have "dress for success" workshops and teach neighbors how to build stronger resumés, and while that might work if you wanted a job at the bank, sitting in a cube staring at a screen, it wasn't the answer for the homeless.

Jobs, when you're without housing, are a whole different matter. You stand out in the waiting room when you only have one outfit, it's wrinkled, and what little you own is in a black plastic trash bag.

One day, Dale stuck his head in the room as I finished my notes from a visit.

"How's it going?"

"Pretty well, Dale, but our people need jobs."

"Yes, but they need housing first, Bruce."

"Well, maybe—but what if we could work on both? Like two sides of the same coin. A roof on one side and income on the other?"

"Interesting," Dale said, dragging out each syllable, before continuing down the hall.

I thought the answer was to find employers willing to give the homeless a hand up, an opportunity, not just a handout. And that would take a unique boss with a spot in his heart for what he could do for the community, not just his bottom line.

I thought about Larry, or Chilly Willy as he was once known. He could have used a job; it would have given him something to do each day other than killin' time. But I had to admit if I were in the personnel department, or HR as they call themselves today, I'd be hard-pressed to hire someone with blond dreadlocks and a Harley Davidson tattoo on his forehead, even if they were dressed for success and had a perfectly crafted resumé.

No, this would need to be different. Someone high up the ladder, maybe at the very top, would need to tell HR that hiring a guy like Larry was more than okay; it was the right thing to do, the thing the CEO wanted to do. And that would take guts.

I thought about it more and more over the next few weeks. I remembered my corporate days and how safe I played each hire. No one sticks their head out when they could get it chopped off. That's why IBM sold so many computers back then; who would recommend an unknown when it was so safe to make the same choice as everyone else? I know I was that way. Every hire followed the rules; understanding past performance was the best indication of the future, so my interview questions always keyed on what the applicant had done, what they had said, what the results had been, and constantly why, why, why.

And while that approach worked for the company and me, it would not work for our neighbors. Unfortunately, their lives had not been a model of success.

But many small business owners are more independent. That's why they're out on their own. They think differently than corner-office executives. They have a higher risk tolerance and, if presented with the right idea, will do the right thing.

I began to sketch out a plan; nothing formal, just ideas. The company would need to hire many, not just one at a time. They would always be looking for workers, even hiring more than required. There's a natural churn to these businesses; maybe 60 to 70 percent of their workforce is stable, but the others come and go, so it's best to have a few extra. It's different, perhaps, but a wiser and broader view when the owner wants to keep things flowing.

It would be best if the company was on a bus line because neighbors use buses, exclusively.

As for those companies only needing one or two people at a time, they'd be fine, and we'd help fill the spot, but we needed to move the needle further, so it was the employers who could take in eight or ten, more even, when they were already full. Those were the ones we would want.

We would need to understand the new software companies used to read resumés. The days of walking in and applying for a job were over, as more and more companies used Applicant Tracking Systems (ATS) to read applications. And that software looked for keywords like *self-starter, motivated, and eager*. The resumé's file format needed to be correct: .docx and .pdf were best. Specific fonts like Arial and Helvetica were easy for computers to read, so forget the rest.

We wanted neighbors to check the right boxes and not check others. The computer reads no further when the box asking about a criminal record has a checkmark. So we would need lawyers who could work without pay, pro bono, to use a process called expungement, a part of Second Chance legislation that allows misdemeanors, even some felonies, to be erased. When the mistake was forgiven and erased from the record, the box didn't need to be checked. It would be better to have the box go away altogether, but expungement was a start.

Next, the neighbor would need all her paperwork in order. A "Real NC ID" was a must. A driver's license was even better but not necessary.

With everything in order, the neighbor would then be job-ready, and there would need to be people reviewing each step to be sure. Because as coach John Wooden said, "If you don't have time to do it right, when will you have time to do it over?"

It was all possible, I thought, but it would take a team, and different roles would have different qualifiers. The volunteers contacting the potential employers would need to know, or have access to, owners. And the owners we needed would not be in the tall towers Uptown; they'd be on the margins, surrounded by everyday people. There's a large group of "small" businesses, and they are not all small. Some employ hundreds, but you wouldn't know it by the cars in the parking lot, only by the lines at the bus stop.

I even started thinking of names. CharlotteWorks was my first choice. It said our city and "Works" said jobs, so it seemed perfect, but that name was taken. I kept at it until I hit on JobWorks. It was a name similar to others used at the Urban Ministry Center, and the more I thought about it, the more I liked the new name.

So my plan was simple: our folks needed an advantage, a leg up, an unleveled playing field that sloped in their favor for a change. "Give a man a fish, and he eats for a day, but teach him to fish, and he eats for a lifetime," wrote Lao Tzu, the contemporary of Confucius. And we wanted our fishermen successful—we'd stock the pond.

After a month of these what-ifs swirling in my head, I was ready to talk to Dale again.

Chapter 53

Paid in Advance

2012

W hen anyone retires, they lose their identity. With no title behind your name, other than "retired," who are you?."

So why not continue with JobWorks? My business was sold, the ten o'clock sharp was finished, and I had the time. Maybe I've always needed a project, something to keep me busy, and something to stand up for. The business had been like that. It was me against the system, the status quo, the norm, and that had turned out well. I had fought against cancer, and now it was gone, so what would be next?

There are fights *against* and fights *for*. Battles *against*, like my fight against cancer, are short, finite; they soon end, one way or the other. But fights *for*, like fighting to build a business, can go on for a long time. Fighting *for* something is a win-win, good for everyone, like an incoming tide.

My battle against cancer was a zero-sum game. I would win, or I would lose. It's an all-consuming fight, and while the doctors, nurses, and techs did their part and I did mine, in the end, at best, I'd be right where I started. I'd break even.

I needed to be engaged in something worthwhile, something *for* and not just *against*.

But this wouldn't be a career like running my company had been. I didn't have time for that, plus there were other things I wanted to do, like spending time with Habitat for Humanity in Charlotte, and more trips to El Salvador. Plus, there was the Porsche; I hadn't driven it in weeks. I could do JobWorks in twelve months, I thought. A year would give me time to set things up, make everything sustainable, and then move on to whatever was next. I never wanted to run the day-to-day, only put it in motion. Stay too long, I reasoned, and the initiative becomes about you and not the good you set out to achieve. Term limits, like horizons, come in different lengths, so I needed to find my replacement in less than a year.

I would be the catalyst, the chemical that comes in, unites the parts, and then steps away, leaving everything different and better than before. I'd work one day each week at the URB and the rest from home. I'd set up and test each process, staff JobWorks with volunteers, and find my replacement in one year.

One thing I'd learned about Dale Mullennix over the years: he listened. Even when he might think the idea seemed crazy, Dale would give it a try.

Maybe it came from his early work in the Jeremiah Seven,

the seven tall steeple churches trying to make a difference in our community in the early 1980s. Christ Episcopal, Myers Park Presbyterian, Myers Park United Methodist, Myers Park Baptist, Covenant Presbyterian, St. Mark's Lutheran, and the Little Church on the Lane were looking for something that would bring the city together. The seven asked a few of their associate ministers to visit Americus, Georgia, and meet with Millard Fuller to learn about a program called Habitat for Humanity.

Habitat was new in the early 1980s, and Dale and the others liked the idea. When they came home, they asked John Crosland to help. Soon Habitat for Humanity was building affordable housing all over Charlotte. Frye Gaillard's book, *If I Were A Carpenter,* recounts the fascinating history of those early days. And even if you don't live in Charlotte and don't know any of the names, you'll enjoy his story of how a small group can make such a big difference.

Dale listened when Ingrid Amols wanted to start ArtWorks 945 and offer the neighbors a studio where they could draw and paint, then sell their work at gallery showings for real money to people who would hang the work in their fancy homes.

He listened to people like Don Boekelheide and then Jack McNeary, who wanted a community garden where neighbors could get their hands in the soil, nurture new life, and watch it grow.

He listened to Peter Fink, who wanted to play soccer in the streets and compete against other homeless soccer players. Just folks who wanted nothing more than to kick a ball around.

Meredith Dolhare wanted the neighbors to run, not away from something but to a better future, for the exercise and confidence-building pride in completing a 10K or marathon. So Running-

Works started, and soon neighbors were running on the streets, between the tall towers, dressed in their familiar blue-and-white RunningWorks T-shirts, dodging the bankers.

Anything love built up was better than things torn down by hate, so Dale was all ears the day we sat down.

Dale liked the idea and wanted others in on the discussions, so he called Barbara and Liz, asking if they could come to his office for a brief meeting. Waiting for them to arrive, I asked Dale about the framed photo of St. Louis's Busch Stadium hanging above his desk. Dale told me how he had attended at least one game in every major league stadium except two, and of all the stadiums he had visited, Busch Stadium was his favorite, along with the St. Louis Cardinals. From then on, my conversations with Dale always started with a few words about the latest box scores.

Barbara arrived first, then Liz. The four of us sat at a round table in the corner of Dale's office. Dale had me go over everything again. He injected a few details, but mostly, Dale let me talk. Barbara had some reservations; Liz was more open to the idea. I'd report to Liz, Dale said.

Next, we met with Beth, the finance manager in the office next to Dale's. She'd gone to the "Zen, Baby" dance program with the others.

Dale wanted me to be a staff member on the payroll. I'd come to meetings, wear a tag with my picture around my neck, and have a title. Dale said name tags were essential to the staff and neighbors. "Plus, when he's out in the community talking to employers, he'll need a card," Dale told Beth.

Beth started pulling out forms and asked Dale what she should put down for a salary. Dale gave her a generous number, then turned to me, "Does that sound right, Bruce?"

I had thought about salary. I knew many around town, like Frank Reed, who started ReStore for Habitat for Humanity and did it all for a few dollars each year.

"A dollar a year will be fine," I said.

With that, Dale reached into his pocket for a handful of change and handed me a quarter. "Okay, since you've said this will take a full year, I'm paying you for three months in advance."

We all laughed.

Liz Clasen-Kelly had been at the URB since she served an internship with them after graduating from Davidson College. She'd held every job there and was now the associate executive director, so when Dale was off raising money, Liz kept things running. Joyce and I had known her from the first day we each volunteered. We'd gone to her wedding to Fred, the reporter with the *Observer*, in the main room of the new building David Furman designed. The room was decorated nicely, nothing fancy, but it all fit, and we'd visited with her parents during the reception. The couple took hyphenated last names: Liz and Fred Clasen-Kelly.

Liz would later become the executive director of the Men's Shelter of Charlotte before they merged with the Urban Ministry Center, forming Roof Above. At the time of the merger, Liz was wisely appointed executive director of the newly combined organization. When Liz wasn't busy, she listened to rap music to help her relax.

I got settled in an office on the first floor of the old train station, near Peter's soccer bunch, at the other end from ArtWorks 945 with

RunningWorks in the middle. It was a plain office with a large piece of glass, like a window, set into one wall. From my office, the glass was a window looking into the main room, but on the other side, a giant mirror. I could spend hours watching people look in the mirror while they combed their hair or picked a piece of something, heaven knows what, from their teeth, but instead, I turned my desk the other way, looking out over the railroad tracks. The occasional freight train rumbling outside my window wasn't as interesting, but it was less distracting.

The office was nothing like my old office on Southside Drive; here none of the furniture matched, the drawers in my small wood desk stuck, my chair squeaked, traffic-worn bright-tangerine and mousey-brown shag carpeting went from wall to wall, and there was barely room for one guest chair. But I had an office and a place to work. And besides, I didn't plan to spend much time there anyway. I already had a list of places to visit.

International Paper had jobs, and job-ready neighbors could leave the Transit Center to make the necessary bus changes along the one-hour route, then walk the remaining mile on Westinghouse Boulevard to the entrance before clocking in. Once on the line, workers would unpack the displays that hadn't been sold in the stores and repack the contents—batteries, toys, vitamins, whatever—into regular cases to return to the stores to restock the shelves. It was a long bus ride, tedious work, and minimum wage, so the dollars weren't much after you divided your paycheck by the hours spent working plus commuting.

Affordable housing near employment centers reduces travel, helps the environment, and leaves workers with more money at the end of the week. But at least International Paper was doing what they could.

A few restaurant chains always needed dishwashers, like Newk's Eatery.

Party Reflections needed help setting up tents for outdoor events like weddings or graduations. But they preferred people who could drive a box truck. They were on Monroe Road then, but they are way out toward Ballantyne these days. Everything's more complicated if you don't own a car. More public transportation is the answer, but if people want only tax dollars used for roads they drive and bridges they cross, there's no political will.

The best employer of all turned out to be my friend, Jamie Gilbert. His company did wood pallets; they'd buy broken pallets and repair them or make new ones if you wanted. Custom Pallet had made the pallets for my building on Southside Drive. Mine were oak, and Jamie made a stencil with our name and logo so we could paint the two flat sides opposite where the forks slide in. While other warehouses had a hodgepodge of pallets in every color and variety of wood, some even plastic, ours all matched. And all said, "McIntyre*Sales*."

Jamie and I talked. "Yes, I'm always hirin', Bruce. Who you got?"

"Well, I've got right many, Jamie. A few are clean and sober, some not so much. Most have records. That a problem?" I asked.

"Nope, no problem."

"You mean any record, like a chainsaw murderer?" I jested.

"Well, we don't have any of those, I don't think, but no, that's not a problem unless he brings his saw." We laughed, then arranged to meet at his office later that week.

I drove to Jamie's on North Graham Street. His building was like many in the older parts of Charlotte, where people had moved further out, leaving things behind. The buildings had all been fine in their day, and while some were a little run-down, most were well-maintained, just not as shiny as the new ones going up in the suburbs.

I admired the tall trees in front of the office, the shade protecting the windows from the afternoon sun. The city made developers add trees to new sites, but I wished the trees developers planted were bigger. It'd be forever before the little ones in the suburbs shaded the new buildings the way Jamie's did now.

Jamie showed me around, and I asked him about things at his church while we were walking back from the production floor.

"I've been right busy, Bruce, but the work I enjoy most is the prison ministry I'm doing in South Carolina. It's rewarding to meet and talk to inmates trying to better themselves, reading the Bible. You ought to give it a try." I said his work sounded wonderful, then thought, *Bettering themselves? That's what the jobs you're creating do for people every day, Jamie.*

Back up front, Jamie introduced me to Yvonne. She did the hiring. We talked about what they called their sweet spot. Those were the people they'd had the best luck with over the years, and now, if people didn't fit the sweet spot, they didn't get hired.

Custom Pallet people needed to be in good shape and have a strong back. They'd be swinging 40-pound pallets all day, less if the pallets were pine, but most were oak, so they needed to be in even better condition than most gym rats hanging out at the Y. They should be between their late twenties and early forties; any younger and they were too immature to handle the group culture. Any older, and they were, well, just too old. Besides that, anything else was fine.

It was piecework, so the more pallets a worker could make in an hour, the more money they took home. Some made $27 an hour, but stay out of their way; get too close, and you'd get hurt. They were strong, and the pallets flew on and off their station quickly.

Jamie excused himself to take a phone call in his office, so Yvonne and I kept talking. I asked her about drugs and alcohol. Was that a problem? "Lordy, yes, it's a problem, Bruce. Every day of the week, but especially on Monday. We pay on Friday, so I'm always the first here on Monday. I leave Belmont way before sunup to beat the traffic and watch 'em walk in the front door. I can usually tell when they clock in, but I know for sure once they're on the shop floor. I'll pull 'em and test in a skinny minute if I think I should. Blow over a 0.08 and I'll send 'em home. Same for drugs, but I have a male supervisor who does the drug testing, and after the third time, you're not allowed back unless you can prove you've gone someplace like the Rescue Mission and worked with Tony Marciano and his crew." Yvonne continued, "I know Jamie may have made it sound different; he puts a happy face on things, but that's how it is."

Yvonne was Jamie's number two, and as I thought about the number two position in any organization, I realized it was only with a strong number two that number one looked good. It was that way with Yvonne, Liz at the URB, and Kristi back at my old shop.

Jamie was back now, and we soon finished up. I thanked them both and said we'd be in touch. "I'm sure we can help," I said, knowing they'd be helping JobWorks more than we'd be helping them.

Wednesday, my one day a week at the URB, was packed. I'd get in early to meet with Liz, then be in my office, but I was now too busy even to watch the trains go by. I'd bring lunch in my yellow bag, the one I'd taken to infusion, and I packed the same things: sliced ham wrapped around mozzarella sticks with some mild Pace Picante Sauce as a dip, tapioca pudding, a small bag of Fritos, and a drink. Afternoons might be spent in the computer lab with John Zika looking at neighbors' resumés to ensure they were job-ready, or out positioning a potential employer for a new kind of hire.

After a protein bar and some green Gatorade as an afternoon snack, I'd put on my warm yellow McIntyre*Sales* jacket and get ready for check-in and loading Room In The Inn guests on the vans to go out for the evening. Room In The Inn was open from December through March, giving neighbors a hot meal, sometimes a shower (even laundry), and a bed for the night. The van drivers could spot my bright jacket as they pulled their large church vans into the narrow drive. I'd get them in position, so we got the right neighbors to the right church (not that we separated Baptist from Methodist, but some places only took men, some women with children, some allowed smoking, some not), then help get the van loaded and off they'd go. The following day, the vans would drop their guests at the transit terminal early, usually after giving them a hot breakfast and a bag lunch.

My favorite van came from St. Peter's Episcopal. They'd started their soup kitchen in '79, and Jerry Blackmon, a small business owner himself, plus a North Carolina Senator and Mecklenburg County Commissioner, was always proud to tell me the role his wife, Irene, played since the beginning. The van's driver was often Lynn Holt, and we'd visit before we got everyone on board. Then I'd tell everyone how lucky they were to be going to St. Peter's for the evening. It was close, and you'd be right Uptown in the morning; besides, you'll get the best meal of your life at St. Peter's.

I was usually home for dinner by about 7:30. I was tired, but it was a good kind of tired.

Other days, I'd work off and on from home. After some tinkering by Paul Hanneman and the URB's IT people, my work emails and phone calls were transferred to my Mac and iPhone, so I could work from anywhere.

That year may have been as rewarding as any in a long while. It was a different environment with different people of varying skills. I wasn't the boss who snapped my fingers, just the catalyst suggesting how the elements could come together. There's a satisfaction to having things happen that way, not the pleasure of building it yourself, but the satisfaction of being part of the team and learning to work together.

The work was making me stronger, and maybe that's the best exercise of all. The initials and words I'd scribbled on my pad that day on the flight to Baltimore were coming to life, and I was happy.

Chapter 54

Stories of Hard Times and Heartbreak

Fall 2012

I was in Ashley's office at the URB on a late October Wednesday, talking about someone she knew at Family Dollar who might be able to offer our neighbors work in his warehouse, when a fellow, younger than me, but not by much, interrupted. He said he was sorry and would only be a minute but needed something from behind the door. I moved out of the way, and he reached for two cans of Carnation—just like mine.

It turned out Charlie had just finished cancer treatment and had been keeping the Carnation VHC in his locker along the back wall of the courtyard when it was time for a locker clean-out. There were only twenty-five lockers available for neighbors to use, and each month there was an announcement to clean them out for an hour and then move back in. That way, lockers no longer being used but still secured with a neighbor's combination lock could be given to the next person on the list. One day, Charlie missed the announcement, and that day he lost his nutrition, extra syringes, journals, and a few favorite books he'd been saving when his lock was cut off, and everything was hauled to the dump.

So now Charlie kept three cases of Carnation behind Ashley's door and would stop by when he needed a meal. He was starting to eat independently, but the feeding tube was still in, and he used it when he got hungry and couldn't find the soft foods he could chew. He told Ashley how exciting it was to be getting a room at Moore Place.

Charlie was sixty-one and had lived on the streets through his entire cancer ordeal. He'd been coughing and had a sore throat for almost a year before his new doctor at C.W. Williams Community Health Center diagnosed him. The doctor sent him to have his teeth pulled because if your teeth aren't good when the radiation starts, the beams take them out along with cancer, so, for folks like Charlie, the doctors just have the dentist pull them all before treatment begins. I was glad our son-in-law had checked mine.

Oral hygiene is difficult for many and impossible when homeless, like Charlie. A long list of health issues is traced to poor oral hygiene: cardiovascular disease, dementia, respiratory infections, diabetes, cancer, and more. Things are being done to provide dental assistance for the homeless and uninsured, but there needs to be more.

I told Charlie I'd had cancer similar to his, and maybe we could talk about it sometime. He said sure and was on his way.

Ashley filled me in and said she thought Charlie could use my help. "He could use more support, Bruce. He's a good guy, and this has been hard to watch. The waiting list is longer at Moore Place than any of us would like, but I'm glad his name finally came up."

A few days later, I saw Charlie when I came out of the monthly staff meeting. He was getting ready to move into Moore Place and was picking up the last of his things from Ashley's office. I offered him a ride over.

He unlocked the door to Room 113, and we went inside. The kitchen was on the right, small, and with everything he needed. There was a table with two chairs. The bed was to the left. Straight ahead, and with a window, was an alcove with a small couch in front of a TV resting on top of an empty bookcase. A bathroom and closet to the far left. The floors were linoleum, and the walls were a pale green. It reminded me of my room in college, but I didn't have a kitchen, a TV, or a private bath. Plus, I had a roommate who stayed up late and left the overhead light on. Charlie's new home was perfect.

We unloaded the things he brought, plus two bags of groceries we'd stopped for. Charlie needed pretty much the same soft foods I'd started with, except he didn't need to worry about being gluten-free. We'd bought puddings, applesauce, Chef Boyardee ravioli, four cans of stewed apples, a jar of jelly (I insisted on Smucker's), some Jif peanut butter, a dozen eggs, milk, and bread.

The people at Moore Place had put together a welcoming kit with kitchen utensils and things for the bathroom. There was a set of new sheets, still in the package, and a blanket lying ready on the bed.

Charlie put the eggs and milk in the refrigerator, left the other groceries on the counter, and walked the few steps to the couch. I pulled up a chair. We talked for a while about what to expect in the next few months, when he could have his tube removed, and if it would hurt. How could he get new teeth? How long would that take? I'd want dentures or dental implants, and the sooner, the better, but when you're homeless, you take what you can get when you can get it.

When he was little, Charlie had been adopted by an older couple, their only child, and had no idea who his real parents might have been. He graduated from Harding High School and then went to North Carolina State. He met a girl, she got pregnant, and they lived in the married dorm until he dropped out.

The marriage lasted about eighteen months before his wife and daughter moved on. His daughter is grown and lives in Charlotte now. She and his ex-wife came to his father's funeral, but they didn't speak to Charlie.

Charlie had been homeless for four years before cancer. He'd owned three homes in Charlotte over the years. Been forced out of them all. Drinking too much, he said. All wasted money. The judge took his license after his last DWI.

"But look, Bruce, there's a bookcase. See there? I bet I'll have it full in no time. I like this place; it'll do fine."

I left him to settle in.

That evening I told Joyce Charlie's story. We imagined how I would have felt undergoing my treatment without her. With no home and no car. No CaringBridge site, no terrace to sit on while I recovered. I'd have to store my Carnation wherever I could and clean the syringe in public restrooms. Have to walk to radiation and chemo and then find a place to sleep at night. The only bench being one in the park, and the police chasing me off after dark. Could that happen? Yes, and it does. I don't know if Charlie knew about Samaritan House or not. It's a small place in Grier Heights that offers a place for the homeless to recover after a hospital stay. Maybe they didn't have room, but it no longer mattered because Charlie had Moore Place to call home.

I was now working with people who had stories of heartbreak and hard times. I told myself to listen to their stories and understand how it's the stories that connect us. Sometimes the stories would be similar, but often not. Like my visit with Charlie in his new home. Rather than me doing the talking, I listened to him. Listen for the culture and the history; those hold the differences that pull us together. The best stories will have texture, layers, and colors; there will be energy, spirit, and excitement that we may not understand; there will be highs and lows lower than any we ever know. When our stories are too similar, they become monochromatic and dull; there's a listless, spiritless cloud overshadowing the joy. The sad part is how unaware we are of the sameness, where nothing stands out. Things should come together, not because they match, but because they don't.

I found my replacement within the first year, and our team had found jobs for over fifty neighbors, with paychecks to help secure housing for most. A few made bad choices with their money, but JobWorks continued to find better ways of connecting people to work.

I helped Darren Ash at Charlotte Family Housing modify the model to fit their needs and helped Tony Marciano at Charlotte Rescue Mission do the same.

Charlie made it for another two years before he died at age sixty-three. The nightmare he suffered is beyond my comprehension. If I had to write the epitaph for Charlie's tombstone, it would say, "He died in bed, with a roof above."

Chapter 55

Southside For Sale

2012

It was time to sell the building. The area along the light rail had continued to develop, and, just as with everything else, no one rings a bell at the top, so why not sell now? On the other hand, the rent checks were arriving like clockwork, and the loan for the building had been paid off, so, with the quad-net lease, I had a good monthly income with no expenses. Yet, someday the lease would expire, or Todd might move on, and where would I be? Needing to find a new tenant for a specialized building is hard. Maybe then I'd want to sell. So, why not sell now, get it over with, and put the money to work elsewhere?

Some people make their living being landlords, but that's not what I wanted. I called H.P. Smith for help. "Smitty," as he is known, answered on the first ring. Gibson Smith Realty is small, but they deal in commercial real estate and are good at what they do.

"Sure, Bruce, I can do that. I'll look into it, take some pictures, maybe go inside if you can arrange it, and take it from there."

Smitty got back to me. "It's a great building, Bruce, on the light rail and in an up-and-coming part of town. I'll gather some comps and work up a listing price, but many of the comps will be from building before upfits, so we'll need to spell that out for any potential buyer. Oh, and do you want a sign?"

"No sign, Smitty. I don't want anyone to get nervous, especially my friends who still work there."

"No problem. Talk soon."

100 Southside Drive, Charlotte, NC 28217, my second home, was now on the market, just like the business had been a few years before. All the emotions returned, except this was only brick and mortar, but still, the building was my legacy. It didn't say McIntyre*Sales* anymore, but it did the same thing, and with most of the same people inside.

I felt a sense of anguish about selling, but it was still the right thing to do. Get it over with, and quickly, I felt. But nothing happened; not even a looker. I'd talk to Smitty every month or so, but still nothing. "Maybe we put up a sign, Smitty. Would that help?"

"No, Bruce. You were right not to put up a sign when we first started. Many don't see that, but I'm glad you did. A sale only needs one buyer, and yours is out there; it's just not his time yet."

"Not his time? How do you mean?"

"Your buyer will do a 1031 swap, and when the clock starts ticking, he'll have only forty-five days to pull it off. You know about 1031 swaps, right?"

"Sure," I lied.

I did some research. A 1031 tax-deferred exchange lets the seller take the money from one investment property and put it into another without paying capital gains, but they need to find the new property within forty-five days of selling the old.

Tax laws always seem to favor a few over others, and while some say the rules are fair for everyone, it's only a question of whose ox is being gored.

Joyce and I were on vacation in Palm Springs when Smitty called. "I've got him, Bruce." Smitty had found a father and son team who had just sold over $30 million in single-family homes. They were all poorly maintained tiny houses in rundown neighborhoods, but they added up to $30 million for a single owner.

"Can you get us inside, fast? Maybe use the same excuse you used when I took the pictures?"

Done and done, and for the full listing price. All with me in California on my mobile phone with a new app to scan papers with its camera.

There had been some discussion about price, but I remembered my conversation with the previous owner when I'd bought the building from him ten years before. "Smitty, you tell your father and son team they can take it or leave it; I don't care." Of course, knowing they only had five of their forty-five days left gave me courage.

I was no longer a landlord.

When Joyce and I returned to Charlotte, we went to Pupuseria Y Restaurante Trust out Central Avenue for the pupusas with cheese and beans. I ordered in Spanish and told Joyce it would soon be time for me to return to El Salvador.

My time in El Salvador was like my time with the homeless at the Urban Ministry Center. Immersing myself in the lives of those so different from myself let me better understand their struggles and forced me to rethink assumptions. I was learning that the best development is always self-development and never something given, but something gained.

Chapter 56

Those Who Travel with the Least Travel Best

My first trip to El Salvador was in October 2005, when a group of sixteen stepped away from otherwise separate lives to spend a week together building Habitat for Humanity homes in the poor Central American country. I didn't sign up with any particular agenda or list of things to accomplish. It just sounded like a fun trip with people who all shared a common interest in affordable housing.

I knew two in our group, Anna Carter and Helen Sanders. Anna had written the construction manual we used to build Habitat for Humanity homes in Charlotte. It was full of photographs she had taken, and her instructions walked the volunteer through each step. I found her DIY guide helpful in my role as house leader when our church built a home each year. Helen was twenty years my senior, a widow who spent summers in New Hampshire and winters in Charlotte working on the Tuesday group of volunteers who had done siding together for years. Helen and I first met when I struggled with fitting the siding where the soffit comes together at a corner. She cupped her hands together, raised them to her mouth, and yelled, "Come down from up there, son, and I'll show you how it's done." She scampered up the ladder and quickly had the corner set properly. "See?" she said, more than asked, as she came down. "These

corners are like everything in life. They're easy once you know how."
From that moment on, Helen was my friend and my role model.

I also knew Meg Robertson, but not well. She was the associate
director of Habitat-Charlotte. I liked the people building homes here
in Charlotte, so I was sure it would be the same in El Salvador.

After Joyce dropped me at the airport early that morning, I
joined a few others as we waited at the gate for our flight to Atlanta.
Our trip leader was Beth Van Gorp, who worked for Habitat as the
volunteer coordinator and, over previous years, had led many to El
Salvador. We were to change planes in Atlanta and board a Delta
flight to San Salvador, the country's capital.

I'd packed lightly, planning to carry everything on board. I had
my backpack with the usual change of underwear, some protein bars
I favored, Cipro, and other medicine. A pen, notebook, whatever
business book I was reading at the time, along with the small toiletry
containers TSA allowed, plus my passport in a secure pouch. My
other bag was a small black zippered duffle with a shoulder strap
that I had planned to store in the overhead rack or stuff under a seat.

Others had checked a bag; in fact, one person checked two when
we arrived at the airport in Charlotte early that crisp morning. So,
with the long walk we'd have in the Atlanta airport, why not? I gave
the Delta agent at the gate my black duffle.

There was the usual getting-to-know-each-other chatter as we
waited to board. Susan Sewell was from Marshall, a small town in
the North Carolina mountains, only thirty miles from my mother's
home state. She seemed to know many in our group, especially Beth,
and we talked. After learning I'd worked in big business and now
owned my own company, Susan pronounced me a Republican. "A

George W. man," she called me. I smiled. "Just look at you," she said. Maybe my Presbyterian neat-and-orderly manner made her say that; I don't know. I only know we had a whole week together, and there would be time to sort that out.

Passport Health had given me a small yellow card, printed in Spanish, with my dietary needs spelled out. *Sin Trigo*, No Wheat, the card began. On the same visit, Passport Health gave me my various shots and Cipro if I consumed any contaminated food or water, which was easy to do, the woman warned.

After we leveled off, I moved to an empty seat next to Beth. I had some questions about what to expect. "It depends, Bruce," was her answer to most. She bent down, rummaged in the bag she had brought on board and pulled out a book. "Here, this may help." She handed me a fat paperback with small print. *The Violence of Love* was a strange title, I thought. It looked tedious. I went back to my seat. By the time we were ready to land, I was well into Óscar Romero's book and had even taken the pen from my backpack to underline a few sentences, not even thinking about how it was Beth's book and not mine.

I didn't know much about the author but soon learned more. Romero's homilies tell the story of transforming from a member of the privileged elite to the most influential voice in the land for the marginalized. The stories tell of rules put in place by a few yet controlling so many. Sermons like those got Archbishop Romero assassinated in hopes of preventing their spread. But voices like Romero's aren't silenced by a bullet. Death only turns up the volume.

The people from Habitat for Humanity in El Salvador were at the airport to meet us. "Hurry up!" Beth shouted. "The van is waiting, and we've got a long drive up the mountain to Santa Ana."

Everyone had their luggage except Anna and me. The carousel now empty, Anna questioned the attendant. "*Lo siento mucho, señorita,*" was his reply. It seemed air cargo was the first priority. Next, bags tagged as "Tour Group." The rest might get unloaded or go further south like Anna's and mine. Our luggage was not Delta's first, or even second, priority. We quickly filled out the missing luggage forms.

I put my backpack over my shoulder, headed through customs, then on to the waiting van.

We stopped for lunch at *Pupuseria Margoth* in the town of Olocuilta. At a long table with the others and with my rice pupusas stuffed with a fresh local flower called *loroco* in front of me, I reached for the large bowl of slaw. Beth quickly said, "Hey guys, remember this slaw was made with lettuce washed in the kitchen with local water. I'd pass if I were you."

In Santa Ana, Beth had the driver pull into a strip mall so Anna and I could rush in and buy some clothes. The small, cluttered shop was nothing like where I shopped back home, but I found a pair of jeans that more or less fit and the plainest shirt in my size. It had a wide collar and broad, ugly stripes going up and down, which, yes, was the plainest they had.

Everyone settled in the Hotel Sahara, agreeing to meet downstairs for dinner at six. My roommate wasn't there yet; he'd be along tomorrow or the day after. He would bring our number to the full sixteen.

Anna and a few others were already there when I went down. She took one look and said, "Oh no, Bruce, that'll never do. You look too, well, I don't know, just too North American. Let me try this."

She pulled out my shirttail, messed up my hair, still wet from the shower, then unbuttoned the top buttons of my new shirt, spreading the already wide collar even further, showing not gold chains but only Anglo-Saxon white skin; she then stepped back to take a more extended look. "Better!" she said. "You look more Salvadoran."

No way I looked Salvadoran, and never would, but everyone got a big chuckle from it all, and the otherwise first night tensions were relaxed. Susan came over saying, "Like your new look."

We rode a bus to the small town southeast of our hotel, *Ciudad de Coatepeque*. We started by digging the foundations with hand tools, then mixing the mortar, called *mezcla* for joints and *chispa* for the filler holding the metal rebar in place. There wasn't a cement mixer, not even the kind with a hand crank. We formed volcano-shaped mounds on the bare dirt with sand or gravel, added the concrete, then gently poured water into the small volcano's mouth. Gradually folding the sides in on themselves with a shovel, hoping the volcano wouldn't open and let everything spill out. And if it did erupt, everyone grabbed a shovel or whatever they could find and frantically put it all back together, saving what they could.

We carried the cinder blocks to the waiting mason, standing in his pink flip-flops, eager to get to work on the 421-square-foot home with one large room and two small bedrooms.

Occasionally the mason might let a *gringo* like me position a cinder block in its chalk-line leveled row. But mostly my job was to use the bottom half of a Kolashampan plastic soda bottle the mason had cut with his pocket knife the day before to scoop the *chispa* from a pail and pour the drippy mixture, more water than gravel and cement, inside the blocks to secure the rebar as it hardened. I later drank a bottle of Kolashampan soda, and while expecting a sugary lemon-lime flavor, it was more like Juicy Fruit chewing gum in a bottle.

Habitat's arrangement with masons was simple. They started with the right amount of sand, gravel, and cement, plus the precise number of cinder blocks. The mason supplied the tools and bought extra material when needed. So letting mortar spill from the volcano or breaking a block came out of his pocket, and the longer it took to finish the house, the longer it would be until he started the next.

We worked alongside the new homeowner and his family, visiting, laughing, exchanging what few words we knew, or using Anna as our interpreter. But it wasn't the words that brought us together; it was the smiles as he and his family put in their sweat-equity hours, and we enjoyed our "vacations."

The house we worked on in the town of Coatepeque was next to another building. So close, there could have been a common wall if that was allowed, but it wasn't, because if an earthquake brought down the neighbor, we didn't want our house dragged down with it. Our house would stand long after the new owner's grandchildren were gone.

The new homeowner still lived in the place he had crafted in the back corner of his lot with his wife and three children before he got the Habitat loan. Using the wall next door on one side and the fence in the back on another, they had built their lives with what they could scavenge. Corner posts were made from tree branches, skinned bare with the husband's machete that, when not in use, was always in its sheath on the wide leather belt looped around his waist. The roof was made of corrugated metal sheets, some wider than others, some overlapping as intended, but some not. A blue tarp would do until they found another piece of corrugated sheeting, even if plastic, to protect them from rain. The walls were mostly cardboard, and a brown tarp covered the front door. It was always tied open, except when it rained. More air could circulate on hot nights that way.

A fire was kept burning outside the front door for cooking and heat when it got cold. The parents slept in the main room, and there was a room off to the side, under the tin roof, with a dry squat toilet in its center, a half-used bag of lime to neutralize odors and ward away flies near where the three young children slept. The couple had one girl and two boys.

The large truck had dumped a whole load of sand in the back of the lot when the cement, rebar, and blocks were delivered, and the three children had begun using the pile of sand as a playground. And, as the new home went up, the new playground went down.

I asked to use the restroom, *baño*, I knew to say. And was pointed to the children's room. I went in the front, past the tied-open brown tarp, and turned right to the bedroom.

There it was. In the center of the small room where the children had fashioned sleeping pallets with old blankets on the dirt floor was the white porcelain oval throne the size and shape of a football, rising about six inches over a hole dug in the ground.

I looked around the children's bedroom; the girl's dresses were hanging on a nail in one of the posts their father had cut with his machete, and there were little cars and trucks the boys had arranged on the floor. My oldest grandson and I played with toys like those when he was about their age, but Kenny kept his in a box under his bed, not next to a toilet. There were a few stuffed animals in one corner. Then my eyes went back to the squat toilet. I decided I could wait.

The new home wouldn't have any closets, and the kitchen and bath were outside, attached to the home and under a roof. The kitchen would have a sink with running water, and the toilet would be in a room by itself where there would be a door you could close, and the toilet would have a handle to flush waste into a septic field before allowing it to reach the aquifer.

Solid but straightforward and the best most would ever have. Plus, it was theirs. They had a clear title to the land and would pay off the mortgage monthly.

The rhythm of our days settled in: breakfast was mashed plantains with fried eggs or scrambled eggs with fried plantains. Sliced avocado, orange juice, and coffee. Then we would top off our bottles with *agua pure* from the five-gallon jug in the hotel's lobby.

We loaded the van, Beth counted heads, and we'd ride the twenty minutes to Coatepeque. Then unload and go to work.

Habitat for Humanity employees brought a lunch we were told was safe to eat to the site, usually laid out in the bed of a pickup. Everyone lined up at the truck, and one of their people would ask if we wanted cheese or beans. I said both, *gracias*. She put two pupusas in a white clamshell container with a scoop of slaw to the side. The next woman dipped a chipped porcelain white-and-blue ladle in a big aluminum pot, filled a plastic bag like the ones my mother used for my sandwich when I was in second grade, with a watery-colored fruit juice, tied a knot in the bag, poked a hole in the bag with a straw, and handed me my drink. A young girl, about eight or nine, gave me a plastic fork.

I walked across the gravel street to the broken curb and joined the mason, his two helpers, the others from Charlotte, the husband, and his wife with their three children, all facing the now halfway complete house. I sat next to the youngest son, who reminded me of Kenny.

We made quite a sight, all of us lined up on the curb with pupusas balanced on our knees, one hand holding the sweet Kool-Aid, the other using the fork, looking like a bunch of mismatched clothes pegs left on the line, ready for the next load of laundry.

There was a morning and afternoon snack of fruit and the same Kool-Aid in your choice of colors, but none unsweetened.

Dinner was in the hotel or at a nearby restaurant. Evenings were spent on the roof of the Hotel Sahara, with a radio playing Salvadoran hip hop and most of us drinking long-neck *cervezas*. I read my new book, underlining more and more as I went. Before bed, I washed out my underwear in the sink, draping it over the towel rack to dry, then looked at that day's shirt and pants to see if tomorrow could be the same or if I'd need to switch to my new striped shirt and ill-fitting jeans. Brush my teeth using the *agua pura* to rinse; then, before flipping the switch that controlled the single overhead bulb, put a shoe in the sink as a reminder not to drink from the tap.

There were many tricks I would learn over the years to not get sick from the water. Like keeping one shoe in the sink and clenching a toothpick between my teeth as I showered so water wouldn't go down my throat. I learned to always order my beverage in a can and never pour it over ice. I would use my bandana to clean the area around the tab because the can had been in a cooler with impure water or ice. And don't forget the lettuce; no matter how healthy it is for you at home, it may have been washed before it got mixed in your salad or put on your sandwich. Best to only eat what the Habitat for Humanity folks said was safe. They knew best, and sick *gringos* made for bad publicity.

That Tuesday afternoon was All Souls Day, or the Day of the Dead, as many called it. The masons and their families visited the cemeteries to honor loved ones who were either dead or missing from the war. They cleaned and painted gravestones and decorated them with plastic flowers.

We walked through one of the cemeteries. It reminded me of my grandfather's garden in Sparta, which he had decorated with gazing balls to ward off evil and bring good luck, adding a mix of white rocks and little cone-shaped dolls with feathers he had won at the fair. Grandpa had the whole thing fixed up, and it looked just like the graves I was walking through on this Day of the Dead, except it would have taken dozens of Grandpa's gardens to make up just one small corner of this crowded cemetery.

Their civil war had been over for thirteen years when I first visited, so the memories of missing loved ones were fresh. Wars are never easy, and battles between your own people must be the hardest of all. Imagine having a family member pulled out of bed and taken with no warning or reason, never to be seen again. I asked Beth which side was right and which was wrong. She paused, then answered, "It depends, Bruce." Then asked, "Are you still reading Óscar Romero's book?"

After dinner on Thursday, Carlos Avalos Valencia arranged a meeting with several local pastors. We went around the table making our introductions, and when it was my turn, I stood to say I was an elder in Myers Park Presbyterian Church and that my church was in "*Charlotte, Carolina del Norte, Estados Unidos.*"

Pastor Rodriguez immediately stood on the other side of the table, walked around, and gave me a hug. He said a few words I didn't understand and then returned to his seat. Embarrassed, I sat down.

After the meeting, Carlos, our interpreter and director of church relations for Habitat, explained how Pastor Rodriguez was Presbyterian, and there were few Protestants, let alone Presbyterians, in this outpost of Rome. Carlos told me the pastor had a small church in Ahuachapán and hoped the two of us could be friends.

Pastor Rodriguez brought me a packet of information about his church to my hotel the next day, but I was off working, so he left it at the desk. Imagine my surprise when I returned that evening to be told I had mail. I don't know if he walked or hitched a ride, but he had come the nineteen miles to deliver a package.

As I walked away from the desk, the manager called me back. "Señor, your bag arrived." Or that's what I think he said as he lifted my missing black duffle to the counter. I thanked him, then took my bag and the sealed envelope to my room. In the envelope were several photographs of what I guess was Pastor Rodriguez's wife and family. A picture of a small piece of land with a tree in the center and several handwritten notes. I would need to have Anna or Beth translate those for me.

The lost bag reminded me of my time at Philmont Scout Ranch years ago when I had lightened my backpack and could see further

301

when I stood up straighter. Those who travel with the least travel best, I remembered. So pack what you need and need what you pack, but leave the rest at home. And if you forgot something, they probably have it there, or something close. And if they don't have it, you may not need it either. Life can be more fulfilling when everything is not so convenient. All I took from my duffle was toothpaste, a razor, and some shaving cream. I zipped it up and didn't open it again until I got home.

I thought about the young family and their toilet, how they would have needed to save to buy the porcelain oval, and how the young couple must have worked together to dig the hole. Did the children help? Probably—because families work together when there's cause.

The next day we said our goodbyes to the masons and others. Our new friends, the homeowners, still puzzled about why we would spend our vacations with them, asked us to return when their new home was finished.

Susan said she'd been wrong about me when we first met and if I was ever in the mountains to stop in for a visit.

It was a wonderful trip. I enjoyed the companionship, but mostly the eye-opening experiences of being immersed in a culture so different from my own. I went home and told Joyce about it. I talked so much that she thought I might be planning to move. I started making plans—not to move—to return.

I had never opened the business book I'd brought and, from then on, traveled with authors like Gustavo Gutierrez, Jon Sobrino, and Robert McAfee Brown.

I got Beth a new copy of the archbishop's sermons.

Chapter 57

Many Crumpled Napkins and Still Not Perfect

2007–2008

My next Habitat for Humanity trip was to El Barro, El Salvador, in July 2007. Then, a week on my own the following summer, to be immersed in Spanish at *Centro de Intercambio y Solidaridad* (Exchange and Solidarity Center). I lived with a local family, speaking only their language. I took the public bus to the school each morning, remembering to have the right coins for the box. The school tested my Spanish on the first day. *Poco* (little), the results said. I was paired with a woman of similar ability from Sweden.

We spent our mornings in a small classroom and then walked, with little conversation, to a neighboring cafe for lunch. We tried to practice the vocabulary we were learning but struggled with the verb tenses. I was thinking in English, and my classmate, no doubt, in her native Svenska.

CIS students were encouraged never to use their first language. It's best to speak, even think, in the second language if you want to make it your own. With time it became more manageable, and as I'd learned from Helen, "Anything is easy, once you know how."

In the afternoon, our guide took the entire group to political, social, or economic points of interest around the large city so we could better understand the Salvadoran culture. When it was time for the day's events to end and for us to return to our separate host families scattered about town, the guide would give us each our directions.

Turning to me, he said, "Bus 28 to the square, then 14 to your stop across from the *Supermercados Super Selectos*, where the guard stands out front with his automatic rifle. Got it?" All in his accelerated Spanish. I'd write the bus numbers in the palm of my hand with my pen and hope they didn't smear as I nervously swung my backpack around front for its security and climbed onto the already overcrowded number 28. I didn't need to make a note about the grocery store with the guard out front. I remembered him and those like him all over town. The armed guards were there to protect the property, make shoppers feel safe, and, I later learned, provide income to the gangs who provided the guards. First, a gang member would ask the shop owner if they wanted a guard to prevent trouble. The owner would say, "No need" because there had been none. Then accidents would start happening, and soon the owner needed a guard. Then the accidents stopped. It's a story that has gone on for ages.

At the end of the week, I packed up what few things I had brought, said goodbye to my host family and their little white dog, then followed my route to *Hábitat para la Humanidad*.

I joined Carlos Avalos and Patty Cordero (who would later become Patty Arcia) for our drive to Ahuachapán.

That weekend, Carlos arranged a visit with Pastor Rodriguez, the Presbyterian minister I had met on my first trip, and his family at the small home they rented in town.

Pastor Rodriguez, then fifty-two, introduced me to his wife, Regina, forty-five, and their three children: Andrea, seventeen; Victor, thirteen; and Habram, nine. The names and ages were written by Pastor Rodriguez on a small slip of paper from my notebook. I taped the list to the back of a picture Carlos snapped that day. The pastor also wrote the names and ages of the other five members of his small congregation. We talked about how he wanted to build a church and how he already owned the lot.

Andrea spoke about teaching the children English while Victor taught crafts and played his guitar. Habram, with his short spiky black hair, didn't speak; instead, he kept his wide brown eyes on me, the fair-skinned North American.

The following week was spent in San Vincente with members of my church, where we built homes on the side of a mountain with great views but giant boulders that needed to be unearthed before we could start the foundations. Joe Fountain, the owner of a landscaping company in Charlotte, talked about how Habitat needed a backhoe until he thought about fuel and repairs and how inexpensive *gringo* volunteers were.

Our church had hired someone fresh out of college to coordinate outreach, and they went off one day with a few from Habitat to buy gifts for the church members who had been significant donors in the recently completed capital campaign. I don't know if the gifts were of value or simply trinkets from the market. I don't know if it was the young coordinator's idea or if they had been told to buy them. It didn't matter. I just thought it odd that some donors got a reward and some did not.

I also learned the people from Habitat had approached the coordinator about our church making a large donation to *Hábitat para la Humanidad* so they could build even more houses around the country. But again, I don't know if they asked or offered, because I wasn't part of any of the conversations.

My time with Bob Breed, the Myers Park Presbyterian Church associate minister of outreach, taught me that mission was about relationships, not money. That a hand-up was better than a hand-out, and how "mission" was done in partnership. I was learning how mission, done Bob's way, was even more transformational for "us" than it was for "them." So, the idea of just writing a big check seemed wrong.

Enrique Sanchez was on the trip, and when we got home, we talked with Bob. Then later, Enrique and I met at Julia's, a coffee shop, to talk about what could come next.

Enrique was born and raised in Corrientes, Argentina, about 300 miles southwest of Iguaza Falls on the border between Brazil, Argentina, and Paraguay, a spot Joyce and I have visited. Enrique had been in the International Economics unit at Bank of America before retiring. In addition to his years of training in economic theory, he had also studied Gustavo Gutiérrez in its original Spanish. Gutiérrez is a Dominican priest from Peru who preaches about our duty, as followers of Christ, to help the poor and oppressed, not only in the church but through involvement in civic and political affairs. Enrique had a head for economics and a heart for theology. And while both Enrique and the ideas he spoke of in his heavy Spanish accent were complicated and difficult for many to grasp, he was brilliant.

Enrique and I picked a table away from the others, hidden in the rows of preowned books sold at Julia's, for our morning meeting. The books Julia's sells are used, just like the furniture next door at ReStore, but the coffee is new and freshly ground by the best baristas in town.

I like to think of the furniture and books as recycled, reclaimed, or repurposed, all better words than *used*. The profits go to build more Habitat for Humanity homes, so why would I browse titles, shop for a bedside table, or meet a friend for coffee anywhere but Julia's?

I must be getting forgetful, I thought. *Who comes to a meeting without a pad of paper?* I picked up some napkins from the front, where they kept the sugar and cream.

Back at our table, I sketched a few ideas on the napkin. Crumpled it up and got another until we had it right.

The Salvadoran Relationship Team was a bold column slightly to the left of the center in our proposed logo. It was vertical, up and down, like it came down from the clouds to meet the earth. Then there were arrows or lines going out to each side, horizontal, not vertical. The boldest of the three arrows on the right was labeled "Education," with four words below: "theology, language, culture, and mission" in parentheses. Above was the arrow: in-country mission. Below that arrow: local mission. The arrow to the left read PC (USA) Mission Network, our church's national governing body.

The entire design looked like a cross, enclosed in multiple circles, not all the same and none precisely round. Enrique called them *ondas*, or ripples. The ripples were the impact the mission would have in different directions and on so many people and for so long.

We wanted the design to accomplish several things. First, we called it Salvadoran, not El Salvador. The relationship was with the people, not the country. The design said, "The Salvadorian Relationship Team seeks to establish a relational ministry honoring the inherent connection between faith, justice, and care of creation."

It took many napkins to complete. Was it perfect? No, because as I would come to understand as I learned more about Archbishop Romero, "Nothing we do is complete, which is a way of saying that the kingdom always lies beyond us."

Chapter 58

Everything Is Better When the Community Is Better

2009

In February of 2009, the year before I started to seriously consider selling my company and the battle with cancer began, I traveled with a group to Ahuachapán. We stayed at Hotel Casa Blanca in the center of town and rode the bus to *Colonia Los Claveles* to build a home for Elvis and his young family.

Steven Eason, our senior pastor, was with us, and we joked about Elvis being the given name of a Salvadoran. Elvis's impact was indeed worldwide. The first evening, after dinner in the hotel, we all walked to Yolanda Ardon's La Neveria shop, just off the square, for ice cream. We all laughed as Steve joked about other names like Elvis that had gone global. Names like Beyoncé and Oprah, and so many more. He said he didn't see any chance of a name like Steve making that list.

That evening, Anna snapped a picture of us gazing up at the sky from the courtyard of the Hotel Casa Blanca. *Under the Same Roof of Stars*, by Anna Gallant Carter, is a collection of her photographs and our stories. It's a book I open often, both for the images and its beautiful words.

Walking back to the hotel, I congratulated Steve on the success-ful capital campaign. I told him how proud everyone was that it had broken all records and how great it was to be spending an equal amount outside the church as within (although there indeed were repairs that needed doing in the sanctuary). I knew the established programs would get extra funding: the Reformed Great Church of Debrecen in Hungary was a favorite with many. Mary Lou Lindsey was its most vocal supporter, and our church choir planned to visit next year. There was Dr. Bill Bradford and his committee's work in Malawi. Fay Grasty's team in the Congo, and the new hope Don Gately was bringing to our neighbors in Grier Heights. Don didn't think it took an overseas flight to help others; he felt it could happen at home, in our own backyard.

Grier Heights is an older, primarily African-American neigh-borhood with absentee owners, and while the majority of homes are rentals, there is a strong group of homeowners who have lived in the community for years. These owners are the leaders in Grier Heights because everything they have is invested in the community, and while that wouldn't be considered much by many, to them, it is everything.

Grier Heights was like the small towns in El Salvador. Each had local leaders but not enough "say" with the powerful. They had churches and a strong faith but not much money. So, like El Salvador, the people of Grier Heights needed someone to walk beside them and be their friend, and Don knew we could be that friend.

Steve and I walked along the narrow sidewalk back to the hotel, and I asked him what he thought of the trip, the people, what we were doing, and all the usual positioning questions leading up to an even bigger ask. "Do you think there would be room in the new budget for El Salvador, Steve?" I finally asked.

"That depends, Bruce."

"Depends on what, exactly, Steve?"

"Well, it would depend on what you planned to do with the money. How would it be used? What would the goals be? How would you know when you reached them, and if you didn't, then what? Would our church have partners, or would we go it alone? When would it end? How would you know when to leave? These are all the questions any Presbyterian committee will ask before writing you a check. That's all."

That may have been all, but that was a lot.

I asked Carlos, the HFH-ES employee overseeing church relations, if we could focus on just one village, not skip around so much, and do more than houses. Maybe work with the children, things like that. Not everyone wants to dig foundations all day, I told him.

Carlos seemed puzzled, saying he would talk to his boss, Kendal Stewart, about it. Kendal, the international donor relations coordinator, was from Raleigh and a Davidson College alumna. In her senior year, she did everything from organizing dance ensembles to raising money to bring a Los Angeles drama team to Charlotte's Urban Ministry Center to "work with the homeless, writing and acting out dramas from their own lives," writes Paul Leonard in his memoir, *Where is Church?*

Kendal often visited with Paul Leonard, a Davidson alumnus and Presbyterian minister, who had mentored Kendal in a leadership program at Davidson. Paul was president of John Crosland in Charlotte and later served as interim executive director of Habitat for Humanity International. He often asked the young people he encountered, "Where is the place you will live, and how will you define its borders?" When Kendal married Carlos Gomez from El Salvador, Paul and Judy visited for a week, and Reverend Leonard officiated at the service.

Paul Leonard knew his Bible and the Book of Jeremiah, where the prophet speaks to his exiled people, telling them they will be in this place for a long time, so they'd better adapt, settle in, and even pray for their oppressors. In Jeremiah 29:7, the prophet tells them not to hate the authorities, "But seek the welfare of the city where I have sent you into exile, and pray to the Lord on its behalf, for in its welfare you will find your welfare."

Allowing all people to flourish, not just the ones with new cinder-block homes, promotes the common good of the entire neighborhood, the whole economy, the schools, and the workplace.

Everything is better when the entire community is better, not just "my life" inside "my walls."

Even without knowing Kendal, the person, I knew how she was raised, so I'd let her work on it for a while, and we'd be okay.

It came time for my first ever Skype call. I was in Charlotte, positioned just as I had been instructed, facing the screen of my computer, when Kendal appeared in front of me. I was in Charlotte, and she was in San Salvador, and we were not only speaking but also looking at each other face to face.

She got down to business. "How can I help?"

I explained how we had worked in several locations around her adopted country, how we liked her work and its mission and wondered if we couldn't do more.

I told Kendal many in our group wanted to return to the same village each trip to see how their new friends were doing, how they decorated their homes, and how much the children had grown. And how there were many in Charlotte who feared the trip would be too hard for them. Were the streets safe? Would the beds be comfortable? Would they be able to eat the food? Was the water safe? I told her about Kae Roberts, a teacher who wanted to spend time with the children, and another volunteer who was interested in diet and wanted to help the people eat better, and a businessman who had ideas for the men (never thinking how the women could start their own businesses, and often do better than the men, a view he later changed). I told her about a doctor who wanted to track the community's medical history. And one congregant who thought, from the pictures she had seen, some of the people, especially the women, needed more exercise.

Kendal laughed. Was what I said funny?

"No, no, Bruce. Everything you're saying is wonderful. It's what our people need. It was just the last part about exercise that made me laugh. Our people work from sunup to sundown, women even longer. They walk for miles, carrying heavy jugs of water on their heads. They fetch firewood, then grind corn into flour on the bare floor. Exercise is the one part I think we're good with, and you can tell your toned Myers Park woman to come work with us for a day, and we'll see who's in shape and who's not."

Kendal told me later she regretted saying the last part, but it was

313

true. She had grown up with so many privileged women, gone to college with them, and later visited in their fashionable homes, all women who could spend hours at a fitness studio but couldn't last a minute in the real world. She added, "Thanks for letting me vent. I need that from time to time."

I told her it was fine, and she was welcome to vent with me whenever she wanted.

"As for all the other things you are asking for, that's a long list. And like Carlos told you, we build houses. So give me a week or so, and we'll set up another call. Oh, and nice to meet you, by the way."

I phoned Enrique and agreed to meet at Julia's again. I invited Jeff Lohr to join us. Jeff had been with Price Waterhouse and was the CFO for a retirement community on Park Road. Jeff and I had gotten to know each other on local Habitat builds and shared a passion for justice in our communities.

We needed to pull our ideas together while Kendal tried to find our answers. That way, we'd have some direction because, like Alice in Wonderland said, "If you don't know where you're going, any road will take you there."

In my next Skype call with Kendal, she told me she had found the perfect spot for us. It was a small *barrio* near Ahuachapán, a city she knew to be safe. Pastor Rodriguez and his family lived nearby in a rental house; the lot he had picked out for his church was there. The Hotel Casa Blanca was there, and above all, there was Yolanda and her La Neveria ice cream. The poor neighborhood we would be working in already had an active homeowners' association and a leader who had managed to get a water treatment plant built nearby. Kendal felt teaming us with Martha de Sanchez, the leader of the homeowners' association, *Asociación para el Desarollo Comunitario* or Community Improvement Association, or ADESCO as we learned to call it, would be the perfect combination to get things done. The community was Getsemaní, named, no doubt, for the garden at the foot of the Mount of Olives in Jerusalem, where Jesus met with his disciples before the Crucifixion and openly shared His sadness and fear. And where He, at His most human, invited their love.

I traveled down with Bob Breed, our outreach associate, and Norie and Enrique Sanchez. Norie was from upstate New York and had been married to Enrique for years; her Spanish may not have been as good as her husband's, but she could hold her own. We'd only be there for a few days, but we would meet with Kendal, Carlos, Martha, and the ADESCO.

Our rickety conference table was on the dirt floor of a vacant lot next to Martha's modest home, the last to eventually undergo renovation. We met under a large blue tarp that served as their conference room's permanent roof. I thought back to the blue tarps covering half the homes in Charlotte after Hurricane Hugo in 1989.

We were seated in a circle on white plastic chairs. They're the ones with arms, and are sold on the sidewalk at Walmart. They can be stacked on top of each other, and if you lean back, they collapse.

Martha's home and our conference room were across the unpaved, puddled road from a large plot of land, holding various pieces of rusty playground equipment that had once been painted a bright blue. It was easy to spot the dirt paths on and off the playground, as the rest of the playground was covered in vines and weeds.

The homeowners' association was made up of all women, except one older man who never spoke. One young woman was breastfeeding her sleeping toddler. Children were playing in the dirt while numerous dogs wandered about; I called them *"Perro del Mundos"* because, like the white chairs, they are all over the world. *Perro del Mundos* are brown in color, medium build, and have short hair. It only takes six breedings to get them looking like this, apparently, no matter what color or size they start, no matter the pedigree.

Everyone in the group was fluent in Spanish, except Bob and me, so it was slow going, with everything needing to be repeated in English.

I was curious why the children weren't in school. They looked old enough. I got some answers I didn't understand and let it slide. We would get to that later, I hoped. Seeing the young children playing in the dirt made me think about my four grandchildren; mine played on green lawns, not in the dirt, and mine were in school. Why weren't these?

Bob wanted us to listen to what the ADESCO members wanted. It took time for the women to open up, but Bob was patient. He sat in his white chair, listened, and didn't lean back. Once they started, the ideas began rushing out.

They needed better housing and ways to earn an income without living in San Salvador or up North. Opportunities for schooling were important. Being able to visit a doctor when sick. Teaching leadership skills to the youth and their parents were on the list. *"Educación en valores,"* one woman said. "Values education," Norie interpreted. And then they would like to learn more about us, about *Estados Unidos*, while we learned about them.

We might have come up with some on our own, but we would have missed others had we not kept quiet and listened. For instance, I wanted pure water that I could drink, but the water from the new plant was pure for those whose bodies had biologically adapted over time.

Maybe I would have thought about jobs for the people in the poor village, but not the simple stay-at-home crafts they wanted. Mine would have been on your own and not in a co-op.

I understood what Albert Camus meant when he said, "Don't walk in front of me . . . I may not follow; Don't walk behind me . . . I may not lead; Walk beside me . . . and just be my friend." It would take time, but many of us would see how it was not about what we, at Myers Park Presbyterian Church, said they needed but about what they, the people of Getsemaní, wanted and were ready to do on their own if only they had someone beside them, a friend.

Martha unrolled a large map she had been keeping under her chair. Spreading it out on the rickety table, she pointed to spots where the various things her members talked about could go. Her map had each parcel marked, showing if there was a clear title or not, along with the home's current conditions. It was marked differently if the lot was for sale or belonged to the city.

By the time we were ready to leave, it was clear Kendal had found an ideal location and the perfect partner for us.

Kendal filled her boss, Jorge Molina, in on the discussion. He wanted to meet these people asking so much of his organization, so Jorge and

Kendal flew to Charlotte and visited our church for Sunday services. Then on Monday, we had lunch at Mama Ricotta's on Kings Drive. Bert Green from Habitat Charlotte and a few of his people were there, along with several from Myers Park Presbyterian Church.

Jorge wondered what Bert thought of building Habitat homes in only one area.

Bert explained how it was "a new way for a new day," as he called it. How it could lift up an entire community, as others followed. Bert went on to say that building a house here and then another somewhere else only created islands. And how, in 1987, Charlotte's struggling Optimist Park neighborhood was transformed into what is now one of the more sought-after in town, all because Habitat for Humanity lifted up the entire community, bringing everyone together.

There was a multiplier effect, where growth becomes exponential. It's not that things just go faster; it's how even the rate of speed accelerates. Think of it like a railroad train struggling for traction until the wheels catch, and the momentum moves everything from the engine to the caboose faster and faster over the track. And once the train is rolling, the acceleration is hard to stop.

Kendal was struggling to keep up. She'd taken notes but was visibly relieved when Enrique stepped in.

"*Crecimiento exponential*," Enrique said. Exponential growth. That was it. Two Spanish words where Bert had used dozens, and it was all coming together.

But Jorge reported to a board that wanted numbers. They wanted houses built, "housing solutions," they called them, not kids in school or classes in nutrition for people they didn't have anything in common with other than sharing the same country.

Jorge and Kendal returned to El Salvador. I thought everything was settled, but there were meetings upon meetings at the church—so many people. There was Norie and Enrique Sanchez, of course. Jeff Lohr and Anna Carter. Kae Roberts, Curt Seifart, Joe Fountain, Tim Leaycraft, Helen Sanders, Natalie Beckett, Jeff Armstrong, Frances Foxworth, Evelyn and Ivan Hinrichs, Ian Frazier, Kelly and Jim Backman, Susan and Bob McKinney, Ed Baesel, Donnie Daugherty, Allan Lewis, Norman Walters, Cooley Walters, Eileen and Allen Woodward, Ann Edgerton, Anna Edgerton, Elsie and Will Barnhardt, Keller and Jim Mulligan, Larry Burton, and Charlie Shaffner. Bob Breed would join from time to time if he wasn't needed in some other church meeting. If Presbyterians do anything well, it's meetings.

We sat around a table in our Charlotte conference room, where the lights came on when we entered and off when we left, while Martha's had no lights at all.

We always sat silently at the start of each meeting to think of our sisters and brothers in Getsemaní, and then one of us would read the prayer by Archbishop Romero.

"It helps, now and then, to step back and take a long view.
The kingdom is not only beyond our efforts,
It is even beyond our vision.

Charles Bruce McIntyre

We accomplish in our lifetime only a tiny fraction
Of the magnificent enterprise that is God's work.
Nothing we do is complete, which is a way of saying
That the kingdom always lies beyond us.
No statement says all that could be said.
No prayer fully expresses our faith.
No confession brings perfection.
No pastoral visit brings wholeness.
No program accomplishes the church's mission.
No set of goals and objectives includes everything.
It may be incomplete,
But it is a beginning, a step along the way,
An opportunity for the Lord's grace to enter and do the rest.
We may never see the end results, but that is the difference
Between the master builder and the worker.
We are workers, not master builders; ministers, not messiahs
We are prophets of a future, not our own.
This is what we are about.
We plant the seeds that one day will grow.
We water seeds already planted,
Knowing that they hold future promise.
We lay foundations that will need further development.
We provide yeast that produces far beyond our capabilities.
We cannot do everything, and there is a sense of liberation
In realizing that. This enables us to do something,
And to do it very well.
Amen."

The prayer humbled me, keeping me grounded. Some said the prayer was composed by a Catholic Bishop in Saginaw, Michigan, but don't say that in El Salvador. The prayer is Archbishop Romero's alone, and on May 23, 2015, during Romero's beatification, Pope Francis declared his "ministry was distinguished by his particular attention to the poorest and marginalized." So for me, the prayer is Romero's, but it doesn't really matter, does it? The words come from much higher.

We pulled out the napkin Enrique and I had drawn that day at Julia's, or a copy of it by now, and talked about all the parts. How could it come together? How would we answer Steve's questions from the night we walked home after ice cream?

This was taking on a life of its own. It was getting big.

Finally, our presentation for the Benevolence Funding committee at church was ready. Jeff Lohr had proofed each word and number. I had the Kinko store on East Boulevard make multiple color copies, carefully binding each.

We met with Jim Abbott and his team on Thursday, July 23, 2009. We'd given each member a copy of the presentation on Monday, so they would have time to prepare.

We had everything spelled out in a PowerPoint presentation, just in case, but there's never a need to read word for word to a group who learned how to do that for themselves years ago.

I provided an overview, positioned the request, and then it was time for Benevolence Funding to make it their own.

The members had done their homework, and I carefully considered who could provide the best answer as the questions started. If the query was financial, about the numbers, I said, "Jeff, would you like to speak on that?" If the question was more cultural, how would the people of Charlotte fit in El Salvador? I turned to Enrique, "Señor Sanchez, you know more than any of us how it feels to live in a culture not your own. What do you think?" For Anna, "Do you feel safe at night, Anna, when we go for ice cream?"

But, if the question was more general or with different parts that could go in another direction, I replied, "That all depends. If this, then that. But if that, then this." All to show we would cross each bridge when we came to it, but no matter the situation, we were prepared.

The financial request came on page twenty-one. We wanted the Benevolence Funding team on board with our vision before asking for the $1.08 million. The project would begin in September 2009 and end in September 2012.

The Salvadoran Relationship Team must have done something right because when our part of the meeting was over, Bob stepped out with us, closed the door, and said, "This shouldn't take long; why not wait in my office?"

About five minutes later, ten at most, Bob walked in with a big smile and a thumbs-up. Bob announced that Benevolence Funding had green-lighted everything, and there was talk about how they wished other groups were as well prepared with their requests.

Chapter 59

Yes, But . . .

August 2009

When I traveled with the next brigade, Carlos arranged a visit to a local museum for our group before we headed up the mountain, but as we were getting on the van, Kendal pulled me aside, saying Jorge would like me to join him for lunch.

The restaurant was close by. There was Jorge, Kendal, and me, along with four members of the HFH-ES board. The board chairman, younger than the others, sat at the end of the table. The chairman and one other wore well-tailored sport coats; the other two did not. Jorge was in his daily uniform of a white laundered shirt with the *Hábitat para la Humanidad* logo embroidered on its chest and his jeans creased down the front and back. And me, looking like the distant cousin who had been invited to dinner but needed to be told which fork to use, dressed in my untucked thrift-store shirt and jet-lagged jeans, carrying a black backpack and wearing a St. Louis Cardinals cap.

My shirts for El Salvador came from the thrift store on South Boulevard. I bought them at the "Two for a Dollar" table because those were the ones the thrift store couldn't sell, and I thought I was doing them a favor. I'd wear them and then donate them to Habitat before I came home so they could sell them to build homes. Plus, I didn't need to worry about them getting lost, and it was less to carry home.

I had a device for my hearing aids to clip on someone's collar or lapel so their voice, boosted by Bluetooth, was louder in my ears. I handed the device to Kendal and asked if she would clip it on the collar of her jacket; up near her throat was best, I said. I also asked her to sit directly across the table from me because I was reading lips more and more these days.

Kendal had the large salad for lunch that day. I remember because I heard her chew each bite. (Not a feature the manufacturer advertised, that I recall.)

The board members, especially the chairman at the end of the table, asked the same questions Jorge had asked Bert in Charlotte.

It all came down to them not understanding why we didn't just give them the money and let them build houses.

I replied to Kendal so she could translate, "Yes, but . . . " And I explained the venture as we had in Charlotte.

"Sí, pero . . . " Kendal translated my plea.

The chairman listed all the other agencies in El Salvador who could handle the other parts we wanted.

I rebutted, "Yes, but why can't we all work together, like a team?"

Now from Kendal, "*Sí, pero . . .* "

I became known as *sí, pero*. I thought I had represented our side well; I wasn't arrogant or insensitive, and I'm sure the board felt the same. It was just that we were coming at the solution from different directions. The board wanted to stay in one silo, while our committee's goal was to bring the silos together. We wanted everyone rubbing shoulders in Getsemaní, everyone working toward a larger purpose. But did it matter? The real winners would be the people of Getsemaní.

By September 2009, Strengthening the Getsemaní Community, as the project was now known, was underway, and our trips began falling into a comfortable routine.

We'd first tour San Salvador, the bustling city with vendors on every street corner with small carts selling everything from a pack of peppermint Chicklets to key chains with a small blue-and-white El Salvador flag dangling from its clasp, to corn-on-the-cob loaded with every imaginable condiment from mayonnaise to chili powder, cheese, cilantro, lime, yellow mustard, and even powdered sugar. *Maíz loco* or "crazy corn" is the most incredible street food I've ever eaten. You can ride a bicycle on a busy street, use a free hand to hold the stick pushed into the cob, and munch away without making a mess. How this is possible, I don't know.

We'd need to step around large openings on the sidewalk or watch for potholes when crossing streets. Some potholes were so deep a Mini Cooper could be at the bottom, and you wouldn't know. And as for orange cones that warn a driver or pedestrian of danger? They don't seem to have made it to San Salvador yet.

Time in the large city helped the group understand the country and the culture.

Then on to the more tranquil setting of Oscar Romero's three-room patio-style home on the grounds of the cancer sanatorium. His dusty black sedan still sat in the carport, where he had switched off the engine that Sunday evening in March before going inside for the night. We'd walk up the hill to the church and speak to the women in the shade of the tree as they peeled potatoes, much as many of the women may have been doing when Archbishop Romero walked past on his way to say mass that Monday morning.

Then inside the Church of the Divine Providence, stand behind the altar and look toward the small narthex with rays of warm sunlight streaming in the open doors; just as it must have been that spring day in 1980 when a lone gunman pulled his dusty red Volkswagen to a stop and carefully aimed his long rifle down the center aisle. They say God lives in these holy places and is always present, but I wonder if He may have stepped out for a moment, but maybe He didn't. Perhaps He saw the whole thing and cried along with the rest at the hate evil can bring to His world.

A solemn bus ride took us to the Cathedral of the Holy Savior and down steps leading to the basement where the poor *campesinas*, peasants, worship at the tomb of the assassinated archbishop.

Next, we would walk to Cuscatlán Park with green urban open areas for family picnics next to the sobering Monument to Memory and Truth, a memorial graphically depicting the country's recent civil war atrocities. Then to the campus of Central American University, where on November 16, 1989, Salvadoran Army soldiers killed six Jesuit priests, along with the wife and daughter of the university's groundskeeper. All murdered in their sleep. The war crime brought international attention and shifted our government's position from supporting El Salvador's military to calling for an immediate settlement.

We headed away from the traffic and up the mountain toward Ahuachapán and the Hotel Casa Blanca. The landscape became more rural, the views ever more spectacular, even though when we looked closer to the road, we saw litter, as if the people looked past it, taking in only nature's beauty.

The trip leader asked the group to notice the poles as we passed through each area. The area was conservative if the utility poles, even tree trunks, were painted red, white, and blue. Most belonged to *ARENA*, the conservative political party. But if the poles were red, the area was progressive and voted for *FMLE* candidates. "It's nice to know if you are in friendly or unfriendly territory," the trip leader would say.

The trip leader would also explain the importance of one word for the week ahead. That word was "flexibility." It's a common word, and perhaps we don't think about it every day, but in places like El Salvador, nothing ever happens exactly the way it's planned. Buses run late, most things don't start on time, and the plan for today quickly becomes the plan for tomorrow. So that one word, flexibility, would be necessary for an enjoyable week.

And the more I've thought about it over the years, either in El Salvador or in Charlotte, it's a pretty good way to greet life. It's okay for me to plan, but it's even better to be flexible and take what life gives me because I never know if what comes along isn't better than what I intended.

Carlos, the incredible one-man band that did it all, greeted us at the hotel entrance, mysteriously knowing the precise time of our arrival, and offered a tall frosty glass of lemonade.

The temperature seemed to drop five degrees as we stepped inside the hotel's courtyard. Maybe it was the shade, the lushness of the plantings, the tile floors, or the slowly whirling fans overhead. Perhaps it was the lemonade, or the peace of feeling at home in a place so different from home.

Inside were tall, comfortable wicker armchairs, and beyond, an open courtyard with a large avocado tree. Discovery is one of the many joys of travel. Even something as simple as finding avocados on a tree rather than on a grocer's shelf can be eye-opening for many.

Vilma Amanya Rodriguez stood beside the desk under the faded movie poster of Bergman and Bogart when they starred in *Casablanca*. She asked us to sign her guest book. You might look back through the pages, seeing names from Charlotte followed by names and cities around the world, and wonder what brought each to this tiny hotel in the middle of nowhere, a place seldom on any traveler's itinerary.

Vilma and her husband ran the Hotel Casa Blanca until he died. The hotel, the surrounding property, and even the abandoned casino across the street had moved from being owned by generations of his family to her.

But the property around the hotel isn't much anymore. There's a barbershop with one chair. A store sells new household items that look like those my mother gave away when she moved to North Carolina in 1984. A room with a single red light bulb left burning all day, hanging from the ceiling where Alcoholics Anonymous gathers in a small circle of chairs each evening, and the casino, looking like a bombed-out Christopher Wren London cathedral after the sirens stopped wailing.

In the roaring 1920s, when my mom and dad were dating, Ahuachapán and Hotel Casa Blanca, with its brightly lit casino, had been at their prime. You could almost hear the scratchy sound of an old phonograph and its worn stylus belting out "Sweet Georgia Brown" as you sat by the now-empty pool in the courtyard that needed weeding.

Room keys were passed out when we arrived, but mine never left the table in my room where I tossed it that first day, never minding to lock my door. Some of the eight rooms had three beds; most had two, so a brigade of twenty took over the hotel.

After dinner, we walked to the town square and Yolanda's for ice cream. For some, it would be their first visit; for others, a warm homecoming.

I would leave my red Nestlé coffee mug near the kitchen in the evening before I went to bed, and early each morning, there would be a quick knock on my door as Carlos walked in and said, "Good morning, Señor Bruce Lee! *Café solo, sin azúcar ni nata, Señor.*" Carlos had grown up on *Enter the Dragon* and other Bruce Lee movies when he was young, and as I was a Bruce, I must be Bruce Lee. At different times each day, Carlos would jump out of a doorway or from behind the avocado tree, surprising me with some martial arts move. My defensive actions were pitiful, but such was the multi-cultured camaraderie of our lasting friendship.

There would be countless "ambushes of Bruce Lee" over the years before I learned his real name was not Carlos at all but, in fact, Douglas Enrique Cosme Chavez. I guess he just felt he was more a Carlos than a Douglas. It would also take time for him to tell me of his mother and her life in Getsemaní, in a home he was embarrassed to visit. Bob said he'd talk to Martha about getting his mother into a Habitat for Humanity home.

Then, before we knew it, the bus was waiting in front, and it was time to load up and be off to a day of digging foundations, carrying blocks, and mixing *chispa* and *mezela*.

The mayor organized a committee to renovate the old casino, and the wealthy town people had raised money. It was slow-going, but with care, the old casino was being transformed into a performing arts center where plays, concerts, and recitals would bring people together. There were spaces for small shops, expanses for art galleries, and community meeting rooms.

In time, Hotel Casa Blanca and the neighborhood would come back.

On later visits, I could walk through the *Centro para la Cultura y las Artes* and see first-hand how the mayor's dream, with the support of the privileged, had brought new life to the city.

Where the town's political rallies had only divided, and different religious festivals had done the same, the arts united the people. Art let the people be together, rub shoulders as they sat enjoying a play, listen to a storyteller, touch finely woven fabric pieces, or enjoy a deafening rock concert. Art brought the city together like politics and religion never did. Art was becoming the community's common ground.

Chapter 60

Drops in the Bucket

February 2010

In February 2010, Strengthening the Getsemaní Community was coming to life. On this trip, we met with Mayor Rafael Moran Orellana and Director of Tourism Señorita Yass Leiva. They introduced us to restaurants and shops where visitors from *Estados Unidos* were always welcome. Yass would load me down with brochures to take back to our group. But I wanted to talk about ways the mayor and his city could help the people of Getsemaní, not us.

Strengthening the Getsemaní Community was getting big. It was growing with Enrique's multiplier effect. Habitat for Humanity El Salvador featured Getsemaní on their website, and Habitat International picked up the story for theirs. People who visited came home with stories, and word spread. Other churches around the country—from Michigan, Florida, and Ohio—sent brigades to build houses. Norie Sanchez collected old sewing machines from people in Charlotte and had them shipped to Getsemaní so people could make curtains for their new homes and later sew items they could sell in the market. Peace Passers of Charlotte boxed up donated soccer equipment and sent it to the children in Getsemaní so they would have the proper gear. Tim Leaycraft volunteered at the Bilingual Preschool in Charlotte, where he helped prepare Spanish-speaking children and those who had moved North for success in a city that favored English.

Getsemaní was changing, its people were changing, and we were changing. We were learning Jim Rohn's wisdom, "Whatever good things we build end up building us."

Dr. Edgar Landaverde staffed the health clinic where a storage shed had once stood. He was part-time, but it was a start. The rundown playground equipment had been cleaned and freshly painted, then relocated to make way for a new community center that Martha and her ADESCO raised the money to have built. The blue tarp was gone; the ADESCO now met in the community center, even if they still sat in the same white plastic chairs.

There was a rabbit ministry that some in Charlotte didn't understand. The rabbits were raised in hutches where they could provide a family pet and protein. The rabbits grew and multiplied on their diet of table scraps, and now there were signs advertising *venta de Conejos*, or "rabbits for sale." Cultures are different, I'd learned, and ours had been much the same not so many years before. I remembered playing with Uncle Thurlo's chickens behind the house on Baroda Avenue and then sitting down to eat one for Sunday dinner.

Jorge's board of directors was beginning to see the value of having so many different ways to get people involved. There were groups from different countries; some wanted to work on housing, while others were nurses and doctors and cared about health. Some were like Kae Roberts and wanted time set aside to teach and play with children. Nancy Losure, from Hamilton, Mississippi, cared about clean water and wanted it available to those of us not from the area. A woman from the International Ministries program of the Presbyterian Church (USA) wanted to talk about food solidarity to have equitable and universal access to healthy food and freedom from hunger for everyone.

These things had nothing to do with how many houses were built in a year, yet they did. Because each visitor, whatever their interest, added visibility and exposure to the Strengthening the Getsemaní Community, which added up to more people bringing more people to build more houses. All just drops in the bucket, and the drops were adding up.

Chapter 61

Heroes Don't Leap Tall Buildings

February 2010

I was in Getsemaní in mid-February 2010, solid and healthy, excited to see the progress being made. On the first day at the hotel, Charlie Shaffner organized a soccer match between our folks and the newly equipped youth from Getsemaní. We had lost to them the previous year, so Charlie wanted to even the score, but with their new gear from Peace Passers, my money was on Getsemaní. Charlie and Pastor Rodriguez's daughter, Andrea, called Yolanda to warn her there would be a packed bus, loaded with both teams, arriving later that day. Ice cream after anything was always welcome, giving everyone a chance to know each other away from the competition.

A group from Ireland, the oldest barely over twenty-five, had already been in town for a week when we arrived. They might leave at the end of this week or even stay longer. The leader was arranging things, and their visas still had time before they expired, so they could be around for a while.

The Irish were a happy bunch, always singing and joking. There were songs for everything: bus rides, walking to the site, digging a trench, or carrying blocks. We had dinner with them one evening at their hostel, and the blessing was a song. The words could have been Jodi Picoult's when she wrote in *Second Glance*:

Heroes don't leap tall buildings or stop bullets with an outstretched hand; they don't wear boots and capes. They bleed, and they bruise, and their superpowers are as simple as listening or loving. Heroes are ordinary people who know that even if their own lives were impossibly knotted, they could untangle someone else's. And maybe that one act can lead someone to rescue you right back.

Then it ended with some "Amens" and "dig-ins."

The house that Curt Seifart and I, along with a few Irish kids, were working on was down a hill, at the intersection of several roads that came together more like old paths crossing in the days before city planners started bringing everything to order. I knew my favorite home at the intersection would need repairs someday, but I hoped its owner would keep the large bougainvillea that had taken over its front. This single plant had grown to over ten meters in height, thriving in the abundant sun, volcanic red soil, and sandy loam.

The bougainvillea's bracts were violet, a regal color that my mind struggled to place in the poor village. Yet its presence and bright color gave me a landmark, letting me know I was at the right place.

During morning and afternoon breaks, Curt and I relaxed with the others, usually sitting on the ground with our backs against a newly finished wall, on an upside-down plastic bucket, or, Curt's favorite, resting in an empty wheelbarrow with his legs sticking out over the wheelbarrow's wood handles. We'd discuss the day and admire the large bougainvillea. One morning, as the sun perfectly framed the plant, one of the Irish girls suggested violet as the official color for Getsemaní. She thought violet had just enough royal purple to give it dignity, with blues to make it calm and serene.

Curt suggested she talk to Martha and the ADESCO.

Chapter 62

Wondrous

December 2010

In the summer of 2010, I had to shift focus from El Salvador to my ten o'clock sharp and selling my company. "We all juggle different balls in life, and it's important to remember which are rubber and which are glass," my daughter, Laura, often said at times like these.

Then, in early October 2010, after Dr. Harley had read the PET scan and pronounced me cancer-free, I got a FedEx envelope from El Salvador. The letter inside said the Board of Directors of Habit for Humanity in El Salvador had awarded me the International Solidarity Award in the individual category. The letter invited my family and me to join in the annual dinner at the *Hotel Sheraton Presidente* on December 3, where the award would be presented and announced publicly.

I talked to Dr. Favaro about it, but I was still too weak to travel. Dr. Favaro explained, "I know the PET scan says you're good, but remember, it was only a few days after Dr. Harley's good news that you needed to go to Presbyterian for two units of blood." He was right. I was too weak to travel.

Instead, Kendal Stewart traveled with Ana Maria Montoya de

Castro, the director for the district including Ahuachapán, to Charlotte—to me.

The award was presented in all four services that December Sunday at Myers Park Presbyterian Church. Kendal said a few words, then interpreted for Ana Maria. It was hard not to choke up when I accepted the award. I thanked them and all of my friends in El Salvador, and then, at each service, I thanked those who worked beside me. I asked those who had been to Getsemaní to join me in standing, then any who had worked here at home. It was absolutely breathtaking—young and old faces I knew and those I had yet to meet rose to face me. It was a wondrous day; almost as memorable as being told I was cancer-free.

Anna Edgerton even rushed up and gave me a big hug as I sat behind the lectern waiting for the first service to begin; not very Presbyterian, perhaps, but heartfelt. Anna taught in the Head Start bilingual program in Oakland, California, and was home for a visit. When she joined us in Getsemaní the year before, Habitat had tried to recruit her away from Head Start for her street-savvy Spanish. Anna's Oakland Spanish was even hipper than any of the hippest youth in San Salvador.

I'd won many awards and been to many ceremonies over the years, but none felt better than this one; not even the national foodservice industry gathering in Palm Springs in 2007 when I received the highest honor our industry presented, the Jerry Waxler Award. That award was given to the individual who had done the most to advance the country's foodservice sales and marketing industry. Even the tall and imposing Jerry Waxler trophy couldn't match my International Solidarity Award from El Salvador.

Chapter 63

Gracias, a Dios

Spring 2011

By the following spring, I was strong enough to travel. So much had happened since my last visit, and while I'd almost forgotten my cancer, Getsemaní certainly had not. Cancer usually doesn't have a happy ending in parts of the world where detection is delayed and treatment postponed or impossible to obtain.

When we got to the community center in Getsemaní, dozens of children had lined up behind a banner welcoming me back. There were hugs and photographs, and I did my best to smile without pulling out my handkerchief.

On Ash Wednesday, I gathered some soot and fine ashes from a cooking fire behind one of the new homes, and Bob Breed led the service. Then, in the afternoon, workers started erecting a stage for a celebration of Getsemaní and a tribute to Archbishop Romero on the anniversary of his assassination. Jorge Molina and a van-load of others arrived, then a van carrying all of the white stacked chairs and instruments for the brass band in a third van. Before long, the once quiet playground that had only hours before held people solemnly standing in line to have ashes used to mark the sign of the cross on their foreheads were treated to lively John Philip Sousa marches.

I was seated on stage next to Pastor Rachel Tune from Thrivent, the Lutheran financial organization that had joined in Strengthening the Getsemaní Community. Pastor Tune gave the opening prayer, and then I said some words about how fortunate Myers Park Presbyterian had been to come alongside our sisters and brothers in Getsemaní to help with the covenants the ADESCO had identified years before. I ended my brief comments by saying how bright the future looked for the children.

On Friday, our last day, we circled some white plastic chairs on the lower part of the dirt playground to say our goodbyes.

Pastor Rodriguez and his family were with us and a few others. From my first meeting with Pastor Rodriguez, I had never seen him without his Bible. His left hand had darkened its brown leather covering over the years by holding it close to his chest. He always read from it and had countless underlined places highlighted in yellow. His Bible was as much a part of him as his smile and 24–7 faith.

While faith in the Northern Hemisphere seems to be spiraling downward, faith in the Southern Hemisphere is headed in the other direction. We in the North can barely focus for one hour on a Sunday morning, but Pastor Rodriguez and his people speak openly of God's grace every day. Pastor Rodriguez's remarks stretched on, as they usually did, but I began to understand where he was leading, even with my poor Spanish. My face was becoming more and more flushed.

Sure enough, he called me to his side and handed me his Bible with a warm embrace. The family had talked about it, and he said I

342

should have it. The Bible would keep my family and me as safe as it had them. This was too much; I couldn't hold back the tears. I cried. Not big sobbing, wailing tears, but enough so you'd notice. I pulled out my bandana, pressed it to my eyes, blew my nose a few times, stumbled back to my spot in the circle, unable to speak, and sank into my white plastic chair.

Regina reached me first, then Andrea, Victor, and Habram. Finally, Pastor Rodriguez was in front of me. I struggled to stand as he bent down to help, then we embraced, and I managed to say, "Gracias a Dios." Thanks be to God.

Sitting back down, I crossed my legs, like old men do when they're tired, pulled my faded St. Louis Cardinal hat down over my eyes, held the Bible in my lap, and bowed my head. I wanted to say, "No, there's been a mistake. This is the Rodriguez Family Bible. It belongs here, not with me." But refusing was unacceptable; it would hurt their feelings, and I didn't want that.

The pastor had purchased the Bible before he was married. He was in seminary in Guatemala City and paid for it in installments. After the final payment was made, the bookstore owner gave him the leather cover. Its hand carving was of the Vatican in Rome, but Pastor Rodriguez didn't know that then, and the owner assumed anyone buying a Bible in Guatemala City must be Catholic.

The cover protected his Bible. It was practical, so he kept it; that was all there was to that.

But now, the Bible that had been Pastor Rodriguez's for all these years was mine, and just like with the cover—that was that.

It had been quite a week, and yes, I was exhausted from the work and the emotion. And, of course, the progress in the community—

more finished homes, more happy children, even more rabbits. Somehow, everyone seemed to have grown a few inches, or were they just standing taller?

I told Joyce about the week when I got home. Then, after dinner, I got the Bible out of my backpack and showed her. "It's in Spanish," she said. It was not like that was a bad thing or strange in any way, more like the obvious question of how could I read it?

I had looked at the Bible closely on the flight home, all of the underlining and yellow highlights, each noting sermons, weddings, baptisms, and funerals. All the history was now in my hands. I put it in a Ziplock bag and placed it on a shelf in my study. It was going back to El Salvador the next time I went, and that was that.

Chapter 64

ADESCO's Vision

Spring 2012

In the spring of 2012, I was ready to return to Ahuachapán. In April, there had been a group for the week before Easter, *Semana Santa*. They told us how the people of Getsemaní had taken part in all the festivals in town. Everyone had spread flower petals in the streets, and even the puddled pavement looked like a fine carpet. They talked about how many in Getsemaní had put altars in their homes to celebrate the resurrection of Christ.

The mood was still festive when we arrived the third week of April. I tried to return the Bible to Pastor Rodriguez a few times, but the timing wasn't right. Then, our group was invited to his new church for a Wednesday evening service. That would be the perfect time.

The new church was airy and open, more like a small theatre than the other churches in town. His didn't have white plastic chairs or even wood pews but raised levels of white stone giving everyone a perfect spot for worship. You could sit forward, lean back on the deck behind you, or stand and raise your open hands to warmly receive

His Holy Word into your body. The area in front had a modest pulpit with a cross behind, and Pastor Rodriguez was free to roam around, like a stage where he preached and played his guitar. There was a Bible on the pulpit, not his, of course. His was in my backpack.

After the service, I tried. We sat together on one of the front levels, and I unzipped my pack, pulled out the Bible, took it out of the Ziplock, and handed it to him.

He pushed it back, looking hurt and insulted. Regina and Andrea came over. They tried to help me understand that the Bible was a link, a tie, a connection between us, and how my returning it would break all that. So no, it was my Bible now, and that was that.

Back in the Ziplock and back in my pack. But I still didn't feel right about it.

Martha and her ADESCO board planned a big Thursday celebration after lunch. The people always had celebrations; the more, the better, and if a brass band was nearby, they would be invited. The community center now had flat grills powered by propane to roll outdoors and prepare pupusas. There was slaw made with pure water and the same overly sweet Kool-Aid in the knotted plastic bags. The women invited us to help prepare lunch. I tried to make pupusas. I put some cornmeal dough in one hand, packed cheese and beans on top, and more dough in the other, then clapped my hands together. I swung back and forth like applauding a rock band and twisting my wrist simultaneously. I'm sure making pupusas is like everything else, easy once you know how, but it was clear I needed more practice when mine fell apart on the grill.

The children were learning to paint. They had fashioned easels with some poles, as an older girl helped them hold the crayons just so and pick the right colors. Colors are different in El Salvador. I'm not sure why, but they are more vibrant and alive than our North American colors; ours look rather sad compared to theirs. *My grand-daughter would love being here*, I thought. Ellie is a young artist and paints with a talent far beyond her years. She would enjoy sharing her love of art with the children.

The rest of us sat around the playground and had lunch. Some pulled chairs under a tree. The groups were not us and them anymore; we were united. Enrique was interpreting in one group while another was getting by with what little Spanglish they could invent. It didn't matter; people were having fun.

There were no brass bands in dusty uniforms that day. There wasn't a stage assembled, just Martha with a single poster listing the six components of the original plan and her new silver pointer a Babson College student had given her to replace the yardstick she'd been using. The pointer could telescope to fifty centimeters, enough to draw your eye.

The Babson student had been there that winter, working with others from his Massachusetts college on micro business and co-op ideas. They had found a greater interest in doing things together, like a co-op, than doing things separately, like an entrepreneur. Every culture's different; they were learning.

Martha had seated her ADESCO board members in the front row. We filled in behind, mixed with the community. Martha began by explaining the vision. Telling everyone how it had been a *gran responsabilidad* and how the town had welcomed the visitors who helped bring new life to their humble village.

Then, she called on women from the front row to speak.

The first speaker talked about how the ADESCO had been strengthened. How she was the assistant to Martha and would take her place someday. There had been training on working with the city officials to get things done. She was confident of a bright future.

The second spoke about health and how Dr. Edgar Landaverde was now staffing *Casa de Salud*. How people were getting care and records were being kept on everyone's health, even children, for the first time. She told us about a group of doctors and nurses from Chicago who had been there a month before to help Dr. Edgar. And how the nurses had blown up their blue rubber examining gloves after they were finished and turned them into dinosaur puppets for the children.

Next came the money part. The words on Martha's poster said, "*Solidaridad economica*." I read that as everyone earning enough to get by. Solidarity, to me, is community interest, or "interest in," so having the best financial interest of your neighbors at heart in a transaction is a good thing.

The speaker said there was a sewing co-op making things to sell, thanks to Norie and her machines. And thanks to Victor, there was a group making bracelets. She went on with other ways people had found to make a living, other than going off to San Salvador for two weeks to be a security guard or up north for months, even years, and sending remittance checks home each Friday.

One woman had started pressing corn tortillas on a large machine, putting them in bags, and selling them to the women who were too busy sewing on Norie's machine to make their own.

The fourth speaker talked about children and youth. Children were starting school at a younger age now that they didn't have to depend on the lottery. The lottery had been needed because of the small number of teachers who wanted to work in the poor neighborhood. But now, more willing teachers meant the lottery was no longer necessary, and children didn't need to wait until their eighth or ninth birthday before entering first grade.

The children were using the community center to study. They had raised money for two computers. They were working with some non-government organizations to read the markings on poles and trees, even buildings, when young boys from other neighborhoods came around to mark or "tag" their gang's territory, so they would know what gangs were present. The older gang members disapproved of the tagging, but the more junior members were eager to show their affiliation and tagged almost anything that didn't move, and Getsemaní wanted it stopped.

She told us about a group in Ohio collecting materials for a Vacation Bible School they planned for the summer. The children were excited to do that again, she said.

Then a woman spoke about cultural exchange. How groups like ours were encouraged to mingle, ask questions, be curious, and how the Getsemaní residents were to do the same.

Now the last speaker. Her name was Evelia, and I remembered seeing her on our first visit, but she hadn't been at the ADESCO meeting under the blue tarp. I had only seen her walking around town.

Years ago, when I first saw Evelia, her head was always down, her spine bent over, and she barely reached Martha's chin. She didn't have a home and lived behind a small grocery in the poor part of an already poor village. She'd walk the streets, collect what had been tossed from cars, and return to her camp. A tossed takeout *Pollo Campero* in its white sack with enough chicken on each piece to make a meal and a used T-shirt with words in English she couldn't read like, "So many men, so little time." It was trash to the people riding by in their cars, but it was a treasure to her.

But then, one day, Ana Maria pulled her truck to the side of the road to talk to Evelia. Evelia recognized the tan pickup; she'd seen it around the new houses being built in Getsemaní. The small truck was a Ford, and the factory called its color Pueblo Gold, but to Evelia, it was tan, about the color of the band uniforms she saw at the many festivals in town. It was perfect for Ana Maria's work with Habitat for Humanity because it always looked clean but not like it was afraid to put in a full day's work.

Ana Maria talked to Evelia about where she was staying and how much better off Evelia would be with a regular home. All of that could be possible if Evelia helped with other houses and then helped with her own. Ana Maria called it *equidad de sudor*, and it was like money, but really wages from hard work. Sweat equity.

Evelia listened and before long was helping on houses, then soon helping on her own. Then she moved in. Evelia didn't have many furnishings at first, just some things from her camp behind the grocery. But she soon had one of Norie's sewing machines. Now Evelia was making things for her home; curtains and a tablecloth for the new table that held the sewing machine where Evelia would sit at night under the electric light and make things to sell in the market. Next, Evelia made clothes for herself, dresses even, and now looked far better than she did when she stayed behind the grocery.

Evelia still walked around town and picked up things like before, but not for herself. Now she would put the trash in a shopping bag and carry it to the community center. Some could be recycled, but not all.

Ana Maria had introduced Evelia to Martha, and now Evelia was becoming known, and people called her by name when they met on the street, saying, *"Buenos días, Evelia, ¿cómo estás?"* And Evelia would reply that she was fine, full of the Good Spirit, and inquire politely about the others' health as well.

Martha nominated Evelia for an open position on the board. Everyone knew she would be a good replacement.

It was now the last board member's turn to speak. Evelia rose effortlessly from her chair, took a few long strides, and turned beside the poster to face the community. She looked taller than the woman I remembered. The face and straight black hair were the same, fresher perhaps, but this woman was a good head taller than the woman I first saw. Her shoulders grew wider as she lengthened the middle of her body, taking a few slow deep breaths. I saw her expand like an umbrella had opened inside her torso. She grew more prominent, more meaningful somehow, with each deliberate breath.

Evelia asked to use Martha's silver pointer. Confidently, she telescoped it out its entire fifty centimeters. She pointed to the line on the poster that read *alojamiento*, housing, and began. She didn't start with the numbers. She didn't count the units and project out how and at what rate Getsemaní would have this many "housing solutions," as Jorge's board called them. Evelia just told her story. Her eyes moved from face to face. They rested on mine for a moment; I hoped they would stay, but they moved on. It wasn't a speech like the others; it was like she was talking to an old friend while they sat by the lake under a tree in the park, sharing a private moment.

Like her grandmother, her name was Evelia, but no one knew her name the way they did her grandmother's. How she had been homeless and living in a tiny shack until the day the woman in the tan truck stopped to visit. Today, she had a home, people knew her name, and they spoke when they met on the street. She said how good it felt to be part of the community, and how proud she was of the work the ADESCO was doing. And how proud she hoped her grandmother would be if she were still alive.

Then, with all of us on the edge of our white plastic chairs, Evelia unrolled the map, the one Martha had used that day under the blue tarp. She taped it to the poster and began to point to houses. She would tap each home with the silver pointer and say who lived there and what they did in the community. It took time because there were so many, but she moved along, ending with *"Gracias por su atención."* Thanks for your attention.

Evelia returned to her seat and the meeting was over. As we mingled about, enjoying our Kool-Aid, I thought about how it had started with Jorge and his board wanting houses. It was fitting for the presentation to end with Evelia and her home and what it had done for her and the community. Sure, it was about houses, but it was about much more.

Señorita Yazz Leiva, from the tourism department, was there that afternoon, and she said the mayor wanted more of the streets paved. She had almost broken an ankle in one of the holes as she walked from where she had parked. I thought she shouldn't have worn such high heels, but I didn't say so. And yes, Mr. Mayor, paved streets would be a good thing, not just for Yazz but for everyone.

Our group had dinner in a nearby artisan village that night. The small town of Ataco is not far from Ahuachapán, yet we were surprised to run into Charlie Shaffner, from church, and his friend, Emily, along with Charlie's sister Caroline. They were in El Salvador to lead a trip of college students the following week. It is indeed a small world.

After dinner, our group walked around the shops. I bought a few things, as did others. It's better to buy from the artist, I think. And I don't haggle over price. Some say it's a game, the way things are done, but I think it's more than a game; it's a livelihood to the artist.

On the bus ride back to the hotel, Bob and I talked about all the trips over all the years. We marveled at how everything had come together so well and how promising the future now seemed for Getsemaní. Then, Bob asked what I was doing tomorrow. "Any meetings?"

"No, I'm just a regular worker tomorrow," I answered.

There was a pause, then Bob said, "Well, I've got one in the morning with Martha, then I'll join you."

Years ago, when it all started, we took a shower after a day's work to remove the sand and dirt. Now we shower in the morning, go to meetings, and call it work. We were starting to look like Jorge, as clean at the end of the day as at the beginning. Bob reminded me of the time late one afternoon when we walked past a group from a sister church in Charlotte. They were just finishing a long day and looked at us, jeering, "You Myers Park boys afraid to get dirty?" We stepped around the corner and splashed muddy water on each other before going further.

The next day, I helped make the first volcano of *mezcla* for the mason. Brother Juan was there. He was seventy-seven years old now but showed no signs of slowing down. I worked with him on almost every trip. He was always at his pastor's side and was as much a part of Pastor Rodriguez as his Bible had been. It was good to see him again. A few were bending wires to hold the rebar together as the masons slid the cinder blocks in place. Joe Fountain from Charlotte, part of more trips than I can remember, was helping them.

Now it was time for a mixture of *chispa*. I may have gotten carried away with the water as the side closest to Juan came loose, spilling the water out in every direction. It was all six of us could do to save some of the mason's *chispa*. He didn't look pleased; we promised to be more careful.

Bob joined us for lunch but said he was sorry, a meeting had come up for the afternoon, so we'd catch up at dinner. I smiled, and he headed away. "Heavy is the head that wears the crown," I thought, knowing he would prefer to be spending the rest of Friday with us.

I sat on a low wall next to Brother Juan for our break. He had always been at Pastor Rodriguez's side, but it was just us today. Pastor Rodriguez was in more meetings too, what with his growing church.

We each had the orange Habitat passed out for our snack and a knotted bag of flavored drink. I offered my limey-green juice to Brother Juan, saying I had water in my blue Nalgene container.

We talked as we peeled and ate our oranges. I let my orange rind and seeds fall to the ground. I'd put everything in the trash later, but

Juan held his in his weathered brown hand. You would have easily spotted the differences if I had held my hand next to his. Brother Juan's hands were calloused and rough; they showed a life of hard work. I'm sure they had a tender touch, but they had been left for too long on the margins, in the hot sun to dry. While my hands, the same age, showed only privilege.

I had given Brother Juan a small Buck knife years earlier, like the one I still carried. A model 55. The small one is just like Buck's famous 110, only half the size. I'd always needed to ask someone in the group who was checking a bag if they'd mind my knife hitching a ride, and I still do. I'd lost one to security and didn't plan to lose another. When the break was almost over, Juan dug in his pocket, pulled out his knife, leaned over, and nudged me with his shoulder as he opened its single blade, his eyes moving between mine and the knife as if to say, "See, I still carry it." He stepped to a nearby hedge-row and cut off a branch. Whittled the stem down to a sharp stick and began to dig holes in the row of tangled bushes. One by one, he planted each seed from his orange, took a small piece of rind he had saved, put it in with the seed, and used the stick to cover the hole. He asked for some of my water and poured it over each freshly planted seed. Then, as we stood, he explained how someday those tiny seeds would grow, and people like us would enjoy an orange and sit to visit together, just as we had today.

I remembered the seeds in Archbishop Romero's prayer.

Back at the hotel, I packed to go home. I put what shirts and pants I'd brought from the thrift store on South Boulevard in a bag for Habitat. They were dirty, but Habitat would wash them and sell them for a few pennies in their store, and all the pennies would add up, like the orange seeds and the drops in the bucket, and soon there would be more homes. Then I put my shoe in the sink and went to bed.

Chapter 65

Regrets and Blackbirds

Spring 2012

On my long flight home the next day, I thought about that week and the weeks before. About my cancer and Dr. Harley. About how easy it would have been for him to stop looking after so many negative biopsies. I thought about how easy it would have been for our church to write a big check and let others do the work, but how much more rewarding it was for us to come alongside the workers. I thought about the doctor who had patiently listened to my reasons for halting the treatment. How many of those stories must he have heard? How many more would there be, and how would he always be kind and understanding? Then, in the end, say he was sorry, but the plan didn't make deals.

I thought about the sale of my company and the work that had gone into getting it built. How devoid of ceremony the handover had been. There was no retirement party. No brass band. No big send-off. No hugs. No new set of golf clubs. Not even two matching rocking chairs for Joyce and me to spend the rest of our days on the porch. I was just gone. Then someone new was at my desk, answering my phone.

What did people think about my selling the company? Did they feel I didn't care? That it had all been a game? I had wanted to visit, to explain, but one thing or another got in the way, and it never happened. Sure, I'd let Laura Bates, along with Kristi and George, spread the word, but it wasn't the same as me telling them in person. I hoped they had figured it out, maybe read CaringBridge, or been told by someone. But as our daughter wrote on the first page of the website, "When cells change, life changes."

I thought about my family and the marks on the doorframe as the grandchildren grew. I thought about Joyce and how understanding she had been over the years. How she had accepted the relocations and then enjoyed staying in one spot. How she had gone without, used samples to save on groceries, fixed dinner for Don and me, and cleaned up after food shows before we were able to hire others.

About our children and their lives, their families, and the success each had become. About their children and if they would find places and people to care about. About Paul Leonard asking, "Where is the place you will live and how will you define its borders?"

I thought back to meeting Jack Wood and his introducing me to Bootie, how he made a blue blazer and khakis the uniform of Charlotte, and the dusty Argentine band uniforms. Jorge and his board, the doctors and their starched white coats, and the different color scrubs. Each is a uniform letting the world know where they fit. I thought about myself with my thrift-store shirts, a white truck, a black sedan, and a red sports car. But what's underneath the uniform counts more, and that takes time to figure out.

I wondered how many other businesses had started like mine. How many owners were all-in, waiting for their ship to arrive? They looked secure, like they had all the answers, when they knew, deep inside, it was all a giant gamble. Everything is not always as it appears.

I thought about my job at the URB and in Getsemaní, and about term limits and how others would take my spot, and how they wouldn't do things my way but how the work would go on, and if it didn't, then maybe it was never meant to be. And I thought about Romero's prayer and how "The kingdom is not only beyond our efforts, it is even beyond our vision."

I thought about all the flights I'd taken over the years, all the destinations for different reasons, looking out the window past the horizon. Looking but not seeing, searching but not finding. There's something about sitting alone in a long silver tube in the sky. Maybe it's the drone of the engines or the oxygen pumped into the cabin. Perhaps it's thinking about how cold it is outside the plane but how warm it is in my seat. It's a type of meditation. When my mind moves to a different place, any thought that doesn't serve me well vanishes with the altitude. Dreams turn out better when they happen in the sky.

Somewhere over the Gulf of Mexico, I put on my headphones and listened to "Morning Has Broken," a 1931 children's hymn made famous by Cat Stevens. I thought about how Getsemaní was only beginning, while my time of being with them had almost come to an end. It was my time to step away, as had been my intention from the beginning, so that fresh thoughts and ideas could come from others. There is a powerful wisdom in the African proverb, "If you want to go fast, go alone. If you want to go far, go together." Building only more and more houses would have been faster, but doing more than houses got us further.

Next on my playlist came "Blackbird," a Beatles favorite written by Paul McCartney, where a blackbird sings in the dead of night, takes its broken wings, and learns to fly.

McCartney wrote his famous song after reading about the civil rights struggles of African-Americans in Little Rock, Arkansas, where I went to Pulaski Heights Elementary and would have been with my classmates at Central High School had we stayed. But we didn't stay, and I wasn't on the other side from those McCartney wrote about, or at least I hoped not. Was the blackbird singing in the dead of night like my screams in the bathroom when I was coughing so hard? Was I waiting for my moment to arise, a moment to take my sunken eyes and see? Was it that very moment that I was ready to be free? And could the blackbird be the people of Getsemaní putting their broken wings in flight, or my neighbors at the Urban Ministry Center doing the same?

But I put all this aside to think about the Bible in my backpack. Could the pastor have given me his because he thought I didn't have one? But I did have a Bible, several in fact, and I was now on my way "from," and not "to" the Rodriquez Family Bible's rightful home.

I got home from El Salvador in time for James's birthday. Our grandson picked Luisa's Brick Oven Pizzeria for his party. Luisa's is a family favorite; we've been going there for years. The owner greeted us at the door wearing his colorful jacket and tie that look like a giant pepperoni pizza. Jeff's smile broadened, and he gave everyone a huge hug and said, "How's the McIntyre family tonight?" We'd been at Luisa's the night before James's big sister, Ellie, was born. We'd been there before his cousin Elizabeth was born and for so many birthdays, anniversaries, Scouting awards, and countless other events.

When we got home, Joyce asked me how I had done in El Salvador. Had I gotten tired? Could I keep up? Was I sorry I went?

I told her I had done okay. Not great, but okay. Most days, when we got back to the hotel, I'd take a nap before dinner. That helped.

For the next few days, I rested on the terrace. Albert Camus's words repeatedly played in my head, like the old phonograph at Hotel Casa Blanca with its stylus stuck in the same groove. "Don't walk in front of me . . . I may not follow; Don't walk behind me . . . I may not lead; Walk beside me . . . and just be my friend."

Chapter 66

Pay It Forward

Three Months Later

Patty Arcia from El Salvador, who was Patty Cordero when we first met, now lived in Charlotte and worked at Myers Park Presbyterian Church. She and her husband, David, had their daughter, Gabby, baptized a few Sundays back, and seemed to have found their forever home in Charlotte. I'd talk to her. She would know what to do about the pastor's Bible.

When we met, she said, "It's no longer the pastor's, Bruce. He gave it to you."

"Yes, but—" I started.

Patty interrupted, "You can't give back a gift. It would be rude." We talked until Patty had an idea. "You can't give it back, but you can pass it on, 'pay it forward,' I hear people say. What if you made a gift of the Bible to someone else? That would be okay, wouldn't it? And what if that person were someone like Andrea Rodriguez, the pastor's oldest daughter? You wouldn't be returning the Bible, not exactly anyway, and in my culture, that would be fine."

On the cover page of the Bible, Pastor Rodriguez had written a message giving the Bible to my family and me. Patty pulled a card from her desk, and we wrote out a note that gave the Bible to Andrea and her family. So that was the answer. We neatly pasted the new message below the old and arranged for Patty to take the Bible with her when she traveled with the youth from our church in a few months.

"Every action of our lives touches on some chord that will vibrate in eternity," wrote Seán O'Casey, the Irish memoirist, and he was right. Pastor Rodriguez had given the Bible to me. I gave it to Andrea, who might give it to her daughter, and then her daughter would give it to someone else through eternity.

Chapter 67

A Rich Life Shuns Apathy

2020

It took "work on it for a while, then I'll be along" to get me here, but I think, years later, I've arrived. Those words did more for me than my parents knew. My dad's parents let him head west to look for gold shortly after finishing grammar school, and he found a lifetime career. My mom's dad let her go to a beach neither of them had seen or heard of, and she found happiness. So it's no wonder they let me begin work when I was ten and go to New Mexico at thirteen.

Perhaps my parents had found a new way to raise children, or maybe they had followed their parents and all the other parents since time began. We would call it co-parenting today, but it's not sharing the role with another couple or even with each other; it's sharing the role with life. It's letting life be as much the teacher as either parent, and co-parenting makes for the best kind of raising. My parents allowed me to learn that gravel hurt my feet when I didn't wear shoes. And if I didn't take a raincoat when the forecast called for rain, I might be wet by the time I got home from school. Things they could have told me, sure, but lessons better learned from life. And as for my Celtic ancestors who came to this country looking for hope, I've never met two better cheerleaders for hope than my mom and dad.

It's been a while since the spring morning in 2010 when this story began, and I've had time to think about the people in the waiting room of the hospital who weren't eager to talk. Maybe they were homeless, like Charlie, or didn't have a black Audi waiting by the curb. Perhaps they would need to find a way to one of the small towns surrounding Charlotte at the end of the day and didn't have a home under the canopy of privilege so close by. Or could they be thinking of today's treatment the same way Delta thought of Anna and my lost luggage, as not their first or second priority at the moment, with other tragic events draining their energy? Maybe when they heard the bell clang for others, it only saddened them, knowing they were simply trying to hold on for a week so they could tell their grandchildren goodbye.

Too many questions, too many maybes. Take time for the answers, I tell myself, they may not be what you expect.

Everyone doesn't have a poster with them at the center. And, when I thought Kristi and George didn't seem grateful, perhaps it was the fear of uncertainty as they went from the known to the unknown. It may not have been about me, and really, when I think about it, it's seldom about me.

"Disrupters," Jean Cauthen had called them when I visited her studio at Dilworth Artisan Station. She was talking about elements in her paintings that allow the static canvas to come to life, to move as your eyes travel in and around the painting's many features, seeing everything from different angles. Maybe it was the smell of the oils in her muddledly comfortable studio or the rooibos tea we were drinking, but my mind went to the sweet bubblegum smell under my mask in those weeks before I rang the bell. Was cancer my disrupter, causing my mind to travel in so many directions and forcing me to look at life from so many intersectional lines and angles?

Yes, cancer is a disrupter; it discombobulates things. It doesn't leave you where it finds you, and because my doctors were going for a cure, I wound up in a better place. Others, like Charlie Patterson, weren't as fortunate.

I'm beginning to like disrupters. No, *like* is not the right word. *Learn from* is better. "What did I learn from the disrupter? What did I do with it?" are the questions to be curious about, but if I am not curious, if I don't care, if I let privilege suffocate me, I've only ignored the disrupters. And ignored disrupters, like untreated cancers, like mendacious political propaganda, only grow stronger. Neglected disrupters add more divided people, sleepless nights, homeless neighbors in Charlotte, and cardboard shacks in El Salvador.

The more substantial the ignored disrupters grow, the more plentiful they become. Then these disrupters divide us even further, shoving us further apart. Because disrupters know that the best way to conquer is to separate, then destroy. And that's what they're doing—if we let them.

Dr. Harley was right when he said, "Things just happen sometimes." We can debate whether it was nature being nature or a divine and predestined act from above, but the one thing we can agree on is that it—good or bad—happened, and it's what we do next that matters. I'll remember that as I "work on it for a while." And just like the old photo of Dad with his prize sailfish, I'm glad they let me figure it out on my own. And when I made up rules for the games I invented in my youth, am I still doing the same as an adult? Or was I only asking "why" and "why not?" because without questions, how can anything, even rules, ever change?

So instead of "My Way," my song would be "The Gambler," made famous by Kenny Rogers. Perhaps you know it? It's about two strangers meeting on a train bound for nowhere, like our pilgrimage in life, you might say. Both are gamblers, and aren't we all, and the older stranger gives the younger stranger his advice. You've got to know when to hold 'em, the song says. Going on to say you need to know when to quit and when to walk away. Then the final advice is not to count your money at the table but to wait, maybe even until life is over, and that's the most difficult part because it's about waiting—delaying gratification—and that's hard.

The song is about poker, yet the song is about life, and life is about choices. So good or bad, the future is controlled by choices.

Walking away from security to start my own business turned out well, so people could say it was a good choice. But had my business failed, the same people would say I was foolish. So it's complicated.

And perhaps if one's life is dealt more winners than losers, they die in their sleep, but they need to wait until the end to find out.

And where does it end, or is this only the beginning? My life has been one big carnival ride, taking me up and down until I'm back at the start. Then I stagger off each ride as Joyce, our children, the community, and my faith carries me on to the next. Yet, in the end, I'm on each ride alone, looking for answers to questions like everyone has always done and will always do.

Perhaps it's not until I ask the question differently, and look at things through a different lens, that I find answers. Maybe it was never about solving the problem but experiencing reality. It's never what happens that matters; it's what happens next. And if I change the way I look at things, things also change. Whether I'm happy or sad is always up to me. Questions go beyond answers, so without them, there is no progress; without progress, there is only stagnation. And with stagnation comes death, peaceful or not.

I'm thankful for the times I took action. Sometimes stepping in and sometimes not, realizing even no action is an action, a decision made. And it's the action that brings certainty to life. Action brings full participation and is always the best way to vitality and happiness. A rich life shuns apathy. Things need to change; they need to be different. "Shake 'um up," Puny said.

I'm also certain of uncertainty and accept that as being fully human. I'm not always in control—seldom, really. And actions bring reactions, and on it goes.

I understand so little, but maybe I've begun to understand Saint Óscar Romero's prayer, "We can not do everything, and there is a

369

sense of liberation in realizing that. This enables us to do something and to do it well. It may be incomplete, but it is a beginning, a step along the way, an opportunity for the Lord's grace to enter and do the rest."

I had thought of myself as average all these years, and I was to other white males of a certain age with a home in Myers Park and, later, a larger home on a private golf course. Just an ordinary college-educated, straight, white male, married to the same wife, with the same background, who had two grown children, each with two of their own. And we all sat in the same pew on Sundays—in a tall, steepled church where each grandchild had been baptized.

But I wasn't ordinary or average to Chilly Willy or Charlie Patterson. I wasn't ordinary to Martha in Getsemaní, and my church home wasn't ordinary to Pastor Rodriguez's congregation. And nothing about me or my life was average to Evelia, even if I did wear thrift-store shirts.

I am privileged, more than I ever imagined. Yes, I had cancer, but I also had a car at the curb and a son who took me fishing. I had a daughter who started a CaringBridge site and a wife who searched the internet until she found something to help. A friend in Jerusalem who lit candles and hundreds that sent cards, letters, and phoned.

I had built a successful business, but only with the help of others like Bootie, Bill, and Tom, and all the others delivering results by being "on time, well prepared, committed to doing what they promised, and enthusiastic—always." I sold that business, but it took a team.

Would I do things differently? That too is complicated. Because, like Paul Frank Baer said, "No one holding four aces wants a new deal."

Would I have walked away from a secure corporate job without the privilege, unconsciously perhaps, of knowing someone like me could easily find another? Would someone without privilege unplug Mouse's phone? And isn't there an implied privilege in even thinking you can negotiate a cancer treatment plan?

Maybe I was like the simple grain of rice. Nurtured from birth in a protected environment before harvest. Then undergoing the pounding that would remove any protection, before being sent back into the world.

I stepped away from golf and the club after thirty-five years, and while it was good once, it had changed, or I had. So instead of golf, Joyce and I have been able to travel, and we've seen things we never imagined. And in our travels, as in my life, I've experienced the meaning of Marcel Proust's words, "The real voyage of discovery consists not in seeking new landscapes but in having new eyes."

I've found more questions than answers, and I'm okay with that. The answers will come, or they won't. It's the questions that matter, and when they stop—living stops.

The End

Epilogue

I saw the doctors for ten years, frequently at first, and then only every six months. The business that I sold grew as it added more people, then merged with a regional broker, and is now part of Waypoint, a national sales and marketing agency headquartered in Tampa, Florida. The building on Southside Drive remains, still doing what it was meant to do and with many of the same people.

The Urban Ministry Center joined forces with the Men's Shelter of Charlotte and is now Roof Above. Their work is even more important than before as they offer a growing spectrum of homeless services and housing programs.

The Getsemaní community in El Salvador is prospering, and members of Myers Park Presbyterian Church and other organizations worldwide visit and continue adding their drops to the bucket. Unfortunantly, Pastor Rodriguez's wife passed away in May 2021. She was sixty-five.

The 1958 Porsche returned to California, where I had found her and where she had belonged all along. Old cars like my 356 are fun, but if I ever have another car as a hobby, it won't be a Porsche; it'll be a 1957 Volkswagen, and just like the blue blazer Jack Wood made the uniform of Charlotte, it will do fine, no matter the occasion. Gone as well is the Audi, replaced by a Subaru. The sedan was perfect for chauffering our Clients and Customers in the business, but the midsize crossover is more practical for errands in retirement.

And when Joyce and I were ready to find a smaller place to live, Mary Beth and K.B. bought our home on Sharon Road. So with Laura and her family in our first house on Hertford and K.B. and his in our second, no matter where we visit at Thanksgiving, I know how to find my way to the dinner table.

The weathered teak bench is still where I left it under the giant oak, waiting for others to relax as the sun fills the sky and they search for their own answers to the unsolvable questions of life. And perhaps, the older woodpecker is doing the same. As for my truck, it's been given free room and board next to the door frame where our son will measure his grandchildren someday.

I still enjoy an occasional nap, especially on a rainy afternoon. So, life is good and better when I savor each part. Not just the good but also the bad; it's all part of the universe, hitched together in ways I'm only beginning to understand.

So, until next time, thanks for listening—we'll visit again soon.

Acknowledgments

This is an impossible task. I will list a few and forget hundreds, but here goes. First to Joyce for her encouragement and for enduring the long hours I spent at my computer.

To our children and grandchildren for reading all or parts and cheering me on to completion. And especially to our daughter Laura, for writing down so much of the story when it happened. Without her notes, much of this story would be missing dates and details.

To the people, many with names, many without, who nurtured me along the way. To childhood friends and pets who came into my life unaware of the difference each made. To my parents, who said, "Work on it, then I'll be along." To my schoolteachers who showed up each day to add drops to my bucket of knowledge, to employers who hired me and allowed me to fail because, without failure, there's no growth. To the man who fired me, forcing my change in direction. To the banker who loaned me money, the one who didn't, and especially the one who extended friendship. And to the many advisors, each an expert in their field, willing to work together to benefit my company and me.

To everyone in healthcare who are there to dust us off, stitch us up, and make us well. Like many in the community, these heroes care more for the good of others than themselves.

Many are named on these pages, but more are not. It's to each that I'm grateful; without them, I wouldn't be who I am, and you wouldn't be reading this story. Believing one does anything on one's own is the greatest mistake of all. It's in not understanding how a power greater than any we know has hitched our universe together, even as I am hitched to you now.

To Sara Vavra, who encouraged me to share my stories and helped improve each. To Tom Petaccia, who understood the technology and flipped the switches so the entire world could follow along in my years of blogging and still keeps me connected to the ever-changing world of technology.

To Kathie Collins, Paul Reali, and the Charlotte Center for Literary Arts for helping writers go beyond the clarity of craft to mold language into art. And to Dr. Lyndall Hare who taught me her native African proverb, "When an old man dies, a library burns to the ground."

To each, I say, "Thank you."

Discussion Questions

1. What one life lesson would the author credit to his parents? Were there others?
2. Was it only cancer that transformed the author, or were there other factors?
3. Was there a time in the story when you felt you were in the scene with the author? If so, how did it feel?
4. Was there anything in the story that shocked you or made you think? If so, what?
5. Is there one central theme that resonates with you throughout the story? If so, can you tell us about it?
6. Do you feel the author was open and sharing, or were there places he was more guarded?
7. What do you think motivated the author to tell his story?
8. How did the memoir make you reflect on your own life?
9. Do you have stories like this to share? Will you do so, and when and how?

References

Allen, James. *As A Man Thinketh,* Self-Published by the author in 1903, now published by Simon & Schuster, New York, New York.

Brown, Robert McAfee. *Reading the Bible with Third World Eyes,* Westminster John Knox Press, Louisville, Kentucky, 1984.

Carroll, Lewis. *Alice's Adventures in Wonderland,* Macmillan Publishers, Ltd, London, 1865.

Carter, Anna Gallant. *Under the Same Roof of Stars,* Published by Anna Gallant Carter, Charlotte, North Carolina, 2010.

Dickens, Charles. *A Christmas Carol,* Chapman & Hall, London, 1843.

Easwaran, Eknath. *Conquest of Mind,* Nilgiri Press, Petaluma, California, 1988.

Eng, Tan Twan. *The Garden of Evening Mists,* Weinstein Books, New York, New York, 2012.

Eng, Tan Twan. *The Gift of Rain,* Weinstein Books, New York, New York, 2008.

Finegan, James W., *Where Golf Is Great: The Finest Courses of Scotland and Ireland,* Artisan Publishing, New York, New York, 2006.

Gaillard, Frye. *If I Were A Carpenter,* John E. Blair, Publisher, Winston-Salem, North Carolina, 1996.

Gutiérrez, Gustavo. *A Theology of Liberation,* Center for Studies and Publications, Lince, Peru, 1971.

Harrelson, Walter J. *The New Interpreter's Study Bible,* Abingdon Press, Nashville, Tennessee, 2003.

Izard, Kathy. *The Hundred Story Home,* Grace Press, Charlotte, North Carolina, 2016.

References

Leonard, Paul. *Where is Church?* Lorimer Press, Davidson, North Carolina, 2012.

Miller, Olive Beaupré (editor), *My Book House*, Published by The Book House for Children, Chicago, Illinois, 1920.

Milne, A.A. *Winnie-the-Pooh*, Methuen & Co. Ltd, London, 1926.

Ming-Dao, Deng. *365 Tao*, HarperCollins, New York, New York, 1992.

Mitchell, Margaret. *Gone With the Wind*, Macmillan Publishers, New York, New York, 1936.

Myers, Ched, Marie Dennis, Joseph Nangle, O.F.M., Cynthia Moe-Lobeda, and Stuart Taylor, *Say to This Mountain*, Orbis Books, Maryknoll, New York, 1996.

National Geographic, *Sacred Places of a Lifetime*, Published by National Geographic, Washington, D.C., 2008.

O'Donohue, John. *Anam Cara*, HarperCollins, New York, New York, 1997.

Picoult, Jodi. *Second Glance*, Atria, New York, New York, 2003.

Proulx, Annie. *The Shipping News*, Scribner, New York, New York, 1993.

Romero, Oscar. *The Violence of Love*, Harper & Row Publishers, San Francisco, 1988.

Servan-Schreiber, David, MD, PhD. *Anticancer, A New Way of Life*, Viking Penguin, New York, NewYork, 2008.

Sobrino, Jon. *Jesus the Liberator*, Orbis Books, Maryknoll, New York, 1994.

Taylor, Barbara Brown. *Learning to Walk in the Dark*, HarperCollins, New York, New York, 2014.

Twain, Mark. *The Adventures Of Tom Sawyer*, Grosset & Dunlap, New York, New York, 1946.

Twain, Mark. *Adventures of Huckleberry Finn*, Chatto & Windus, London, 1884.

About the Illustration and Makeup of This Book

The art director for the book was Diana Wade. The text is 11-point Minion Pro, designed by font designer Robert Slimbach and inspired by Renaissance-era type. It is intended for body text and extended reading. The book was printed on demand to reduce environmental impact, using eco-friendly paper, not sourced from endangered old-growth forests, forests of exceptional conservation value, or the Amazon Basin.

The developmental editor was Betsy Thorpe, and the copyeditor was Katherine Bartis. Kathy Brown was the proofreader, and Jeff Cravotta was the photographer. Tom Petaccia and Hannah Larrew continue to contribute to the book's publicity.

Artist Darcy Wade used watercolors and ink for her drawing on the book's cover.

About the Author

Charles Bruce McIntyre, or "Bruce" to anyone who knows him, is a retired business owner and cancer survivor. He was born in St. Louis, Missouri, in 1941 and often moved while growing up. After spending seventeen years in corporate America, Bruce founded and managed a foodservice sales and marketing agency for thirty years.

There Are No Answers Here, Only Questions is his first published work. In his writing, Bruce shows his ability to successfully move from transmitting boring business memos to the art of telling a good story.

Bruce and his wife Joyce have been married since 1967 and have two grown children and four grandchildren. The couple share their retirement cottage with a gregarious golden retriever and a shy indoor cat. All call Charlotte, North Carolina, home.

CPSIA information can be obtained
at www.ICGtesting.com
Printed in the USA
BVHW032347150223
658592BV00012B/347/J